STUMBLING HOME

MY LIFE AS AN IMPOSTER

Beatrice Starr, Ph.D

Lifeline Press

Stumbling Home
My Life as an Imposter
All Rights Reserved.
Copyright © 2020 Beatrice Starr, Ph.D
v5.0

The opinions expressed in this manuscript are solely the opinions of the author and do not represent the opinions or thoughts of the publisher. The author has represented and warranted full ownership and/or legal right to publish all the materials in this book.

This book may not be reproduced, transmitted, or stored in whole or in part by any means, including graphic, electronic, or mechanical without the express written consent of the publisher except in the case of brief quotations embodied in critical articles and reviews.

Lifeline Press

Paperback ISBN: 978-0-578-22678-1
Hardback ISBN: 978-0-578-22679-8

Cover Photo © 2020 Beatrice Starr, Ph.D. All rights reserved - used with permission.

PRINTED IN THE UNITED STATES OF AMERICA

For my darling Son and Daughter
For my brother whom I love dearly,
For Grace, Rhoda, and Ettie,
For Samuel, and Chawe
For my daughter-in-law, son-in-law and sisters-in law
For my cousins, nieces and nephews

and for
M. L. R

A special thanks goes to;

Nanci P, Eileen S, Ya'akov G, Mark P
Leatrice P, Shoshana S, Morrie L, Arn P.
Meryl M, Mark S., David S, Dr. Betty H.

Ketty M, Gloria N, Jo M, & Lisa P.
and Carole King

(Most names in this manuscript including the author's name have been changed to protect the innocent…and the not so innocent).

CHILDHOOD

BROOKLYN, 1958. MAYBE you thought it was a real cool place to live -- The Brooklyn Dodgers, Barbra Streisand, Coney Island? But that just proves a phoenix can rise from the ashes -- but it's ash, just the same. Brooklyn was a bitch. I don't care what you've been told. You know how people describe driving cross-country? It's great till you get to the Great Plains: Iowa, Kansas, Nebraska. Then you'll be driving forever, mile after mile after mile with nothing for as far as the eye can see but flat, monotonous land -- nothing on it, nothing alive -- not like life is supposed to look anyway. You'll drop dead before you get through the Plains. They're a real bitch. Not even a nice place to visit!

That was Brooklyn in l958. Death in slow motion, and I was one of those dying. Single-family homes attached to each other endlessly like a camera gone berserk, repeating one mediocre image after another, ad nauseam. Everything and everyone the same, an endless hum of white noise trying to convince you it's a concerto. Well, I wasn't convinced. I knew that Brooklyn was Kansas with an edge.

No one had an anxiety attack where I grew up. Not that anxiety attacks were good things to have, mind you, or that their existence said anything important about a whole population. It's just interesting to note that they didn't exist. Or maybe it would be better to say that they didn't APPEAR to exist. Yes, that would be more accurate. Maybe Brooklyn was just a massive anxiety attack trying to pass itself off as a stupor. That's what the craving for upward mobility and assimilation did to us -- or to *THEM*, to be more precise. *THEY* needed to be indistinguishable. God forbid someone brought attention to herself. Even positive attention was wrapped in a vague, unstated disquiet. *Don't be different! Above all, don't be different!* That was the ticket.

Maybe it was the war and the not-so-distant reminders of what could happen if you were different and the slowly emerging images of ovens and emaciated Jews. Maybe it was the moaning of the dead just a continent away but a thousand light years from Brooklyn............. or the post-war prosperity that everybody wanted a piece of -- that could only be had if you got with the program. Maybe it was Anti-Semitism that could suck you into the flames of Sobibor if it caught you in its sight or maybe it was just the dread of the internal cataclysm that *all* people want to avoid no matter where they live -- or when.

This guy down the street from us -- he was only a few years older than me. One night the whole neighborhood was twitching. Agitated whispers from one Partridge family to the next. The guy hung himself in his bathroom and before the ambulance could even take his body away it was understood that he died in a *"car crash!"* Not another word said. No. Everything was just fine. Maybe that's the only real difference between Brooklyn and the Great Plains. At least when you're talking about The Plains, everyone agrees if you stay too long it'll kill you. In 1958, I was 16 and dying in Brooklyn and no one had a clue.

Sundays were the worst. All the girls hung out at the local candy store pretending they were Sandra Dee or some other Gwyneth Paltrow of later days, blonde, blue-eyed, lithe, clearly not of Eastern European stock. But me? Imagine a fat Morticia. All I wanted in the whole damned world was to look like Sandra Dee -- or at least bear some familial resemblance to the gene pool. But no! I had to be dark complected with dark hair and a long nose like my mother and hers. When people tell you have a great personality, you know you look nothing like Sandra Dee. I had to be born from some Siberian outpost genophyle bearing no resemblance whatsoever to American

CHILDHOOD

icons of the 50's. A fat Charlie Chaplain in drag.

What does it mean when people whisper to your mother that you're *"interesting looking," "Slavic," "Hebraic." "She's got such a nice face if only she'd lose some weight.* I wanted them to say I was light as a feather -- *"and so pretty with her blue eyes and lovely blonde hair. She's really angelic, isn't she? Graceful as a swan."* But here was a fat Morticia pirouetting across a ballet stage in a pink tutu trying her damnedest to look like a bird. Why did they make me  take ballet? What were they thinking? *"Hey, Beastress!"* my brother screamed out to me from the audience at my first dance recital. *"Over here, Beastress, over here!"*

"Pleasingly plump, cheerfully chubby and fantastically fat!" That's what he called me, especially when our paths crossed in the corridors at school. *"Thar she blows. It's a bird. It's a plane. No. It's Beastress!"* What was I supposed to do? Argue that I wasn't *"Beastress?"* Should I run home and tell my mother? A lot of good that would do. Even if she wanted to listen, which, of course, she didn't, she was clinically deaf. And this was the 40's. Hearing aides were primitive. She wore this metal contraption across her head like a radar device connected to a tiny receiver pinned to the inside of her bra. If you wanted to speak to her you had to talk into her cleavage.

But even if she could have heard, she wouldn't have. Some people quote the scriptures – it organizes the world and makes sense of it:

STUMBLING HOME

"How you doin since 'ole Henry died?"
"Well, 'the Lord giveth and the Lord taketh away'."

These people aren't what you'd call "emotionally accessible!" But it wasn't the scriptures my mother quoted. If she wasn't scaring the shit out of me with "The Jews, the Jews, they're killing us over there," in those brief, unembellished moments of authenticity and terror, she was morphing into the safety of poetry, her alter self, her *Art*, where this complicated, frightened, woman found her mouthpiece. The focus on the war in Europe saturated the air, not only in our home, but, I suppose, in the homes of many Jews, especially immigrant Jews, which my parents were, she from Russia and my father from…………………*wherever*. Yiddish was their language at home, though their English was of the King's variety, 19th century to be exact, and their knowledge of poetry, all poetry and literature, was unparalleled. Here was this plain-Jane woman whom you'd never notice in a million years, who never did anything wrong or offended a living soul, who had a slight smile on her face no matter what was going on, and she refused to speak a word of plain English, the English of Brooklyn, of 20th century America. Except, as I said, when the lava of the authentic self erupted into a flood of anguish about the plight of the Jews in Europe. But in either case, whether she was hiding out in her deafness and the poetry of Keats or submerged in the here and now where annihilation and doom spilled from her lips, she was deaf to me. But that didn't stop me from trying to reach her. I kept plugging away -- for just one word that was real. The more distant she appeared, the more relentless I became.

"Mama, did you have a boyfriend before you married daddy?" No response. *"MAMA, DID YOU HAVE A BOYFRIEND BEFORE YOU MARRIED DADDY?"* No response. Right into the cleavage! *"**A BOYFRIEND**?"* Hands flailing. *"**B-O-Y-F-R-I-E-N-D**!"* Aha! A look of recognition. Maybe she'll let me in. I strained to hear.

"When I was one and twenty," she whispered,
"I heard a wise man say,
Give crowns and pounds and guineas,
But not your heart away.
Give pearls away and rubies,
But keep your fancy free,
But I was one and twenty, no use to talk to me.
When I was one and twenty..."

To add to my confusion, my father said she was a saint! And he believed it, too. Maybe I believed it, most of all. Not a vulgar word or impulse in her being. Not a moment of harshness, not a human emotion other than the ones she borrowed from the poets or the moments when she unwittingly tried to prepare me for the world as she saw it, for another Holocaust looming just around the corner. My mother even looked like a saint: her slight, timid presence, unnoticeable if you didn't know she was there, fragile-looking with not a drop of make-up nor obvious concern for her gray and thinning hair, tentative movements as if to not disturb the grown-up world around her. She was childlike and perplexed. No! That's a lie. She was ancient, rigid, moralistic, ever-present, scanning the universe with invisible eyes, always knowing when I was "naughty or nice." That's it! Santa Claus! That's who my mother was! Santa Claus, but thin, Jewish, without laughter or gifts or good cheer. Santa -- after she'd hit the skids.

People invariably mistook my mother for my grandmother. I hated that but understood why. She was much older than the other mothers and made no attempt to hide it. She wasn't anything like them. And that's the way she wanted it. She was out of the loop. What she lost in sensuality, she gained in status. Other women were *devious, cunning, vain*. Not my mother -- with the radar antenna around her head. She was special. She was a saint. And my father agreed. He was safe with her. She would never hurt him like the rest of them. To the contrary, she revered him. *He* was a *great* poet. She idealized him. She quoted

HIS poetry too. Never mind that he beat the shit out of us if the stock market closed down a point or two. *"It was only a tap,* "she'd say. *"Daddy didn't mean it. He loves you. Daddy's not like other men. He's an artist, and sometimes artists get carried away. We have to be patient. We have to turn the other cheek!"*

Isn't it amazing how two people manage to find their perfect mates in a universe of infinite possibilities? She was his greatest audience. She had married a "very special man." Special like herself, a poet, not a *devious, cunning, vain* man with ants in his pants like the rest of them who'll fuck you and move on. He was interested in more *important* things. He was above the fold. Actually, the stock market was HIS whore. But no one knew that he *dallied* in the market. That wouldn't be fitting the Good Lefty he was, who just happened to make money in the stock market and by selling rare books for profits that would make Lenin blush. He'd sneak out in the morning to follow the ticker tape and return at noon filled with bravado, bigger than life, *when the market went his way.* How my brother and I loved him *then* and knew everything was O.K. --- Or, he'd return, ready for war, gunning for his two smallest foes. And we knew there was no place to hide. It was just a question of time.

Like the day I was riding my little tricycle. My brother decided he wanted it so he grabbed my arm and threw me to the ground. I fell hard and began to cry. I lay there sobbing, all by myself, holding my broken arm -- and no one came. *No one!* Now mind you, my mother might not have heard me, and even if she had, she probably wouldn't have thought it very important. After all, it wasn't Proust crying. It was just me. Finally, when I realized she wasn't coming, I pulled my hurt, little body up and ran to her room where she was reading, as usual.

By the time I got there, my arm had begun to swell.

"Oh, Sissy, he didn't hurt you," she said, after I told her what my brother had done. "It's just a little bruise."

"No, mommy. It really hurts."

"Sissy, you're such a little actress. We have to put you on the stage."

"Mommy," I cried. "Please. It hurts me bad."

"**Badly**," she corrected, returning to her book. I tugged at her skirt tearfully, but she'd already tuned me out.

"Mommy, please. He hurt me!" Again, no response. You would have sworn I wasn't there. I was pulling on her skirt, holding my broken arm, crying my little eyes out but she didn't move. It's not that she willfully ignored me. She had simply made me invisible. I was no longer there. Oh, but I was -- and there was no escape --- because a minute later, I heard the heavy footsteps coming from downstairs.

"What the hell's going on up there," my father roared. "What are you damn kids doing now?" I didn't know where my brother was -- but then I saw him -- racing through the house for cover -- and I wasn't far behind, swollen arm and all.

"Where are you, you impudent little pups? Where's your brother?"

"He pushed me," I screamed, as I ran away as fast as I could. Maybe he'll leave me alone this time because it wasn't my fault. "It wasn't my fault, daddy. It wasn't my fault."

"You ungrateful kids. I can't get a moment's peace around here!"

God, was he mad! I was so scared I tried to hide under my bed, even though I couldn't fit. Then I heard my brother cry. *He got him!* I thought. *Good! Maybe he'll stop at that.* No! It wasn't good. I was scared to death but I felt bad for my brother -- even though he always beat me up. Then I heard him yell:

"I hate you, daddy, I hate you."

I begged him in my mind to be quiet. *Don't say it. Don't say it. He'll kill you.* But he kept saying it, over and over. I could hear my father's belt cut through its path. But my brother didn't stop. He kept yelling and crying and my father kept whipping. *Why doesn't he shut up? If only he'd stop being fresh, maybe daddy would go away. Please don't be fresh!. Don't be fresh. He'll kill you!*

Then I heard the footsteps again. He was done with my brother. *Where now? He's going to find me!* I squeezed under the bed as far as I could and prayed he wouldn't see me. I wrapped my body into the smallest ball I could and pulled my shirt over my face like gauze, as my little body shook uncontrollably in the blackness of my tomb. Then I heard him near me -- and I knew it was no use. *You big, fat pig!* I chided myself in silence. *He couldn't get you if you fit under the bed!*

And I couldn't have been older than six! Where was my mother when that belt whipped through our hides? What was she doing that couldn't wait?

When my father had finally purged the market's decline and left, I remember my mother sitting awkwardly at the foot of my bed, as if she had something very important to say but wasn't quite sure just what it was.

"It was only a tap, Sissy," she said, as she spoke to me in the most consoling voice she could muster up. *"It was only a tap."*

Let me up the ante to make my point. I don't recall the exact date, but I must have been about five (and my brother a year older) when we moved from one house in Brooklyn to another just a few blocks away. In the first home, my parents had a bedroom and my brother and I shared the other, the way children often do. But as we got older, my parents decided it wasn't appropriate for a little girl to share a bedroom with a little boy, and so they bought a larger house with three bedrooms.

I remember being thrilled that I would have my own room. My parents even bought me a new bedroom set for a real "girls" room, white furniture as pretty and feminine as could be. I was so happy. *Now I'll be a girl like the other girls.* Only one thing confused me. As the new furniture was being set up in my room, two beds were brought in, identical twin beds placed on either side of a small night table. *How odd,* I thought. *I don't need two beds.*

"Mommy," I asked, innocently enough. "How come I have two beds?"
"You don't," she said, matter-of-factly. "*One is for you and one is for me.*"
"You're going to sleep in **my** room?" I asked in disbelief.
"In **our** room," she said, "**our** room."

I wish I could tell you what I felt at the time, but I can't. Except I do remember that it was hard to breathe -- the way it had been hard to breathe sometimes when my father beat me.
"But, why, mommy? Why will we have the same room?"
"Daddy likes to go to sleep before me," she explained. "He doesn't want the light on."
Oh! That made sense. She can't read late. O.K. I get it. But why can't I catch my breath?
"So daddy will sleep in **his** own room?" I asked. She nodded. "And Manny will have **his** room, too?" She nodded again. "But how come Manny can have his own room and I can't?"
"Because he's a boy and we only have three bedrooms."

What else can I tell you about this peculiar arrangement? It just was. But what I do remember, as if it were yesterday, is this: When I got into my new bed that night for the very first time, my mother was already in hers. The light on the night table between us was on and my mother was reading. I was tired and asked her if we could close the light. She didn't hear me. I asked again, louder. She still didn't hear me. I reached across to her bed and tapped her on the leg. She looked at me, obviously not hearing what I had said and began adjusting her hearing aid. I asked her again if we could close the light. The hearing aid emitted piercing tones until she finally found the right frequency.

"In a minute," she said sweetly, as she returned to her book.

I waited and waited, trying to sleep in spite of the bright light. It was impossible. I asked a third time and again she didn't hear me. Again I reached over, tapped her on the leg and again she adjusted her hearing aid.

"Just one more minute," she said in the gentlest voice with eyes beseeching me to be patient for just a second longer.

Of course I'll be patient. She's so kind. I have to be patient. I have to try and sleep, despite the light. I closed my five-year-old eyelids as tight as I could while my face tensed like a statue in terror and tried to force myself to sleep. I tried and tried for hours. But, the longer I did, the more awake I became and the more my frustration slapped me in my fat face and belittled me for being such a nasty little child with bad, bad feelings that normal little children don't have. Yet despite my self, I had to sleep.

"Please turn out the light, mommy," I sobbed, exhausted with hate and self-contempt.

"I'm almost done, Sissy. I'm almost done," her angelic voice pleaded, as she smiled at me with such tenderness I could kill.

And then the most amazing thing happened, something that felt eerily familiar yet had never happened in quite this way before. As I lay in my bed with my eyes shut tight, I saw myself in a coffin, underground. Above the earth people were walking and talking, completely unaware that I was just beneath them, buried alive, screaming to be heard. Of course they didn't hear me, yet I continued to scream in the absolute blackness of my coffin, shaking with unimaginable terror. Nothing I did that night could alter my living death, no image I tried to evoke, no fantasy, no thought however lovely or appealing could rescue me. It was only with the first ray of daylight that the image finally passed and it was only then that I could sleep. And as it happened, this vision, this living death, this most vivid of all waking night-mares continued to haunt me every night of my young life as I laid my head on my pillow hoping to sleep.

CHILDHOOD

And every night was the same, my mother reading by the light of the lamp between us until the wee hours of the morning, her gentle voice repeating the same words, unaware that I trembled not two feet away in a tomb I could not escape. And there was no escape, until sunrise -- when the vision would pass. Yet I knew it was only a question of time before another night came, before I was again, inexorably buried alive. And so when each and every daylight came I resolved to kill myself before the next darkness sucked me back into the tomb. The thought of suicide was my only hope. But of course, when darkness came again, death was no longer death. It was a waking death for all eternity -- and in its grip, I plotted again for my suicide the following day. And these plans, these desperate, agonizing ruminations in the mind of a child who had barely started to live!

I remember, years later, as an adult, reading about the nightmare at Babi Yar. While there's much I want to say here -- and *will* do so a bit later, suffice it to say now that at that moment, the ditches were not only filled with the nude and bloodied bodies of men and women but the bodies of children, as well. I remember the photos of mangled and mutilated corpses piled one a-top the other as far as the eye could see, rail-thin arms and legs protruding from the mound as if unattached to a body that housed a mind and a heart. In one photo, just below the top layer of Nazi "garbage," a child could be seen as if squirming, not yet dead but yet unable to break free. Apparently there were many such scenes, people too damaged to wiggle out of the trap set by man yet too irrelevant to be granted the mercy of death. I imagined that the wails of this child could be heard only if one knew they were the wails of a child and not the vague and unidentifiable sounds of a wounded and dying animal caught in a poacher's trap, twisting feverishly to stay alive. I knew immediately when I saw this child that she and I were connected --- not in the usual ways we identify similarity but in the subjective experience of utter hopelessness. Who is to say that a mother who looses both of her two children in a hurricane is twice as devastated as the mother who loses her one and only child. Who is to say that a child dying in the rubble of a Ukrainian killing field is any more pained than the child waiting to die in post-war Brooklyn?

That child in Brooklyn, wishing that death would take her when the sun rose in the morning, was as close to Babi Yar as I would get, me the child of a Ukrainian immigrant screaming into the oblivion of a deaf and indifferent universe, a child who had no real future for she assumed she was already dead and the child of an immigrant from a place I'd yet to learn.

Of course, I didn't know it at the time, the seed of escape had been planted in those sleepless nights – in my soundless voice, in the paralysis of negation ……and the remaining years of childhood became preparation for eventual flight. It wasn't until I ran away from home at sixteen that I fell asleep in peace for the very first time.

MOMMY

MY MOTHER (TOP right) hadn't always been deaf. As I understand it, a high fever claimed her hearing at 18 -- but she had, long before that, lost the ability to hear. The earlier trauma is much more difficult to pinpoint because it wasn't a disease or an accident or a twist of fate. It wasn't even in her ears. Let me tell you what I know.

As a child, my mother was anything but sickly. To the contrary, as the stories go, she was a terror on wheels. In fact, she had such color and spunk that they called her *Gypsy*. (Of course, my brother and I weren't born until she was in her forties, so this woman known as *Gypsy* had long since disappeared.) But the photos and family tales bear witness to the fact that, indeed, Gypsy had once lived. She'd strut her stuff in Brownsville and embarrass the hell out of her orthodox mother and her father who was a *Rabbi, no less*. *Gypsy* even rode a bike! Now this was the early 1920's in an immigrant ghetto where kids worked twelve and fourteen hours a day in sweatshops to help make ends meet. And when they weren't working, young girls weren't riding around on bicycles -- in pants! But she was the runt of the litter so she got to do a lot of things her older brothers and sisters couldn't. They were the ones who had to work so she could go to school and learn English and prosper. That was her mother's dream, my grandmother, Brucha.)

I never met my grandmother, but I'm named after her. All I know of her was told to me by my mother, so don't make book on it.

STUMBLING HOME

My grandmother's family was killed by the Cossacks in a Russian pogrom in 1886. Alone, and virtually homeless, she was married off at 12 to an old widower, Staradubski, in a Russian *shtetl*. It was a coup, the story went, assuring her of a place in the world and assuring him of a caretaker for the remainder of his life. It was an uncomplicated marriage centered around survival, the birth and survival of their four children (Ethel, Yudi, Nathan & Monya) and their heroic, if not uncommon, efforts to ward off the anti-Semitism that engulfed the continent. But when *Brucha's* aging husband died, and she again became invisible (as did all unattached women of the day), she married a Talmudic teacher who brought with him respectability, but little money. Conditions were difficult, at best, especially for Jews. Yet, *Brucha* and her new husband, *Nossen*, managed to eke out a life for themselves and their children. By the time their last child, my mother, was born in Kiev in 1902, the family had grown to nine (an older sister, Lena, an older brother Sammy and my mother, Ettie, all born of this second marriage), and were determined to move to America, which they ultimately did a decade later.

And so, that's how my mother came to occupy a special place in her mother's consciousness. She was the only one whose childhood was shaped by *The New World*, by all its promises and contradictions. She was the one who came to embody them and to suffer their uniquely disparate voices. In her was housed the old mandates and the new, the traditional and the revolutionary, and sometimes the collision of the two was unavoidable. It was *my* mother who learned to speak English, who saw *her* mother keep the family afloat, sewing in the middle of the night for pennies while her father "studied" the Talmud. And it was my mother, Gypsie, as she came to be called, who took to riding a bicycle in her orthodox Brooklyn neighborhood, covered in bright colors and fabrics to the great displeasure of the elders who frowned upon such heresy and disrespect. Dark clothing hemmed below the calves, unobtrusively, that was the order of the day but somehow Gypsy just wasn't into becoming invisible.

In Russia there were students to learn what *Nossen* had to teach -- but in America, Talmudic study just wasn't a high ticket item. You'd think there'd be a simple lesson to be learned from this -- something about supply and demand. But, no. The lesson was far more profound. Surprisingly, As *Nossen's* wage-earning abilities decreased, his status seemed to increase. In Kiev, he was a *"Rabbi"* with a meager income. In New York he was a *"scholar"*. And when income couldn't nourish his ego, his wife could.

By the time I was born, years after both my grandparents were dead, my mother had already mastered her lessons well. Her father, she told me, couldn't earn a living in America because he didn't speak English -- *"but he was a very important man",* she said, *"a Rabbi, a scholar."* Grandma *Brucha* even made her kids tip-toe around their apartment because *Nossen* was studying very important things and shouldn't be disturbed! And my grandmother, raising seven children virtually alone colluded in this! Maybe she even authored it! *Damn! How do you get to be an unemployed Talmud teacher? That's what I want to be!*

And *my* mother learned her lessons at *her* mother's knee -- and learned her lessons well: you study, strive, marry, take a fall, surrender, and go underground, or else! And that's exactly what *Gypsy* did.

She studied hard, learned English and even managed to go to college, flaunting her colors like a peacock. This was a girl who could fly. And she did. A rebel of the first order, a *Gypsy*, a Lefty, a poet, a bicycle-riding Bolshevik in pants. *God, how I would have loved that girl I never knew!* (The woman in this photo I never knew. The mother I knew NEVER, never would have sat with her legs apart!)

STUMBLING HOME

She was going as far and as fast as she could go. She even fell madly in love with a Spanish professor, the love of her life, I suspect, but was prohibited from marrying him because he had been divorced, a fact of life her orthodox parents just couldn't abide. And while she pined for him, her heartbreak was evidence of that part of her that was rooted in the new world, that embraced the many cultures and cultural differences that existed and she turned her back on the culture of her birth.

It would be years, in fact, before she'd fully re-connect with her roots, until the blistering soil of Hitler's Europe scared the shit out of her and made her take notice. And along the way, as if to hasten the process of regression and attachment, she met the second love of her life, my father. And it was her very own mother (who'd once invested in her the breadth of achievement and possibility) who implored her to drop out of college or risk the consequences of threatening the ego of this fine young man who had no formal education. *Never, ever be smarter than your man!* And Gypsy obeyed and her colors began to fade. (The only one of the seven children, fluent in English, it was she who got to go to College, Hunter College, and then forced to abandon her dreams for herself so as not to rock the boat.) And that's how she finally took her rightful place in the oblivion of deafness and silence.

Now I don't mean to imply that this was my father's fault, because it wasn't. He just happened to have been the kind of guy that young girls fell for, with poems that could seduce any Bolshevik biker. He didn't try to be sexy. But he was. Not just his looks, though, his sadness, too. God, did that make the girls swoon. He was really a lost soul, my dad, until my mother rescued him and made him God.

DADDY

SAMUEL STARR. OH, boy. Let me think about this for a minute. I want to get it right -- not just so you'll understand him better, but because when I describe my father, I'm also describing parts of myself. I'm like him a lot, I think. Maybe I'm also like my mother, but that feels more elusive............ at least at the moment. Anyway, my father:

Sam Starr was an orphan. That's important to know. Not an orphan like we think of orphans today, but "orphans" like they existed at the turn of the century in Europe, kids living in no-man's land.

Sam Starr was orphaned in London in 1906. As best I could gather, my father had been born in England four years earlier* (a point I'll return to a bit later), the first child of Russian (*) immigrants who had fled their homeland to escape persecution. But since life in England didn't prove much better than in Russia*, his father, *Moishe*, decided to come to America to make his fortune. When he had saved enough money, he thought, he'd send for his young son and his wife whom he adored. What my grandfather didn't know at the time was that his beautiful wife, Annie, was apparently already pregnant with their second child when he decided to leave for the New World. When he suspected her "condition," he waited till the birth of his child, a second son, Jossel, and then made his way to America, arriving in Philadelphia in 1906. By the time he got news of his family, Annie had died in England from complications of pneumonia. My father and his infant brother, Joey, were placed in the care of a Jewish orphanage in London until *Moishe* was able to pay their fare to America.

STUMBLING HOME

Annie was buried in a pauper's cemetery somewhere in London, it's exact location to remain a mystery for the next six decades.

As it happened, it would be years before my father and Joey were beckoned to make the transatlantic journey, and by that time Joey was sick and very frail. Conditions in the orphanage had taken their toll. When he and my father finally arrived in New York they were met by two strangers, their father and the woman he had married solely to care for his sons.

Mary, the new wife, was a bitter woman I was told, a "widower" with a club foot who had lost her husband and her infant child, rendering her "unmarriageable" until *Moishe* came along. She, more than anyone, understood the truth of her marital arrangement and resented the two boys she had agreed to raise. Not only were they wounded and difficult children, they were constant reminders of her husband's real love -- as they were for *Moishe* as well. In an effort to placate his new wife and minimize the pain of his own vivid memories, Moishe resolved never to speak of Annie again, despite my father's hunger to keep her memory alive. She was dead! It was over. *Moishe* had to shut her out -- and in so doing, shut out his young sons, too. Her name would never be uttered in his home again.

And so my father and little Joey lived as outsiders in their father's home. Their short history had not been his. Theirs was still across the ocean and in their dreams and nightmares. It was history in the present tense. London was all around them.......... Sam clung to his mother, Annie, as if she'd never left. In his heart he was still hiding under her shabby coat, peeking out at the cobblestone streets every now and again until the cold and the dark warned him to return to his home against her body. He had no fears under that coat -- and neither did she. They were wealthy and in love, Sam and his mother. The rest of the world could go straight clear to hell. Four feet scurried below her hem-line -- two so small and awkward they had to be kept in line by the others. Strangers smiled in recognition. They too had once hidden out in this safest spot of all. Annie smiled back and cocked her head with pride. She was the only mother on earth. The London streets belonged to her, this young, lovely, dark-haired creature with four legs -- who made Sam giggle when she swung her hips this way and that, especially when he wasn't ready. That was the best - when she'd stop in her tracks and he'd lunge forth right into the Tower of Babel not half a foot in front of him. And when his little legs gave out -- the way they do with little half-pints all the time, he'd tug on the back of her skirt and she'd know, as if he'd spoken reams. He'd peek out his sweet little face from under her coat and tease her with his eyes. He was certain she had no idea where he'd been.

"*So there you are!,*" she'd say with utter surprise -- and he'd laugh with sheer delight. He, just a pip-squeak, could pull the wool over her eyes, again! Then he'd poise his ten-foot tall body, erect and triumphant and stretch his little arms high above his head. And she knew the signal from a hundred dress rehearsals. She'd bend down low, pregnancy and all, and he'd crawl up her back till her arms were clasped beneath him and he'd rest his sleepy head on her shoulder as she carried her angel home. Now if this wasn't heaven, what was? This was an act you could take on the road, Annie, barely a woman and her precious son, Sam -- ready to be called at any moment by the promises ahead. Who could have known that the laughter would be so brief.

In the middle of some pitch-black night that could hardly be otherwise recalled, Annie gave birth to Jossel amid screams and wails that chimed in my father's ears for the rest of his life. Something was terribly wrong!

When daylight finally came, strangers filled the dismal London flat with whispers and tears. Annie was dead. And that was that.

And then there was *Moishe's* home. Not a pretty sight either.

"Enough of your damn whining -- or I'll give you the back of me hand!" Moishe would roar when his sons misbehaved.

The stories my father told made my head spin:

Tyrants and Edicts and Edicts and tyrants -- and bitter gimps who are really spinsters in disguise. But, I've got their number. I know what's cooking here. A bunch of crap, that's what. Not an honest god-damned word. You, Moishe, deaf and mute, playing house in a mausoleum, ready to erupt at the drop of a hat. And you, Mary, dragging your club foot to club these orphans to kingdom-come. Joey, sick as a child could be, hiding under my father's coat -- four little feet scurrying this way and that as fast as they could with nowhere to go. Got you! You little so and so! The jig is up!

Joey was sickly and weakening by the day as children did in early America. Nothing could be done for his frail health, so the story went. Fevers took the children - a dime a dozen.

Joey lingered in his father's Brooklyn home. That's the way it was. His sickly body was eating itself up, as his tiny frame dwindled before his brother's eyes. My father nursed his dear little Joey, his shadow from that other hell to this. They were inseparable, these two lost boys. They were all they had. My father tried to fix him up -- the way one pathetic creature fixes up another. He tried to make his coat-tails long, but they were a sorry sight. If the truth be told, Samuel Starr couldn't do a thing to help his mother -- and in the second *Kristallnacht* of his young life, he couldn't do a thing for Joe.

And so, on an August night in 1913, seven-year-old Joey died and returned to his mother he'd never known

And that was that -- again! So, what was Moisha to do? Pretend Joey never existed *either*? Flog anyone who uttered HIS name? Not so easy this time. His name stuck to Sam's tongue like molasses. Every word out of his mouth drifted through it like a tunnel. Joey. Joey and Ana. What else was there? If Sam had been difficult before Joey's death, he was toxic now. He had his father's temper -- and his depression too. But also his passion for books and THE UNION.

Moishe was a union organizer. You didn't mess with his politics or his books. At least other people didn't. But my father was chomping at his bit. The older my father got, the more fiercely he challenged Moishe. Everything was riding on it. In the end, Samuel Starr didn't go down easy. But he did go down -- at least to a private world on the written page -- and there was no bringing him back. When Mary *gave* Moishe four other children and a *bono fide* new family, Sam's fate was sealed. Mary, *Moishe*, Al, Ruthie, Betty and Lou. Oh yes, and Samuel Starr.

It wasn't much later that my father went out to work to earn his keep, a messenger, I was told. He was twelve at the time, or maybe eleven, or maybe even younger. A blessing in disguise. He had some place to be -- and he knew it was his ticket out. His errands took him all over town, to new places and new people and something was resurrected in him that had been long gone. Maybe it was hope -- or maybe it was that feisty streak that made his mother swoon. Whatever it was, it was easy to see and hard to resist. He had charisma. That he did. He was more than just a handsome lad, tall and dark with ice-blue eyes that brought you to your knees. He was soulful. And sexy, too. But he was also smart -- at first just the kind of street-smarts you're never sure will hit pay dirt, the kind of smarts that can go either way -- a Boston strangler or a Samuel Beckett. Fortunately, he took the latter turn, to the poets and anarchists, union organizers like his father, actors and dancers and *literati* he met along the way -- and he gradually found his niche.

Now Sam Starr was a complicated guy, so when I say he found his *niche,* what I'm really trying to say is that he found it -- and he didn't find it! Let me explain. Just before my father died in 1982, I was going through a stack of old photos I'd never seen before -- the way you clean house when you know you're about to vacate -- for the very last time. In the pile was an old black and white snapshot of a young woman with a child on her knee. They were beautiful, the two of them, especially the child. I wasn't sure if it was a little girl or a little boy because the features were so angelic.

"Who is this?" I asked my father, pointing to the child.

"It's me," he said, "and that's my mother."

"Annie?" I asked, my eyes widening in disbelief. He nodded.

"It's the only picture I have of her. Chawe was her given name but everyone called her Annie."

I could hardly believe it! I had no idea that she looked like that. Dark hair and eyes like a rainbow, beautiful eyes, not blue-white like Sam's but hazel as if they were undecided..........and her olive skin, like mine, "Hebrew" skin.

"She looked like you," he smiled, handing me the photo. "It's yours. Keep it."

I was speechless. *I look like Annie? How could it be?* I never looked like anyone. I was the kid they thought was adopted. *And besides, this woman is lovely. He's got to be pulling my leg.*

But there was a resemblance. Not that I was pretty like she, but the coloring, the long, dark hair parted down the middle. But the real similarity was something else. It was her mystery, her somber poise --- which could, if you weren't searching her soul, be mistaken for the tone, the formality of all turn-of-the-century snapshots. This was a woman in 1904 who looked like I was trying to look in 1958, yet whom I'd never seen, a woman who's stateliness might have been dismissed as an artifact of the medium. Maybe it's projection on my part but I had the sense this was not a woman you'd approach frivolously. Maybe if you wanted to know the origins of time or something profound like that.

Anyway, that wasn't really my point. My point was that Samuel Starr was a complicated guy and things weren't always as they seemed. Like the word "Warsaw" stamped on the bottom of the photograph.

"How could this picture have been taken in Poland?" I asked my father. It didn't make any sense. My father was born in England. He couldn't have been more than two when the photo was taken. And his mother must have died soon afterwards. When did they go to Poland, and why?

"It was taken in Poland," he said with great hesitation.

"Why did you go to Poland," I asked, perplexed.

There was a long silence. He seemed to be looking for words. It was so unlike him. Words were his stock and trade. He leaned towards me, slowly, tentatively, as though a bomb might explode if he made the wrong movement.

"You're the only person I've ever told this to," he began, his eyes alert, checking me out as you would a stranger you'd come upon in a war zone. *"I was born in Poland."*

"You were born in Poland? How could that be? You were born in England. That's what you've always told me. That's what you've always told everyone. I don't understand." I reached for a book of his poetry and pointed to the picture of him on the back cover with the short bio underneath: *"Samuel Starr, born in London, England........."*

"That's what I always said, but it's not true."

"I don't understand. Why would you say you were born in England if you were born in Poland?" His eyes began to change -- as if he realized I wasn't the enemy and that his suspicions had been misplaced.

"I never wanted to be associated with immigrants, with the shtetels," he said sheepishly, confessing his misdeeds. *"Not with Poland nor with pushcarts. I wanted to be associated with England......... with literature."*

"Are you telling me it's all been a lie?" My face tightened as if ready to scold him. The frightened child was holding her ground before the bogey man, seeing him for the first time --- or seeing herself.

"I was born in Poland..........We moved to England just after this

picture was taken -- when I was two."

"How could mommy go along with this lie?" I asked incredulously. Silence. Dead silence.

"She doesn't know."

My mother wasn't the prettiest in the crowd but she had her own magic. It was just packaged differently. She ate books. Her politics were radical and she wasn't afraid to flaunt them in your face. My father learned from her and she from him. Though, on first glance, one might have thought his currency far richer than hers, but that would have been a mistake.

Gypsy had something invaluable that Sam Starr couldn't resist.... She could take him under *her* wing and pretend she was under his and put any Geisha to shame. It was an offer he couldn't refuse.... and she had all the equipment to pull it off: the soft, gentle voice, so well rehearsed you never knew it was screaming in your ear -- the large, embracing family, hungry for a real patriarch -- that took this orphan to its bosom and gave him the helm. After all, Samuel Starr was a published poet! He was going to restore the rightful status of these *special* people who just happened to have fallen on hard times. Yes, it's true. They worked with their hands, most of them, anyway. But not my grandfather, *Nossen*. He didn't work at all. NO! That's not true. He was thinking and *scholaring* all of the time. What could be more important? O.K., so it didn't pay the rent. But he couldn't speak English! But Sam Starr. Ah! That's a different story! He spoke the language of kings. (He was born in England, don't forget. No wonder he was so articulate). *Brucha*, my mother's mother, couldn't wait till *The Jewish Daily Forward* hit the newsstands to look for another poem by her daughter's beau. And when she found one, all was right in the universe for there, in print, right before her eyes for all to see, was *Samuel Starr*, the next Keats.

So Etta (Staradubski, Polenofski expunged the loss of her Spanish professor's love whose divorce rendered him damaged goods and found, instead, a *REAL* man with the perfect configuration of attributes (and shortcomings) to hit the jackpot.

Samuel was handsome (but only incidentally; not consciously handsome the way Jewish men are not supposed to be, not the kind of man who primps over himself but the kind who is sexy in spite of himself); Samuel was smart the way a *real* man was supposed to be, not too smart in the real world who might make a ton of money and embarrass his socialist cronies, but book smart, articulate, impressive as they come, a man who could hold court with the best of them, who could quote the sages and poets at will, whose worth was vetted by the poems he published and the philosophers he hoarded. And probably just as importantly, Samuel Starr was not a believer. He was, after all, not HER father's son. He had no use for religion of any ilk nor the people who did. His was the God of Spinoza; the god of intellectuals; the god of the secular world. While he was a man of the book like her own father, they were the *right* books; the books of the contemporary world. He was as towering in her mind, as the list of books he'd mastered with barely a minimum of formal education. She bowed before him as she was taught to do and happy to do so.

Now, I'm not implying that my mother wanted to take a fall, that she was masochistic or self-reproaching. To the contrary, I think it was just the way things were. In her eyes, you surrender. And when you do, you become a *real* woman, assuming you surrender to a *real* man. But even if you surrender to a flop, you'll still achieve your genetic potential. People may call him a flop, but they'll also say, *"He's so lucky to have her. She's such a fine, devoted woman, poor thing."* And what's more womanly than that! *She stuck by the bastard, didn't she?* What were the alternatives? To become a *spinster*, an *old maid*? This was the 1920's. So if every woman had to have a man, my father was the pick of the litter. She didn't see her *surrender* as her *fall*. She saw it as her ascension. And he, an orphan in a storm, was more than happy to occupy the throne. Oh, except for one thing. He left the part about Poland out.

ELLIE

HAD I NOT met Ellie, escape might never have come. It's the first day of junior high school and the new students, flaunting their just-bought clothes, sat nervously in the school's auditorium awaiting the arrival of faculty. Directly in front of me a ponytail dangled like a marionette, swaying gracefully with each imperceptible movement of the girl's head. Certainly, I could never have a ringlet like that. It wasn't just that my hair was straight. It was deeper than that. Somehow, I knew I wasn't programmed with **any** of the qualities that carried much cachet in the 1950's. God had simply tripped up. It was the kind of assessment that proved formative, like coming to know oneself as "female," or "male," or "white" or "black." I came to *know* I was different. And that perfect pony-tail came to symbolize the chasm between me and *all* the rest.

And yet she wasn't a **real** *Gwyneth Paltrow*. Her features weren't perfect, (though she was pretty enough). Her hair wasn't pure blonde, but auburn and she appeared to be taller and a bit more "ethnic" than the usual Nordic and Germanic beauties. But even so, she had radiance about her and a larcenous laughter that let you know she was ruling the roost, at least to me. And there was an edge to her, too. She was sassy and unafraid to shock you with her wit and her willingness to push the boundaries of propriety. She was not your typical *Gwyneth Paltrow*, for sure, though everyone seemed to admire her as much as I, but for very different reasons. They saw the parts of her that were like themselves: she was pretty, popular and trendy and had enough of that central European tone to make them feel she was one of them. I saw all that (and was duly impressed) but I also saw a bit of a renegade, an "artiness" that reminded me of my own status on the outside. It was that strange mixture of the "in" and the "out," that ambiguity she seemed to flaunt, that made her intriguing and seductive at the same time.

Actually, her name wasn't Ellie. It was *Eleanora*. Not *Ellen*, or even *Eleanore*. It was *Eleanora* -- as if Fellini were calling her from the Italian countryside. "*Eleanora*," regal, superior. Not what you'd expect from the projects in Brooklyn. Not what you'd have expected her parents to have come up with. *Dottie*, perhaps, *Mertyl* but *Eleanora?* Where did it come from in these parents of hers from the other side of the tracks, from an old, shabby kook and his fat wife with no teeth? What was beneath the surface of these two dilapidated old souls? What had they once anticipated for their lives before depression and poverty took them down?

Ellie's apartment was utterly bleak. Old, dreary furnishings collected and arranged haphazardly as if no one had lived there for decades. It was the carelessness of the place that struck me the most, and the fact that in spite of such dankness and indifference, a child could thrive. Ellie's room was testament to that. It was nothing like the rest of the apartment -- with its rich colors and fabrics that transformed poverty into whimsy and delight. Her talents and sparkle were everywhere, in her drawings, her music, in the uniqueness of every object she handpicked and adorned. It was a room of life, of adventure. It was the room of a young girl free to explore her own inclinations. And I took to it as I did to Ellie, for oxygen.

I don't know where her parents were, but they were rarely home. It's not like they had any real important business outside. Ellie's mother had some low-level clerical job she hated, where it didn't matter if she was fat and had no teeth. But her father, that was different. He had big plans. He always had some scheme up his sleeve that was going to take him over the top. Her parents were old, like mine, so her father must have had had plenty of time to hit the jackpot, but hadn't. That didn't stop him, though. There was always tomorrow. A real Willy Loman, he was. Whenever I saw him, he'd grab my ear and carry on and on about some new-fangled invention or device that was going to make him rich. Her mother would roll her eyes back and just laugh in his face, like, *"you stupid old fool."* Sometimes she'd even say it straight out. She never gave him the time of day. I was sure he was going to just turn around and crack her one, like in my house. You'd never, ever dismiss MY father. But Ellie's father didn't seem to care. He'd just keep on talking without skipping a beat, as if she hadn't said a word. And I'd listen and *oow* and *ah* and make him feel like a million bucks. I think I was his best audience. I loved that old guy. I didn't care if he was full of it. It just blew my mind that every time I thought he was going to whack her one, he didn't. I wanted to give him a great big hug whenever that happened, which was a lot. It made me smile from ear to ear. And I loved Ellie's mother, too. Even though she was really shot to shit. This fat old woman would just get in his face and call him an old fart!

Who ever said, *"fart,"* anyway? Not in my house. But here was this Jewish woman who had no front teeth, telling dirty jokes and laughing so hard she'd make the floor shake. Dirty jokes? Sex? Farting? Not like any Jew in MY family. She could bring down my blood pressure so fast you'd have thought I was a sprinter. Especially when we talked about boys. We could talk to her about anything, boys, periods, necking, anything – and not be afraid. Not that we had any experience with stuff like that -- but boy, were we interested. And she wouldn't even bat an eye. We'd just sit around the kitchen table and talk, like three old girlfriends just shooting the breeze. And sometimes, out of nowhere, she'd just reach over and give us a hug, for no damned reason at all, just a big hug, out of the blue. I don't know why. Maybe she just liked us. I could have sat there for the rest of my life.

But, of course, Ellie didn't feel the same way. She couldn't wait to hit the road when her parents were around. She'd get real restless and snippy and give me all these signals like, *"let's get out of here, NOW!"* She'd kick me under the table or stare me down or pinch my arm when no one was looking till she knew I got the hint. And then we'd have to leave, which of course, I didn't want to do. I don't know why she couldn't stand being around them. I think she was ashamed -- because she'd always make me look at this one picture she had hanging on her wall. It was her parent's wedding picture I think -- and every time I was there, she'd ask me, *"Did you ever see this picture over here?"* which, of course, I'd seen a thousand times. But she'd make a real point of it, anyway. Like she wanted to be sure I knew how they used to look. Clark Gable and Lana Turner look-alikes. You'd never believe that these were the same two people. I didn't really care, though. I thought they were great just the way they were.

We'd leave her apartment and cross over Nostrand Avenue, which was kind of the dividing line between the *"haves"* and the *"have-nots"* and go to my house because that's where **she** wanted to be. Of course, it was the last place I'd have chosen, but I'd give in because I was so proud she was my friend.

But every time we'd enter my house, all of a sudden, as if some switch went on, Ellie would start talking different. She'd sound older and kind of English -- and she'd comment about this painting or this sculpture or this book as if she were a museum curator or a literary critic, as if she knew about every piece of art because that's *exactly* what she had in **her** house! That really bothered me, when she'd start putting on airs. I thought she was the best - but when she put on all those airs, I felt left out. Of course, I didn't know they were airs. I thought she really loved my parents because they were probably lovable -- and I just didn't see it because I was crazy. I thought she appreciated them and spoke their language because she was special like they were. I was the odd one. There was something very wrong with **me**. Why else would I love **her** parents?

And, certainly it seemed my parents loved *her*. Actually, my mother could have cared less. She probably never even knew we were there. But my father thought Ellie was really something. The two of them would start talking about books or poetry and I'd sit there like a bump on a log wishing **her** mother was there, just shooting the bull the way she did. I don't really think Ellie knew what she was talking about, though, but it sounded good and my father was duly impressed. Maybe she read a poem or two or the first few lines of a book here and there, but I don't think she cared about it any more than I did. Of course, I could talk the same way if I wanted. After all, it was **my** house and I'd lived there all my life and I knew how it was done. God knows, I'd done it often enough! But that's not what I wanted to do. For me, just gabbing with Ellie's mom was as close to happiness as I'd come.

Anyway, when Ellie would start all that superior stuff, I'd get really annoyed, especially when she did it with *MY* parents. But I'd never say anything because most of the time she was just like me, and I loved her. Even when we went to Bernie Eisner's apartment in the East Village and she'd pretend she was 20 and a great writer or something, it didn't seem to bother me, maybe because I was pretending, too. Anyway, those Sunday afternoons at Bernie Eisner's blew me into the cosmos.

BERNIE'S PLACE

BERNIE'S PLACE WAS on the top floor of a fifth-floor walk-up tenement on East 6th Street and 2nd Avenue, far off our beaten path on what was then called the *Lower East Side*, long before realtors decided a name change would spike the profits; a name change for the area settled by immigrants, refugees and the poor from the turn of the century to "The East Village". But somehow we'd managed to find it -- and knowing I'd be there every Sunday afternoon helped me through the week like plasma.

Bernie was only about 18 when I met him, three years older than me, though I never told *him* that. He wasn't handsome or anything. Actually, he was kind of awkward yet still attractive, and he had his **own apartment** where, on Sunday afternoons, as dependably as clockwork, you could find just about any *poet* -- or any fat Morticia from the suburbs wanting to stretch her wings.

Bernie Eisner's was the hottest ticket in town. And I was proud to be there. And so was Ellie – with all the cool beatniks and wannabes who could squeeze in and find a spot on the mattresses that lined the floors. Everyone was welcomed -- for as long as they wished to stay. Some people stayed for days, some even longer than that, and Bernie didn't seem to mind, especially if they brought a guitar or a bottle of cheap mountain wine. Crowds of beautiful young *poets* and *artists* of every race and color pressed against one another like asparagus stalks within the small, antiquated space. And then there was Ellie and me, awe-struck, grateful and itching for flight.

Ellie really knew how to work the room. She could have any guy she wanted, not that she did a whole lot with them, *or so I thought*. But I'd always see her holding court with a bunch of them or necking in a corner with one or the other till it was time for us to head back to Brooklyn. It wasn't the same for me, of course, being fat and all, but just being there was enough and, who knows, I reminded myself, *maybe if I try real hard, my luck will change*.

I stood in a corner seductively with a cigarette holder dangling from my lips. The guy next to me moved his head and got burnt on the face. *Damn!* I thought. *Ashes, all over my dress. Now I'll have to move!* Just when I'd finally gotten the cleavage right! *What a klutz he is!* I said to myself. *What a klutz!*

"Oh, I'm so sorry. Are you O.K.?" I ask.

"It's hep," he says, indifferently. "Don't worry. It happens all the time."

Jesus, I thought. *He's so sexy*. "Like Sisyphus," I added, knowingly, as he begins to turn his head away again.

"Huh?"

"Sisyphus, you know. He carries the rock up the mountain but it keeps falling down."

"Yeah, ugh, right," he mutters, scratching his head and returning to his book.

How the hell can he read? I wondered. *It's so dark in here.*

"Are you sure you're all right? Let me get you a little water for that burn." I turn slowly, trying to maintain the cleavage, holding my stomach in tight, trying to keep the cigarette holder in my mouth without hitting anybody else.

"No. I don't need any," he answers. "But since you're getting up, can you grab that gallon of wine over there?"

"Sure. No problem." I reach behind several heads, stretching out my body in a graceful arabesque.

"Thanks," he says, as he places his thumb through the loop at the bottle's neck and hoists the gallon over his wrist.

I marveled and wished he'd marry me.

"Want a slug?," he asks.

God, did I! If only so my lips would touch what his lips had. I didn't care about the wine. *Jews don't drink, anyway.* At least not the Jews I knew. But to have my lips touch that bottle!

"Sure," I said, lifting the wine with my thumb as he had, suffering the weight of the gallon in silence.

"Here. Let me help you," he offers, raising the bottle with ease.

I pursed my lips over the neck of the bottle just right, luscious, red Angelina Jolie lips, careful to sip as a Presbyterian would, properly, without evidence of thirst, knowing full well that Brooklyn was peeking her indelicate head out of the bag.

"Have another swig," he suggests. I comply. "How 'bout another?" I comply again. And once more. My head begins to whirl.

"This wine is quite nice," I slurred.

"Nice? Let me tell you something. This wine is about as bad as it gets."

"Well, let me tell **YOU** something," I say coyly, leaning my body towards him as if to whisper in his ear. "Umm……." I stammer, forgetting what I was about to say. "Umm……"

"Yes?." he asks.

"Umm…….Let me tell you……umm…………..The history of world ideas."

He stares at me blankly, scratching his head again.

"The history of world ideas," I repeat, proud as a peacock.

"The first idea wasn't an idea at all," he shot back without skipping a beat. *"The first idea was an instinct."*

I tensed my spine, lest my body melt. I could barely contain my awe. He was sexier than Jimmy Dean, about the coolest boy I'd ever met. I looked him straight in the eyes, the sexiest look I could summon, then lowered my head so my hair draped over one eye like Rita Hayworth and chuckled knowingly, as if half bored, half amused. I lit another cigarette and sucked the air teasingly, staring him down. He stared back -- reaching over and taking the cigarette from my lips and putting it between his.

STUMBLING HOME

Light-headedness overcame me. My heart threatened to break through my chest. His eyes were glued to mine as I felt him reach across my body and lay his hand on my breast, his fingers reaching into the cleavage that had taken such effort to create. I feared I was going to pass out. I could barely breathe. *Ellie, eat your heart out!* I thought. I tried to pull away, seductively, of course, but pull away, nonetheless. I wanted to stay there more than anything in the world. But I couldn't. I knew I'd die if he reached into my bra and felt the socks. I'd just die.

"You know, I really like you," I said coyly, as I moved his hand away, *"but I really have to leave. It's getting very late."*

"Leave? Don't tell me you have to go home to mommy in the burbs?"

"Hah, not exactly," I flustered. *"Uh...... I have a Nietzsche class tonight. I hate to miss it."*

"Nietzsche? Sunday night?"

"Uh, yeah," I stumbled. *"It's a special kind of thing."*

"Come on, a few more minutes." He reached over, cradling my face in his hands and pressed his lips tightly against mine. The ground beneath me began to sway.

"Ellie," I screamed awkwardly. *"We've got to leave!"* The room was a maze of people. I couldn't see her. *"Ellie,"*

I screamed out again, pushing him away in the nick of time. "We have to go!"

"O.K., O.K.," I heard her respond. *"Meet me at the door."*

It was later than usual when we left Bernie's that night. Much later. Not minutes later or hours, but decades later, generations, light years. At least for me. Ellie seemed the same, just a little annoyed that I made her leave. But she was flying, just like me. We were always flying when we came from Bernie's -- the long walk to the train station seemed over before it began. There was always so much to say. Mostly it was Ellie who'd talk about this guy she'd met or that, and he said this and she said that and blah blah blah! I loved her stories. She could talk to me for hours. I always wanted to hear more. I was never bored. Never. She was my idol. And when she'd tell me that this one kissed her or that one, and he did this and she did that, God! I thought she was a different species. And even though I never had those kinds of stories to tell, it didn't seem to bother her. She was just high as a kite and happy to share it with me and I was happy to listen. Of course, I wished it had been me. But I was never jealous. Not the way you're jealous of someone who has something you *should* have had or *could* have had. That was never a possibility. Kind of like a kid sister watching her big sister get ready for the prom. She's happy for her. She's not jealous. She couldn't go to the prom now even if her big sister didn't -- so she enjoys it with her. That was me. Except that night, when I left Bernie's house, I wasn't a kid sister any more. I wasn't the same as Ellie but I was flying too.

I couldn't get the guy out of my mind. *He touched me! He kissed me. Me! Beastress! This guy kissed ME. He could have kissed anyone but he kissed* **ME**. Nothing would be the same again.

Ellie didn't ask me if anything special happened that night. I suppose there was no reason to assume anything had... So she talked and I listened, the way we'd always done until the train finally came. I hated that train. I hated waiting on the platform for the Brooklyn-bound BMT train that would take us home. I hated *going* home, especially that night. But when the train did come and we started our long trip back, I suddenly understood why I'd labored to graduate early, why I'd labored to waitress in the Catskills for every penny I could save while other girls slow-danced to The Platters.

My mother's face surfaced in my mind as the train wobbled toward Brooklyn. The ride had always been filled with pain - but on that particular night something new emerged. It wasn't the anger I'd felt before or the frustration or even the awe but an overwhelming sorrow, as perplexing as it was unfamiliar. My mother's voice surrounded me. I tried to reach it. Her deafness exploded. I wasn't repelled. Instead, I felt myself press through the rubble towards her. She was a saint, my father said…and I was left to wobble like the train – in confusion, in an abyss of what could only be called homesickness. It was then I knew that my days at THAT home were numbered. I would run away, I resolved, and Ellie, as eager as I, would come, too.

It was that day that convinced me to loose weight and to have a *"nose job."* So many girls in my neighborhood had *"nose jobs"* and I was certain my mother would agree. While she was utterly deaf to my feelings, she was totally aware that a girl needed to be thin and to have a straight nose if she was ever to attract a man. Cartoons that appeared in Germany before and during the war, where sinister, dark complected men, hunched over with large hooked noses, made it clear that these men were the work of the devil and needed to be eliminated. I needn't have to say a word!

That winter we'd gone to Florida, as we usually did, and it was on that vacation that I decided to "fast." I would finally make myself thin.... For almost a month I ate nothing, NOTHING and drank only water.... and the pounds flew off. When I saw my friends a month later, I was thin, wearing "peddle pushers" that were popular at the time but which I'd never worn. My mother, in fact, was apparently so pleased by my transformation that she took me shopping and ALLOWED ME to pick out my own clothes, which she'd never done. A few weeks later she told my father that I was going to have a nose job, which I did! He asked why, saying I was beautiful just the way I was!! In some ways, he was as unconscious as my moth

The transformation was quite startling. I knew I was fat; I knew I had a "hooked nose" but I never realized just how pronounced these two features were until I remedied both of them. Running into my friends on my first day back at school you would have thought I was a visiting movie star. I was absolutely smiling from ear to ear…..and my mother as well. (I had met Ellie at the local diner the day before and she was a bit confused. While she repeatedly said how terrific I looked, I sensed there was more to her reaction….maybe she was a bit jealous. I'm not sure. I'd never experienced any of those competitive feelings in her but, then again, there was never a competition. She was always, indisputably the more talented, the prettier, the one whom boys would absolutely have preferred. But now apparently something had changed.

PREPARING FOR FLIGHT

THE MORE CERTAIN I grew of running away, the more hypnotic the months became. Ellie and I crammed to graduate early. Whatever had motivated us before, the urgency was now clear. We were heading for something that was pulling us toward it with the force of gravity and we willingly surrendered. When the day came, we thought, we'd simply leave and head for Bernie's. The rest would take care of itself. Bernie Eisner, after-all, was our friend and, like the only kid in the suburbs who has a car, his apartment brought him status and rank. Not only would he let us *crash*, he'd help us find our way.

I was looking out at the universe from where I'd once lived, as if I'd been in a terrible accident and had, somehow, been thrown free, unscathed, staring back at the wreckage with utter relief that I'd survived, yet I was still in it, but without pain. I was just a passenger there, just passing through.

In the wake of such mercy the pounds kept slipping away and "*Beastress*" was being transformed, a cross between Morticia and Cher, theatrical and very exotic. I was in a transcendent place, like how a mother must feel just after childbirth -- except I was the child being born.

My knapsack was packed, filled with the only necessities a sixteen year-old run-away would need: one outfit and enough make-up to last in perpetuity: A long black crepe dress falling just above the ankles, hugging my new thin figure like a 1930's couture ad and a black shawl to be draped haphazardly over one shoulder. That's all I'd need. It would serve me well at Bernie's. But it was the black silk opera-length gloves that I'd come to wear routinely on my trips to *The Village* that distinguished the outfit from the ones more conventional girls might choose. On first glance one might have thought of Garbo or Dietrich. But that would have been only a cursory look. Beneath the surface the waist-high cotton underpants and white cotton bra, size 34AA (with a pair of socks to fill the cups), could reveal the true age and station of the wearer.

These items, in and of themselves, weighed little. But it was the shoe-box filled with make-up that made the knapsack heavy: black eye shadows, black eyeliners and black mascara, false eyelashes, white theatrical make-up, hairspray and an assortment of lipsticks limited in colors to white, brown and fire-engine red.

Lest one think I was childish and superficial, my knapsack also contained a pack of Kent cigarettes, a long black cigarette holder, "The Dialogues of Plato," "A New Anthology of Modern Poetry," and "The Living Thoughts of Spinoza." And then there was my guitar. This was no plain Jane, after all, from the suburbs. This was her father's daughter, a very special girl, indeed.

I should clarify: I never read these books and had no intention of ever reading them. I may have "looked them over" occasionally (if my father was nearby), but actually READING them? Never. If I'd had my choice, which, of course, I didn't, I'd have read The Enquirer or some Hollywood gossip rag, but that would have been sacrilegious. I was supposed to read Heine or Goethe or Keats, or as my knapsack attested, The Dialogues of Plato which clearly I was preparing to do!

Liberation began ominously with the first winter storm! Single digits, bleak, overcast skies, frigid winds and occasional flurries of rain and hale. It didn't matter. I was ready for flight. I called Ellie one last time. I could barely stop my hands from shaking or hold back the giggles. Her phone rang. No answer. I tried again. Finally her voice!

"Did you tell them?" I asked, bursting into laughter. *"Did you tell*

them yet?"

"Bea..." She hesitated. "Bea....I..........."

"What? Tell me. Do your parents know you're leaving?"

"I didn't tell them, " she struggled. "I can't................I can't go."

For a moment I froze. The future I'd seen and planned for in my fantasies was falling out of reach. The skies were getting dark again -- and I feared the coffin would shut the way it did every night before. My knapsack and guitar sat at my feet like two lost children waiting for mommy to pick them up and take them home. But there was no mommy but me.

What now? I asked myself as my mind reeled dangerously out of control the way it did when the stakes were just too high. How could she? How could she back out? For all her beauty and smarts, Ellie was a coward. She couldn't leave the sorry sight of mediocrity, *the apex of nowhere, dead center in the bosom of Kansas. Maybe it was different for her. Maybe she didn't die in her parent's home. But for me, the option to stay was no option at all. In my parent's house there was no way home! Not a soul within ear shot, even if you screamed bloody-murder through the whole damned Plains. Not a house, not a person. You could scream till the cows come home and it wouldn't make a shit-load of difference.*

When I finally understood that, like the day my brother broke my arm and no one came to help, I finally understood that this was not my home and no one would make it so, I reached for my knapsack and guitar to find my place, alone, fortified by the $20.00 bill my father had slipped into my pocket.

The drive was quick. Uneventful. Just another lift to the station. No mention of anything out of the ordinary. My brother had gone off to college the year before and was never missed. It's not like he'd joined the army or anything. God forbid! Now *that* would have been a calamity! He was off to *college* -- and one day he'd become a great doctor. What could be more impressive? So he just left and that was that and no one seemed to notice he was even gone.

Like the time we were seven or eight and my parents took us to the Grand Canyon. We all stood on the precipice, overlooking the great expanse, then returned to the car and took off for California. Twenty minutes down the highway I asked where Manny was. Damn! We'd left him at the Canyon! No one even realized, except for me. We had to drive all the way back with my father cursing and sputtering because of the inconvenience. An *"impudent little pup,"* he kept howling. Whatever the hell **that** meant!

My mother was crying her eyes out. I think she really cared for Manny, even *loved* him, as much as she was able. Maybe she saw him as powerless, like herself -- because my father always beat the hell out of him. But me? No sir. I was my father's girl, she'd mock. Once, when I was six or seven, she taunted me because she said I knew just how to wrap him round my little finger. And the way she said it. God! You'd have thought I was Lady Macbeth -- and only six years old! It's true I tried to be cute and funny to keep his rage at bay (which my brother didn't seem able or willing to do). But that couldn't be what she was referring to, or could it? I wasn't very good at it, after all. It's not like I didn't get my share of whippings. I think it was more that I was just female, one of those *manipulative, flirtatious, deceitful* creatures who could sway men any way they pleased, like the women who came on to my father -- the women who thought my mother couldn't hear a word they were saying to him. God! She hated them. And the more they flirted, the more she renounced *womanhood* and flaunted her gray hair and *finer* thoughts. That was her ace in the hole. She wasn't a woman like other woman; she wasn't like me. Maybe that's the way she saw it.

So if I ran away, I didn't think I'd be terribly missed. She'd rant and rave for a while. *How could I do this to* **her***? Embarrass* **her** *this way? What would her family think? What boy would want a girl who's been* **"around".**

But my father would help her see the light. *It was a tribute to*

them, he'd say, that their daughter left. He even drove her to the train, after all! She's ***"a chip off the old block,"*** he'd remind her. It's not like she was running away from home because they were bad parents or anything. She wasn't *running **away*** at all. She was going off to write a great novel, and only 16 years old! *She must be very gifted, from a very impressive family. What a special young woman from such special parents.* Yes, that's how I supposed it would be put to rest.

My mother's face haunted me as I took the train, one last time from Sheepshead Bay for Manhattan. What I'd imagined would be a blissful journey felt only like sorrow and loss, a terrifying detour through fragile terrain, back through the unfinished business in my head. *But now was not the time,* I told myself. *Forget about them!* But it was no use.

My body rocked with the graceless movement of the antiquated train - and my mind spun dangerously to its depths. *Why do they let the trains get as vulgar as this?* Bumping and grinding like an old vaudeville stripper who no longer gives a damn how her act is received. She just takes the money and runs. Too many years giving her all when she believed something might come of it -- and now, with hope gone, there's nothing left but bitterness and jaded old bones, creaking off-tempo to music that's as "has-been" as she, the music that was trash to begin with because it was meant for this crowd alone. Know your audience! That's what they say, like the trains that take you from one strip club to the next.

Why are the trains so bad? Because I've got no money? Because I'm just a kid -- trying to move on. My father was right! It's a world for the rich. To hell with the poor slobs who ride the trains. They're lucky they have a train to ride in in the first place. Now they're gonna whine about the dirt and the noise and corruption at City Hall? Let 'em walk!

I couldn't get my mother's face out of my mind as I wobbled back and forth on the train to my liberation. *She was leaning over me, pulling the blanket to my neck as I was just about to sleep, there in that dirty, old train. Her face was soft. Her eyes were quick and piercing. She could see much more than she chose to see. I knew it as she looked down at me -- that she could see deep into my thoughts, but that she wouldn't, anymore than she would search her own with wonder and despise. Sometimes I thought she saw me, for a second, just for a second, then threw the image into oblivion with disgust! Ever so often I sensed that what she saw in me, in that instant, she tossed into the garbage dump with all repellent notions that plagued her in herself. It made me ashamed and guarded of her powers -- that I was what I shouldn't be, and she knew it. In her eyes she saw it -- because she had been there once and bore me from her self.*

Why does she look at me with such contempt? Why do I think of things she wouldn't? Why do I want what I shouldn't? Why am I her anger and desire? How I wished that she would fall, that she would be corrupted in her virtue, tainted, like I. I saw it in her face, her righteousness. She never did what she shouldn't. But I, in the heap of her desires, feeling them for her, with all their confusion and constraints -- I, whom she gave birth to as if evacuating her self of her humanity in one, huge, agonizing movement in the shit-hole! And she was done with it at last. But I, how I cried when she looked at me that way, like the stench she'd swiftly cleansed away, then beat to death with piercing, punishing eyes for ever having been inside. I tried to look away. She leaned over me with her soft, plain face and magic eyes. She frightened me, such a plain and gentle face. I was confused by the horror in her eyes -- as she kissed me, separated from me by the vast and sterile distance she put between all the good and evil within herself. And by the time I reached the city, never to return again, I wondered if I was like her.

Greenwich Village: 1958. The bitter cold had silenced the city and overcast skies hovered as if in mourning. Not a good day for running away, I thought, as if any days were good enough for that kind of thing. Another girl, a *normal* girl, might have prepared for the winter storm. But not me -- in my little black ballet slippers and fishnet hose, wading through the frozen streets, shivering to the bone. It didn't matter, though. My feet looked dainty in those black *Capezio's*. *"So feminine…So light on her feet,"* they'd whisper if they saw me that day.

The closer I got to Bernie's place, the more I surfaced. I'd left a girl behind whom I'd inhabited without choice. I could feel myself coming to life, coming out of a play where I'd been terribly miscast, regaining some energy that only existed when I was far away from home. Bernie would take me in. He'd promised. I'd died and gone to heaven. Galoshes weren't worn at the Pearly Gates.

My knapsack and guitar tugged on my shoulders as I waited in the street for him to return. As the hours past, my skin trembled under my thin, black shawl, wet and defenseless by the time the sun began to set. Bernie was always home. That's how Bohemians were. They slept a lot. But not that day. Not the day that mattered. Finally, I walked crosstown to McDougal St. and 3rd, to Figaro's, a corner café where lost souls like me could play a game of chess to occupy the time before life occurred. I was only sixteen but I played a mean game of chess. I loved playing with the old geezers and whipping their pants off as strangers watched and marveled at this very special girl child. I played for hours that day and only stopped long after darkness had fallen and the late dinner crowd converged on Figaro's.

Then I knew it was time again to leave. But where to? Where would I go? How long would it take me to get there? Who would greet me when I arrived? What would become of me? Who would know what had occurred? I shuddered….and thought of going home, just for a moment, till suicide reappeared, full-bodied, in my mind. Home was not my home. That was clear. Nothing in that cold night could force me to return. Nothing frightened me like the thought of going back. There was no choice. I packed up my belongings and walked out aimlessly into the frigid night air, walking from one street to the next, stopping now and then to call Bernie. When my body could barely tolerate the winds a moment longer, I stepped into a doorway for cover.

There, above the door, I noticed a sign, ambiguous and understated: "JUDSON STUDENT HOUSE," like the sight of Jesus for a Catholic on his deathbed. *Student House*. A safe harbor. An honorable place for a Jew. I could rest here a while as I waited for Bernie to return. I knocked on the door. Students. Of course they'd let me in. The door opened. A tall, staid man in his thirties greeted me.

"Can I help you," he asked, kindly, as he motioned me into the foyer.

Before I could answer, a telephone rang. He closed the door behind me to shut out the cold and motioned for me to wait in the foyer as he took the call in a room off to my right. There, from the alcove, I could see it was an office, unremarkable by any standards, the way offices usually are, but to my left. Ah. That was a different story. To my left was a room unlike any I'd ever seen.

The room was ordinary enough, maybe a bit more dilapidated than most. But it wasn't the condition that caught my eye. It was a young Indian woman sitting at a dinning table, laughing as she reached unselfconsciously *with her fingers* for a platter of food in the center. I flinched instinctively as if she'd belched. Her eyes glittered and fixed on several Indian men who seemed to be competing good-naturedly for her attentions, indifferent to or unaware of her peculiar manners. Then I realized that others, perhaps all of the dozen or so people in the room, were doing the very same thing, talking and laughing as they ate. It wasn't the talk that made my brow rise. It was the laughter. Everything else was incidental.

I'd never seen a dinner with laughter, at least not in my home. Make yourself invisible. That was the point. Stay out of the line of fire. One false move and the axe falls. Isn't that the way it is? Stuffing spinach down your mouth or he'll beat the shit out of you!

Yes, Daddy. No, Daddy. Thank you, Daddy. Please. And even then, you'd never know if the stock market closed up or down. You'd never know if the spinach would stay put in your stomach or high tail it out of your small intestines! *An inhospitable environment.* That's what they said at the Salem Witch Trials: make the body so uninviting that even the devil leaves. That's why they burnt them alive, poor souls. Damn! Even my spinach ran away! How bad must a body feel to scare the hell out of spinach!

But not here. Not in this peculiar place. I stared at the dining room like a kid with her nose in the pastry-shop window. I knew immediately it was where I belonged. In the foyer of JUDSON STUDENT HOUSE, on the coldest day of the year, I had come home. *It **must** become my home. And why not? I could be a student again. What safer route could I take?* My heart raced. *If only he'd get off the phone and invite me into his family.* The seconds passed endlessly. My body that had been so cold just moments before. was now warm as a baby, as I waited for him to return. I scanned every inch of the room with utter delight, until another sign, directly overhead, caught my eye: *"Judson Student House,"* the notice read, *"An **International** Residence for 25 **foreign** students from around the world!"*

I shuddered. It was over as quickly as it had begun! For a moment there'd been hope, a marker on an unfamiliar road. And then it disappeared, like a forest fire incinerating the oxygen in its path. *Foreign students! They're all foreign students and I'm just a kid from Brooklyn!*

I had barely regrouped when the man returned.

"I'm Reverend Moody," he announced, gently. "How can I help you?"

Suddenly the disappointment vanished without any apparent reason. I remember regaining my composure and smiling though I had no idea why. I had transcended my self………..gone where the conscious mind forbids ---yet a sense of inestimable well-being accompanied me and lit me up like a beacon in the darkest tunnel of hell.

"I…uh……. Beatricia," I said reflexively like the movement of the hands when you're about to fall. "Beatricia, how you say, from…uh uh…. ˞˞˞˞˞˞˞˞˞˞˞˞˞˞˞˞˞˞˞da Ukraine."

JUDSON

"THE UKRAINE! HOW interesting! Reverend Moody gushed as his face piqued with curiosity. *What are you doing in New York?"*

"I...uh... I exchange student."

"Really! We don't see many Soviet students these days." I smiled in agreement. *"Where are you studying?"*

"Da university...uh....Queens College," I said, cautiously, flirting with the sounds of my childhood, the Russian sounds, Yiddish sounds, the sounds my parents spoke at home - telling the stories of the other side, the Ukraine, the pogroms, the war. It was part of me. It just needed dusting. And had I been asked at the time, in confidence, I probably might have said it was merely the demands of circumstance that brought these sounds to my lips. Yet, even then, I would have known, somewhere in the clutter of history, that there was more at stake, some great pressure to claim this foreign voice as my own, some inclination, however unrefined, to speak a convoluted truth. Like the time, years before, when we'd left the unveiling for fat Aunt Bertha. *Damn! I couldn't stand Aunt Bertha. Always mean and nasty if you sat on the wrong chair or the sofa without the plastic. And her cheap coins on your birthday, like she was some kind of sport. And I was supposed to thank her and kiss her on her fat old face. Damn! Didn't she ever hear of electrolysis? It's O.K.* I wanted to scream out as we left the cemetery. *She's really dead and gone. You can all stop acting like you care. You can start laughing again and being yourself. O.K. now. Who gets the lamp -- and the*

silver plate? Who's going through the bank accounts? Where's the bagels and lox?

"I study...uh... art history, " I continued without faltering.

"Wonderful. Come in here to my office. I'll give you an application. We actually **do** have a room available. You're very lucky because it's rare that we do."

"Oh! I so...uh...How you say.....uh....excited."

"Well, it will be wonderful for Judson. I'm sure everyone will have a million questions to ask you about Russia. It's so unusual these days to meet someone from the Soviet Union, what with the Cold War and all. I didn't know they were allowing any exchange of students. This is very exciting. We'll have much to talk about."

Damn! I said to myself! *The Cold War?* I'd heard something about a cold war but given the tumult that was my life, I hadn't thought it necessary to inquire.

"Why don't you take the application with you and return it tomorrow. You can move in then, if it's not too soon."

"Oh! Not too soon at all."

"Where are you staying now, by the way?"

"Well...um...I ...uh... staying with some...uh relatives in Brooklyn. I come to...uh... New York today to find room because...uh..it is long...uh..long trip to the University. You know, it is....uh... like Kiev here......... very...um...cold."

"Yes, indeed. You picked a bad day to be looking around. You must have a lot of stamina."

"I not..uh...understand."

"Stamina. Energy."

"Nyet. Uh...I mean... No. I don't," I said with obvious fatigue.

"Well, look, Beatricia..."

"Beatricia," I interrupted. "'Beatricia' it is good."

"O.K., Beatricia. If you'd rather not go back to Brooklyn this late in the evening, I could give you the room tonight. It's empty now, so *there wouldn't be any problem. Would you prefer that?"*

"Oh! Dis is…. uh… so kind of you… But…I don't want to…uh… make difficult."

"It's not difficult at all. You'd just have to complete the application and give me the first week's rent in advance."

My body froze then thawed the next moment when he completed the sentence.

"It's only $15.00 a week -- and that includes your meals. I can explain everything to you once your settled and introduce you to all the other students. I'm sure they'll be thrilled to meet you. What do you think?"

"Oh…uh…Reverend Moody," I sighed with relief. *"I so happy. Dis would be wonderful."*

"Yes. I think so, too. Welcome to our home."

"I so happy to be here…It has taken….uh…. long time."

"I'm sure it has."

"Oh," I said coyly. *"You can't imagine."*

You know how some people just seem to be lucky? Things come to them without great pain or heartache. They don't have to suffer to get where they're going. They don't have to beg. They don't have to pay the piper with blood. They don't have to fight to hold back the tears. They just seem to have been blessed -- like a house, untouched by a raging fire that levels every home around it. It's just the luck of the draw. Some people are born into war, into carnage, some are born infirmed, some are born with bad genes that make them think insects are creeping into their eyeballs, some are born with pleasant dispositions and rarely get mad or rattled, some are born high-strung and get mad if it's raining in Jersey, some are born into wealth, into the right country, the right race, the right moment in history. Others aren't so lucky and wait to be resurrected to get another shot at the brass rings. When I opened the door in Greenwich Village to that 7 by 9 foot room on the corner of Thompson and 3rd, I was one of the blessed.

My room at Judson was smaller than Ellie's room in Brooklyn, 7 by 9, at most, a second floor room with a window on to the fire escape. If I leaned out, I could almost touch the street below. The old and rickety furniture was on its last legs. The walls hadn't been painted in years. I suppose some people might have been disappointed in the room, its size and condition and closeness to the street. But, for me, there was nothing more perfect, more beautiful in the entire world.

I unpacked my few belongings, arranging them like precious jewels in a Tiffany window then returned downstairs where Reverend Moody and my new family awaited me: Sinai, Amir, Alfredo, Juan, Suri, from countries whose names I'd never heard before -- more peculiar names and faces and national dress than I could ever recall, more schools and courses of study than I knew existed. I was dumbstruck in their midst, awed and overwhelmed.

They invited me to join them for dinner. I graciously declined. Not that I wasn't hungry. I was. I'd eaten nothing all day for fear of depleting the little money I had. And furthermore, I thought, *I'm far too delicate to eat, too angelic. I hoped they'd realize. I eat like a bird, like a young Slavic dove. I've hardly any appetite at all. Don't let my hips deceive you. This isn't fat. It's muscle from good peasant stock and hours in the fields. I'm dainty. Can't you see? Watch how I move my hands. These are the hands of a tragic child who's wandered aimlessly through the camps of Displaced Persons and lost souls. These are the fragile hands of a child of the War. Take her in. She won't trouble you at all. She'll give -- and take nothing in return, not even your food. She'll entertain and amuse you and make you feel ten feet tall. Just ask. She'll be whomever you wish. It's as simple as that. It's your call.*

"Your accent is so interesting," Sinai said. "I've never heard one like it. Is it Polish or Czech or maybe Rumanian?"

"Vell.....It is many dialects. Ve moved so much during da war."

"How did you manage to get here? I heard Russia stopped sending students to America."

"Oh! It is such long story. I left my home during the var. I vas in DP camp. I don't like to talk about dis." I bowed my head.

This is heavy stuff I told them silently. You have to understand. I've had a terrible life. War, havoc, DP camps. Excuse me, but DP WHAT? Displaced Persons, you fool. Don't you know anything about the war? Oh! DP camps, sure. My parents used to talk about them when I was a kid. They even got some family out of Europe who were displaced during and after the war. God! They had it rough! Their families killed, their homes destroyed. Look, this isn't easy stuff to talk about. I can't just open up at the drop of a hat. Could you, if you'd been through what I've been through?

They understood without a word spoken. They saw it when I bowed my head, how inappropriate it is to question the victim of such horror, especially over the dinner table. *How would you feel about a reporter sticking a microphone in your face if your kid's just been decapitated before your eyes?*

"Excuse me, ma'am. But could you tell us how it feels to look for your kid's head? Did you see it roll? Was it upsetting?"

They all got it and held their tongues -- except for Sinai, the older guy with a turban and piercing black eyes. He thought I looked Indian, he said. He could have sworn I had Indian blood. *Was I certain of my ancestry?* He asked. *I looked just like his cousin from Bengal, like an Indian princess. Sinai,* I thought. *Come on! Tell me, what you're up to? Haven't you ever seen a young Russian gypsy? They **all** look like Morticia when she was a kid.* Jeez, he was persistent. *O.K., if you must know, I **am** part Indian, but I can't go into it now. I really can't.* I bowed my head again. Alfredo, the handsome young Spaniard, came to my rescue.

"Sinai, she just got here. Give her a chance."

Sinai speared him with his eyes, a look of a thousand words.

STUMBLING HOME

What's this? A duel over ME? Not possible. Maybe Sinai is interested. Sure. He's middle-aged with a long nose and a turban. But Alfredo? Never! He's much too handsome! But either way, it didn't matter, for they talked to me late into the night, protectively, as if I were the last born and most vulnerable of their clan, as if I were the baby sheep who'd gotten separated from the herd and had somehow found her way home. I glowed. If the world tried to hurt me, Alfredo or Sinai would take my back. I knew it the minute I bowed my head.

So I guess it's no wonder that I slept sound as a baby for the very first time, in my very own room, with not a single coffin in sight.

REBIRTH

IN THE MORNING, light poured through my window, as if by magic, and I knew I'd gotten a reprieve. There'd be no more begging or pleading or gasping for air. There'd be no more punishment. All I had to do now was survive. Oddly enough, the logistics of **that,** of getting by, didn't phase me in the least. It had something to do with neglect. Let me explain:

Someone once told me that if you want to make kids crazy, tell them that what they see, they don't. Now, they can be poor or persecuted or mistreated, but that won't necessarily make them nuts. They might be so poor or so persecuted or so mistreated that they hate and rage -- or even kill, but they won't necessarily be nuts. If you want to make kids nuts, tell them what they see, they don't. I was *almost* one of those kids. But I had a saving grace. No one was *bent* on making me crazy. That wasn't in the cards. My parents were far too busy with their own illusions to focus that kind of energy on me. For the most part, I was just invisible. And even if they weren't too busy, they weren't diabolical. That's not what they were about. They weren't knowingly cruel.

Like this boy I'd read about in the paper. His mother raised him in a chicken coop on some remote farm in Appalachia where no one even knew they existed. She put him in this coop when he was a kid and he grew up in it with all the other chickens. Well, he didn't really grow **up** in it. He **aged** in it and he grew bent and misshapen, like a chicken -- and he made sounds like a chicken, like all the other chickens! Some townspeople finally discovered him but it was far too late to undo the damage.

Now **this** mother had a plan! There was nothing uncertain about that. God knows why. Maybe she thought she was a chicken, too. Who knows? The point is, she was hell-bent on a course of action -- and he was it! So even if he wanted to, he couldn't *chicken out*, so to speak!

And that's the difference. I could. I wasn't anybody's course of action. Neglect has its virtue. When I caught the crap it was because I was in the wrong place at the wrong time. My mother didn't *try* and make me crazy by keeping the light on all night. She just wasn't thinking about me. Maybe if some psychologist shook her and said, *"Look, you're hurting this child by what you're doing,"* she probably would have turned the light off. That's not to say she would have been responsive to anything else. She wouldn't have been, unless you shook her again and lectured her about the next infraction -- every step of the way. You can't make someone think about you when they're not interested. That's just the way it is.

And my father didn't plot and scheme to beat the shit out of us like some sadistic serial killer. We were just in his way. So he struck out like you do when you kick a chair that you've just tripped over. *Damn chair! I'll fix you!*

Now I don't want it to seem that I'm defending them or excusing them or trivializing the pain they created, because I'm not. We all know the road to hell is paved with good intentions. I'm just trying to highlight the fact of their indifference, that I wasn't on anyone's mind or in anyone's thoughts -- and that saved the day -- for if that hadn't been so, it would have meant being raised as a chicken and I'd rather take the indifference.

Of course, I had no choice anyway. But getting back to my original point: The task of "survival" didn't phase me in the least for one of the consequences of my parent's indifference was that I had to fend for myself and become resourceful, and that I did.

Maybe I was crazy, maybe I was psychotically depressed, maybe I was even the cause of my own pain, but I **was** resourceful. I could do things that most kids my age couldn't even imagine. Not a lot of fun things, mind you, like getting a date for the prom or feeling good about myself. Those things were inconceivable, so far out of reach. They were part of another vocabulary in another person's life. But I was resourceful in other ways. I could build things, fix things, or get a job, most any job, and keep it if I had to. If they wanted a salesgirl, I could be a salesgirl. If they wanted a waitress, I could be a waitress. If they wanted a switchboard operator, I could be a switchboard operator. I learned fast. I could look at a map and figure out how to get from A to B in a heartbeat. I could check out a puzzle and know the solution before most people even knew it was a puzzle.

So, when I awoke Monday morning, the task of providing for myself didn't seem difficult. I left Judson early and headed for an employment agency that booked kitchen staff for Catskill resorts. After a few minor *corrections* on my birth certificate I had a weekend job as a waitress at the Concord Hotel in upstate New York. Next, I took two subways and a bus and enrolled with ease in Queens College. It was only reality, after all. It was only real.

Sinai was at my door when I returned, ready to paint my room. *Clearly the room was a mess, but why was he going to paint it?* I didn't understand. *Was this **his** job at Judson?* I wondered. *Hadn't he told me the night before that he was working on a Ph.D in economics, his 'second doctorate,'* he said, *whatever the hell **that** was? How come he's a house painter? And at his age! It was sad, a grown man, almost middle-aged, having to work for his keep.*

I thanked him but, *no, it wasn't necessary*. The last thing I needed was to spend money for someone to paint my room. I could do that myself. That was part of my resourcefulness, too. But he kept insisting, as if it weren't open to discussion -- and I kept thanking him but declining, till he simply opened the can of paint and began the job, like I hadn't said a word – like a guy on the Bowery with a squeegee brush and a bucket of water. *Damn! Now what am I supposed to do now? How much will **this** cost? But how could I argue? That would be so gauche. If I had enough money to get me here -- all the way from the Ukraine, I must have enough money to paint my dirty walls.*

I tried to work with him, thinking it would lower the price, but he wouldn't hear of it. *Damn!* He had me. I was a sitting duck. The night before he had seemed so caring, so protective. But, of course, it was too good to be true! He was just another capitalist out to make a buck off the back of a peon! See! When the chips are down, it's every man for him self! *How could you fall for this nonsense about watching your back? It's a dangerous world, girl. You better wise up.*

Then Alfredo walked in, too, with a brush in **HIS** hand. So not only didn't I have a say about getting my room painted, I didn't seem to have a say in who got hired to do the job! *Shit! Alfredo and Sinai!* I thought. *They're both on the take! And here Alfredo had told me his father was a real big-shot, a Minister of State or something! He's got some nerve trying to squeeze a few dollars out of a kid who'd escaped from a DP camp! Some people have no heart!* I turned away in disillusion just as there was a knock on my door. It was the Danish political science student.

"Let me help," she said kindly.

"Nyet! Nyet!, "I urged. "Everything is fine. It almost done."

"There must be **something** I can do. How can I help?" she asked, as Subaga walked in with a bouquet of flowers.

"Welcome, Beatricia," they said in unison.

"*Vus es dus? I mean... vhat is dis?*" I asked, dumbfounded.

"For you. We're so happy you're with us. We want to help also. Here, I brought a broom from downstairs. I'll sweep. Lisandros will be up after school. They're going to wax the floor. Shulamit is doing the window. Everybody will be home for dinner tonight for a proper welcome."

I stood motionless without saying a word. Not even a "thank you " emerged from my lips. They might have thought me ungrateful had they not noticed the tears streaming down my cheeks.

HOW TO MAKE A DEAF SAINT

SUCH A SIMPLE act of kindness. Yet I couldn't shake the bewilderment it unleashed, the unalterable return in my mind to the family I'd never really left, to the questions that pressed for answers. And the greater the kindness, the greater my confusion.

I doubt that my brother had experienced as much neglect as I, at least not in the same way - for I sensed that the kindness I was shown that first day at Judson would not have felt as foreign to him. I could be wrong. Maybe it had to do with gender, that boys had always been more valued. He would probably have disagreed. (It's not that he didn't get his share of whippings. He did, maybe even worse than me and he was, after all, our father's son. That brought with it its own unique pain that I didn't understand until years later. And when I did I was able to forgive him and love him).

Maybe neither of us was truly wanted. Maybe our parent's marriage left no room for that sort of thing. They'd waited, after all, so long to have children. Why? I knew so little of the circumstances surrounding our births, so little of who our parents were before we were born, only bits and pieces, mythologies, no doubt, from subjective sources who had a stake in the narratives they endorsed.

STUMBLING HOME

What I do know is that Samuel and (Gypsy) were married in 1926, give or take a year. They settled in The Village and, with their only wealth, their books, they opened a small, second-hand bookshop on Eighth Street and Fourth Avenue in what was then *The Bible House*. They lined the shelves of *"Camelot Books"* with their trousseaux, their own obscure and treasured volumes that had been their closest friends and their potential. So it's no surprise that New York's intellectual elite claimed the shop as their home or that my father's wit and charm kept them coming -- to talk books and poetry and politics and buy what couldn't be bought anywhere else. And it's no surprise that Gypsy, timid and soft-spoken as she may have later become, took her rightful place beside him -- above the fray, the high priest and priestess of the left.

In short order they opened a second bookshop, then a third and a fourth -- from 57th Street to Eighth. My father wrote, as if on a freight train headed for a cliff, needing to leave some record of what had been. His plays marked him as a man to watch. For fourteen years they prospered and traveled the world. The only problem in their idyllic lives seems to have been the fact that they couldn't have children, a problem later minimized by my mother when we spoke, the way she'd minimized the wallop of my father's hand.

The issue of childlessness needs some elaboration. Several years after I ran away from home, after I left Judson, I went to see a therapist. I was eighteen at the time and in a tailspin. The early sessions focused on family history, how wonderful my parents were, how special, how perfect their lives had been, how incongruous it was that two such remarkable people should have such a confused and despondent daughter. My analyst suggested there was more to the story than met the eye. But I was stolid --- until one day when he told me my mother had called him.

"WHAT!!!" I gasped, shuddering as if invaded by a hostile tribe.
"She wanted to know why you're coming here............."

"What did you tell her?" I asked incredulously.
"That I couldn't discuss it with her."
"What did she say?"
"She didn't like that at all."
"She must have been r e a l l y mad!"
"But not in the way I would have expected…………………" he added.
"What do you mean?"
"……………………..Why didn't you tell me your mother was a bitch?"

I probably would never have returned to his office except that something was unraveling – and I knew it. I was in trouble, now more than ever. *How dare he! How dare he!* Something was coming apart inside of me. I wanted to tell him I was never coming back, that I didn't like him anymore, that it wasn't safe. But something held me back.

It wasn't the call itself, he explained, that raised his eyebrows. It was the tone of my mother's voice. This wasn't the gentle, tentative, unobtrusive woman I'd described to him again and again. A woman at peace. This wasn't a voice of powerlessness. To the contrary, he said. Even *he* got the willies. So what was this discrepancy about, he asked. One of us was misreading her. Is it possible, just possible, he posed, that what I saw as her timidity was a steely power, a rage, insidious and unassailable, a power that ultimately exerted far more influence over me than my father's belt?

When you're hit with a belt, he said, *you know it's a belt. The enemy is clear. My mother's belt was elusive. I couldn't see it. I didn't even know it was a belt. I thought it was my own fist.* So when the pain from this invisible enemy tore through me, it was worse than a belt -- for I couldn't fight back or even lick my wounds. I couldn't even find them -- nor could anyone else. The only evidence of their existence was as hidden as the weapon itself, a relentless, gnawing self-hate and a tango with the fantasy of death.

STUMBLING HOME

This was the prison he wanted to dismantle when he called my mother a "bitch." *But if it were true,* he said, *why was it true? Who was she? How could I not know her? How could she not let me know?*

I went to my father for answers. Despite his discomfort, despite his unassailable belief that all this "therapy" was voodoo, that it was the fad of the day, the vacuous new religion for the masses, he sensed my urgency and pain and did what he'd done several times before, let me know that I was heard and entitled to his respect.

"Things weren't always perfect," he said with great hesitation. They'd had their share of problems. My mother couldn't have children and it tore away at the foundation of their marriage.

"She had a condition, " he went on, awkwardly, as if he were walking on hot coals, *"called vaginismus,"* where the muscles of the vagina contract and prevent penetration. They'd never had sex, he claimed. Not really. So when my mother got her young cousin out from Europe at the start of the war and came to live with them, my father succumbed to his arousal and they had an affair and ran off together. To say I was dumb struck would have been an understatement, like finding out at 40 that you were adopted or that you had three other siblings.

I thought suddenly of my mother. She seemed changed, as if she'd unclenched her fist and extended her opened palm. My mother begged him to come home, he explained. But he wanted children desperately and knew he could never have them with her. He returned only briefly, to formalize their separation. And it was then, as if governed by some destiny or chance, that they had sex for the very first time and she conceived. Just like that! JUST LIKE THAT!! It was what he longed for and all plans for divorce were curtailed. My brother was born in 1941 and just months later she was pregnant **again**, with me. For a man who'd known such loss, these gifts were immeasurable.

I was startled by what he said, that I was my mother's daughter and yet I never knew these things, never was privy to her wounds. It's not like she'd broken her arm, after all, and was out of commission for a month. These were years and years of disappointment, years and years of all it meant in the 30's and the 40's to be **barren**! What did she do with that woman, with **Barren Etta?** *Why didn't she tell me where she'd been? Why didn't she let me in?* She was ashamed, my father said, too ashamed to let anyone know. No one knew the truth of it.

I had a thousand questions, as if a dam had ruptured. I was hungry for answers and, knowing my father's moodiness, I wondered if I'd ever have another such opportunity. I plowed forward. They left the city after Manny was born (named for Moishe, our father's father), he continued, and they took an apartment in Brooklyn. It's what immigrants did with the first flush of prosperity, the flight from the cities and the beginnings of a middle class.

"Wasn't that hard for you, giving up The Village?"

"Yes" my father went on. But they were old for parents and their lives had profoundly changed. They needed to conform, to live like other parents, to do what was *"best for the children."*

"'The Village' is no place to raise a family," my grandfather, the Rabbi, would remind them, with all the rebels and bohemians and *immigrants*. It was time to settle down the way **proper** parents did, to leave their Bohemian lifestyle behind. And so they sold their stores and moved to Brooklyn and embarked on a whole new chapter in their lives.

I couldn't imagine the change. The logic escaped me. Brooklyn, the place I'd run from. The Great Plains. Why would someone **choose** that route? Didn't they see the pitfalls in the road? I was caught off guard. It was important to me to see them as *Bohemians*, as if that somehow exonerated them.

"Artists are different," my mother would say. *"You have to excuse them and be patient."*

But it wasn't only the conformity that scared me. It wasn't just

Brooklyn and its colorlessness. It wasn't a judgment. It wasn't cerebral. It was sadness I felt, empathy for my mother, as if she were about to be crushed and I assumed it was Brooklyn that would chop her up.

I thought of Gypsy, the first girl in her family to wear knickers, the first girl in her family to ride a bicycle. That was very bold in those days, so *unladylike*. I thought of her reading poetry at The Russian Bear. She was different from the other girls. That's what I'd been told. She was a ball of fire, with her long braids down her back and the brightest colors you could imagine. That's why they called her "Gypsy" after all. I thought how hard it must have been to "settle down." I knew she had been an atheist, a socialist, a non-conformist. But the woman I knew as "mother" was a distant, unrecognizable mutation of that woman who once had been.

The body is amazing, isn't it? That it can do what it has to do to preserve itself, that it has its own alarms that can set off the sprinkler before you even know there's a fire. Maybe it's called "vaginismus." Maybe it's what women of the 30's and 40's contracted when they weren't sure if they wanted to be mothers. And maybe it was only "cured" when their men were about to stray.

You know the stories of the frail mother who lifts a car to save her child pinned beneath it? Yes, the mind can do amazing things when it must.

So it shouldn't have surprised me what my father said, the logic of it. Had my mother wanted children in the first place? Did she want the stage my father occupied as a mere birthright? I suspect my brother's birth had been the price she willingly paid to preserve her marriage. And that baby was a boy, after-all. The first son of the first son. A price well worth it. His birth was accompanied by great celebration and praise for my mother. But **MY** birth, a year later, a *daughter*, a *second* child? That was a different story. I was superfluous.

A chord had been struck by my father's tale. I knew in my heart that the story was true. It made my head reel with an ancient memory I'd somehow preserved for safekeeping. I could see my mother standing over my crib, her long braids reaching down far enough that I could touch them, grabbing them in my little fist and pulling them as a rider does a horse's reins, this way and that, fast then slow, then fast again, at will. And she, my mother, moving her head with each tug as if to let me lead the way – then shaking her head to tease me with her long braids dangling just out of reach. And I laughed and laughed and laughed. I couldn't have been more than a year old. *Was it a dream? This playful mother and her child? Could it have been real?*

I can see us. I can see her, her bright colors, radiant and unrestrained. I can see the braids -- thick with life and prosperity, longer than any braids I've ever seen since. Can she be real, this Gypsy? Is it just a dream? Her braids reminded me of………..of……………something, something long ago….and dazzling.

There she is again, sitting at the foot of my bed. I must be two now…….or three, at most. Her braids are gone. Her hair is short, close-cropped and the smile is gone from her face. Her clothes are staid and proper, starched as if by the weight of a thousand old-world Rabbis. She's reading me Emily Dickinson. I don't understand -- but I want to. I should. She wants me to. Culture is important!

Oh! Momma. What happened to your lovely hair? Why don't you tease me anymore? Why is your face so sad? Are you mad at me, momma? Please talk to me. Did I do something wrong? Can you hear me, momma? Can you hear? Are you sorry I was born? Please say something, momma. I'm here! -------- *Oh! I'm sorry. Emily Dickinson! I'll try to understand. Poetry matters!*

It was her deafness I heard most on the Great Plains of Brooklyn – the Plains that stole her life and stuffed it in its mediocrity – The Great Plains to which she *gave* her self unwittingly. I heard her deafness but I also heard the swish of my father's belt when he came to sense that the elusive "normalcy" he'd hungered for had arrived, like a flesh-eating bacteria that invades silently, unannounced, from nowhere, from a mere nothing to consume him and his devoted Gypsy. And in the place of these characters created from grandiosity, pathos and mere fatigue, created from the best and the worst of them, came two peculiar souls running blindly into the blade of a rotary saw.

Samuel continued his writing as the very real parameters of his life gradually revealed themselves to his utter dismay. And his once soft-spoken bohemian Gypsy, the custodian of every poem ever written, became, without warning or notice, a warrior for propriety, for mediocrity, at least as it appeared to the outside world. But that passionate spirit of her youth had not really died. It had merely been transformed. She clung to her ordinariness as a lifeline. She grabbed what was expected of her with the tenacity of a martyr. Just as some middle-aged man whose dreams had been shattered might become a warrior for Christ and alert the populace to the dangers of sin and blasphemy, my mother became a warrior for the Jews. Maybe it was all she was learning about what had occurred in Europe, what all America was learning about the unimaginable. Maybe it was her parent's deaths that left her searching for them in her obvious roots. Or maybe it was merely the suburbs and the shattering of narcissism that invariably accompanies age and the awareness of mortality.

Where once she too had been a poet, a rebel, a Bolshevik, now she'd become an armed guard, guarding her family from the anti-Semitism that loomed just below the surface. "Be careful," she'd say to me when I resisted the obvious adherence to religiosity. "You may not call yourself a Jew but the world will!" As deaf as she was, she could hear the whispers of anti-Semitism from another town, from another dimension, from the curious expression on a stranger's face…. and she'd be right. Yet she had no idea that my avoidance also came from my fear of Jewishness, my fear of the reality that accompanied every Jew in the 1940's and '50.s, from the confusion I felt when this otherwise soft spoken woman, seemingly unresponsive to events of the real world, would erupt in paroxysmal outbursts as the news followed events in Europe.

And, with the auditory acuity of a barn owl, she could also hear the lecherous plans of adolescent boys to get into a girl's pants. As invisible as I'd always been, as mute as she'd always been with me, in these two edicts her voice was loud and unrelenting. *The world* will always hate you because you're a Jew and *boys* will always want to get in your pants because you're a girl. This was her legacy to me. This was the ash that was left of her when the fire went out……at least, so I thought, in the confusion of my youth.

Had only someone explained to me her plight, the plight of a smart woman with spunk in 1940's America. And had only someone explained that I might be next! But no one did. Instead, I was *"lucky to be Sam Starr's daughter,"* and *"lucky to have such a saint for a mother! You must be a very proud little girl."* And I believed it too. Maybe more than anyone else. He only beat us because he's great and she only speaks in tongues because real words elude her. Yes, they were very special people, my mom and dad. It was I who was nuts!

SETTLING IN

I DIDN'T KNOW it at Judson, in those early days of magic, that my course had already been set, that sorrow hid imperceptibly behind the moment – behind the mere pause in the evolutionary script. The moment -- a bleep in the biological path ways that were constructed generations before and would make their way through me on their way to their genetic end, a conduit for the evolution of pain. That's all I was, or so I once thought, as if its destination had a life of its own. Sadness was in me as it had been for my parents and perhaps there was nothing to be done about it.

Is it the truth? I wondered. *Is this Displaced Person nothing more than a strip of road, faceless, interchangeable, upon which pain plows through to the next hapless sucker down the pike? Is she just a sitting duck for a biological inheritance so heartless, so indifferent to the road that carries it that it can pummel a Displaced Person as easily as it can a queen?*

Is destiny some hot-shot dancer who grabs her round the waist then pulls her weightless body to surrender in a choreography of triumph and control? Is she putty in his hands, moving this way and that with the slightest pressure of his lead, nothing but inadvertent blacktop upon which he would do what he was meant to do? Or can she change the dance? Can she push and shove, quicken and recoil, Cha Cha though he's bent on a Tango?

SETTLING IN

Maybe my course was set in stone, as perhaps it had been for my parents. Maybe there was something about "imposters" that held a clue to our collective pain and needed to be exposed. Maybe there was nothing we could have done to change a thing. Maybe it was just the luck of the draw. But in those early months at Judson, illusion or not, magic was in the air and I was a kid mesmerized by the slight of hand.

I think it was Mencken who said, *"You are who you choose to be so be careful who you choose."* Well, I didn't think I had *chosen,* per se, at least not deliberately. But, as time went on, I did become a foreign student, a Displaced Person, a (sometimes) orphan, a sometimes *anything* that was called for to stay the course. Yet despite these deceptions, nothing in my life **before** Judson had ever felt as authentic. Maybe **that's** what's crazy! Maybe it was Bea **from Brooklyn** who was the imposter, whose life was filled with pretense and mythology and half-truths. Bea Starr, a Displaced Person from the Ukraine, was far closer to the truth of my experience, far closer to what it **felt** like to be me.

Of course, I could never have put that together in my head at the time, that some greater truth was, inadvertently, making itself known. But it was, nonetheless, and it filled me with vitality and the hope to go on. There was fear, too, of course, the fear of exposure -- and shame that I was really crazy! But they were nothing new. I'd lived with them all my life.

I sat on the ledge of my opened window at Judson as if it were a saddle, two stories up, one leg *dangling* over the side, strumming my guitar to songs of the Red Army Chorus while people gathered on the street below. It was the music of my childhood and I'd mastered it well. No Bobby Daren for me. Russian gypsy songs, Communist marches, Paul Robeson, *Negro* spirituals, Mahalia Jackson, Burl Ives, songs of the I.W.O., songs of protest and liberation. That was **my** repertoire.

Passer-bys applauded and asked for more.

STUMBLING HOME

"I can't believe your voice," they'd yell up. *"It's so amazing...so deep."* I'd heard that all my life and I suppose there was something to be said for it. But if I could have chosen, I'd have chosen the voice of a *blonde*, a lyrical voice, a soprano, a voice that could sing the *female* lead in Oscar and Hammerstein. But I was a contralto, like a tuba at a Slavic wake! You'd have sworn I was Black -- and male. "Which Side Are You On?" That was **my** song. "'Ole Man River." Another perky musical hit. Dirges were my stock and trade. I was Odetta before I'd ever heard her name. I could belt out a spiritual that would make you lift your arms to the heavens and shout "Hallelujah."

Ditties. That 's the word. I never sang a ditty. Mine were songs of oceanic depth, mourning, loss, the suffering of the human race. I'd learned them from my father who loved *humanity* (but hated *people*). If it played at a malt shop, it wasn't a song for me. If Elvis sang it, I didn't. That's how I picked my songs.

I remember one afternoon belting out a song in Washington Square Park. There were dozens of us: runaways, throwaways, minstrels from here to L.A. You'd find us near the fountain in the center of the park with our guitars and fiddles and bath-tub drums. If it made a sound, someone sang to its music.

I was singing to a great audience in my mind when some guy standing next to me starts ranting and raving and drowning me out. *And his voice! Had he no shame? How could he sing in public with a voice like he'd swallowed bleach? Frank Sinatra he wasn't. And where was the melody? Isn't a song supposed to have one?*

I stopped singing and approached him gingerly to ask him if he could *graciously* just tone it down a bit, just a bit............ when I realized it wasn't a song he was singing after all, at least not the kind of song I'd ever heard of. The words jolted me like an electric shock. I stood humbled in the shadow of this "boy." His outrage shamed me in my silly plight and his vision brought me to my knees. I knew I was in the presence of greatness and I never sang quite so willingly again. Remembering back years later, it must have been, I suspect now, Bob Dylan.

And then there was Cedar Tavern where famous artists hugged the bar, dueling with their alcoholic wit and bickering like children -- ready to deck each other for some imagined slight that occurred twenty years before.
I tried to look mysterious, to catch the eye of one of these icons.
Once I managed to get Franz Klein's attention. I think I stepped on his toe *by accident.* "*Don't you know who that is?*" someone scolded. "*It's Franz Klein.*" How should I have known. He offered me a drink. I accepted, then followed it with several more because that's how we drank in the Ukraine.
I tried to step on de Kooning's toe *by accident* but he was real paranoid about his feet. I think it was de Kooning, anyway. That was the buzz, but he could have fooled me. They all just looked like sloppy old farts .

Most of the time I went to Cedar alone so no one would cramp my style. If Sinai came along -- or Alfredo, that was O.K., too, but it made for a different script. With Sinai, people stared at us, maybe because of his turban or maybe because we looked so odd, a forty-something Hindu and his chalk-faced *Hindu* girl. But I thought they stared because I looked so gorgeous in my sari -- with the dot on my forehead. -- that they stared to eat up the royalty and magnificence in their midst.
He was so proud of me, my dear Sinai, and so attentive. Once he took me to hear Malcolm X speak. He knew a lot of important people, yet he always seemed proud to introduce *them* to *me*. He said I was his *"princess"* and I tried to fit the bill, except when Dan Wakefield came to Judson and Sinai would hiss because he knew I was sweet on Dan and, of course, he was right -- though I think Wakefield had my number but was too much of a gentleman to let on.

STUMBLING HOME

For whatever the minor disappointments, this time at Judson was a gift I never could have anticipated nor ever could repay. It was a time of love and restoration, dues paid to indemnify a long-overdue claim. And even though my claim was rightful and just, I never expected it to be paid.

ALFREDO

EVEN ALFREDO LOVED me. If you ask me why he felt that way, I couldn't answer. Every night, as predictably as dusk, he'd come to my room armed with the poetry of seduction and read to me for hours. Lorca, of course, *in Spanish* -- and though I didn't understand a word, I was seduced -- maybe just by the idea: the voice, the flowers, his eyes staring as they did into my own. It didn't take long for him and Lorca to wear me down.

He was otherworldly, this handsome son of wealth and status. But who hits on a girl with *Blood Wedding*? **He** wasn't one of those guys my mother had warned me about, the ones who take *liberties* then zip up and zip out. The man read me poetry! In Spanish! He never took a "liberty", except for the first amendment. And it was no secret to anyone that he was in love with me. Can you imagine what it was like, knowing that everyone knew and saw his adoration? It would be different if he loved me in private. That would have been like winning the *Miss America* pageant without it being televised! But they all knew about Alfredo. He made it a point. My stock must have gone through the roof - or so it felt. And I just ate it up. But I never let on. I was even a bit blasé. *It's just the way it is when they fall at your feet. I was just born that way. They dropped like flies before me.*

STUMBLING HOME

Now Alfredo was handsome, gorgeous, some said. But if you really want to know the truth, I wasn't that impressed. Yes, he was tall and dark and good looking, but not the kind of *good-looking* that brought **me** to my knees. He was too pretty for a girl whose father beat her, too polished, too articulate. Brando, in *On The Waterfront, Streetcar Named Desire*. That's my kind of man! Stupid! That's what boiled my water. Stupid in a dirty *tee*. Clark Gable, kicking in the door to Vivian Leigh: *"They'll be no locks or bolts between us!"* Who cares about Lorca when you can have a guy who's an idiot! Macho. That's what it's called -- and Alfredo just didn't fit the mold. So I didn't fall down dead with heart palpitations. I was rather indifferent to him, a bit detached, if the truth be told, but I loved the attention and the public display. I never so much as kissed him. That'll tell you how he ranked!

Alfredo was all over me. It was late, well past the time he should have left my room. The candles flickered in my small sanctuary, filled, like a Hindu temple, with scents and artifacts, Indian bedspreads, tapestries, beads hanging from the ceiling. Flowers and books and incense, Rachmaninoff, for effect, and wine for the shabbos of the mind. *How worldly can you get?* Alfredo agreed. He was trying to stick his tongue down my mouth. *Is he nuts? What the hell is he doing? I don't even like him.*

Just then there was a knock at the door. *Who the hell is knocking at this hour?* I stood up, straightened my dress and opened the door just far enough to see who was there. Melissa, one of the few American students at Judson, chubby, slovenly, from the mid-west, getting a Ph.D in something or other and the one person in the house who never said a word to me. *What does she have against me?* I'd ask myself. *Who knows? Who cares? She's weird, anyway. She probably doesn't like foreigners.*

She asked me to step into the hall. It was important, she said. She had something to ask me. I hadn't a clue what it could be about, nor did I care......until she said that she knew Alfredo was in my room. That certainly piqued my interest in the most disarming way. Had she known we'd kissed? How could she have known that? But if she did, what would she think of me? Would I be one of those loose women my mother abhorred? The thought was intolerable. I stepped out into the hall and closed the door behind me.

"Beatricia. This is very hard for me to say, but I've got to ask you. You can have any guy you want. I've wanted Alfredo since before you ever came here. I've been in love with him for a long time. Please let him go. Please let me have him. You can have anybody you want."

The tears wet her cheeks and I could see that she was very sad. *But this is crazy!* I thought. *CRAZY! I can have anyone I want?? She's asking ME for a guy? ME? BEASTRESS?* It scared me. She was so humbled. I didn't want her to be humbled. I'd been there too often. I couldn't bear for her to beg me. *I don't have any power. I don't have anything that anyone could want! Don't you see?* I didn't even know she liked him! I knew he liked me, but he didn't *REALLY* like me. It was just some game, some pretense. He couldn't like *ME. What is she talking about? This is crazy!*

"Please, Beatricia," she repeated. "Please let me have him."

"I don't know vhat to say to you, Melissa. I feel so bad..."

"Just leave him alone," she cried, as she ran from me down the hall. *"Just leave him alone."*

I couldn't go back to my room. I had to make sense out of this, out of how she saw me. I wasn't one of the bad *guys*. No one had **ever** seen me like that. I wasn't one of those women my mother detested. I was the good *guy*. I was the girl who'd give you the shirt off her back. I was the cat who had no claws. Whatever one might have thought of me, too fat, too ugly, you **NEVER** would have said I was the girl other girls wanted to be! It was very upsetting to me, that she saw me that way. You'd think it would have been men I was so wary of, and of course I was, but a woman? Why? Women are powerless. *Aren't they?* Maybe it was guilt I felt. I tried to understand -- but I knew in the pit of my stomach it was also fear, not that I could have verbalized it then. I KNEW I was frightened, frightened that if she didn't like me, she'd hurt me. I couldn't figure out how, but it was imminent. Somehow, she'd make me disappear. I ran after her down the hall and threw my arms around her, as if she held my fate in her hands and begged her to forgive me. I had no idea, I told her. She needn't worry. I really didn't like him anyway.

She looked at me -- weak and defeated, as if to thank me for my kindness -- for giving such a Displaced Person as herself a little crumb of bread. I knew that place so well, where she lived. I lived there too -- until I had the good fortune to emigrate.

As I returned to my room, I decided not to mention the conversation to Alfredo. I would simply ask him to leave. It was late. I was tired. He'd understand. And besides, I wasn't really attracted to him anyway. He wasn't my type. It's not like I was giving up something I really wanted. It was an easy price to pay -- to ensure that I wouldn't be vaporized. I opened the door to find Alfredo lying on my bed. There was something strangely unfamiliar about the scene.

Something had changed. Something was very different. I could see it in the mirror. I was prettier than when I'd left -- and taller too. It made no sense but that's the way it was. Alfredo was different too. He'd become sexy in a moment in time. I looked at him, at his body draped across my bed, his newly rugged frame waiting to take me on, waiting to mold my body to his. My heart began to race. The man in front of me was a stranger, someone I'd never seen before, dark and powerful, commanding the room, commanding my submission. I could barely silence the thunder in my heart. I knew what was about to happen, though it had never happened before. He reached for my hand and took me to him, half-asking, half-insisting I followed his lead. He unzipped my dress and pulled it to the floor. I lay down beside him, staring into the oblivion of his eyes, faint, delirious with hunger. My chest rose and fell with each deep breath as he covered my body with his and forced me to yield to every movement of his will.

Without a word said, my childhood ended, as if it had never been. Gone, without a whimper, without regret, without nostalgia for what never was. In its place, the flag of the conquering navigator imbedded itself in my consciousness, and I was now his.

In the vernacular of the times, we went *all the way*. Or did we? I wasn't sure. I didn't know what *all the way* should feel like. It had never happened before. I knew there was thunder and lightening, but I didn't know if it had stormed. Don't ask. Don't tell -- like sex is supposed to be, at least when I was a kid. Maybe this sounds absurd, but I didn't know if he was even inside me. Maybe because my body was so electric, so charged, I couldn't distinguish one feeling from the next. My whole body was pulsating. Every neuron was firing at once. I knew there was no epiphany, though. The man never touched me. He just did what he did that he needed to do with his *you know what*. That's how sex is. He fucks you and you love it because he's chosen *you*. That's what's erotic. At least it was then. Girls don't care about sex, per se. They care that *he* cares. They enjoy it because *he* enjoys it. It's a vicarious thing. That's what we were taught. And it's her responsibility to make **sure** he enjoys it. Besides, girls don't have **organisms**, anyway, at least not *nice* girls. But if you're a bad girl, and you *happen* to have an **organism,** it's purely by luck (or the lack of it, as the case may be). Boys were taught that, too, that girls just love those things they have. The mere sight of one excites her. And the bigger it is, the more excited she gets. You'll have to strap her down to control her libido. Show her a big penis and she's yours. Let it touch her private parts and she'll turn into a moron.

It's such a primitive delusion, this belief men have about their genitals: since he gets such a kick out of it, she must too. It's the kind of primitive perception you'd expect from an infant, that he is the world, that he and the world are indistinguishable and what he feels, the world feels as well. The concept that she may feel differently is anathema. But, if the truth be told, while boys were learning one thing, girls were learning something very different, at least the girls in Brooklyn in the '1940's.

Yuk! That's what I was taught. Just spread your legs and bear it. Boys have this silly appendage that has a life of its own, that makes them say and do all sorts of peculiar things, that makes them lie and cheat and even kill, that governs their choices throughout their lives -- this hairy twit of a thing that he takes more seriously than God, that **is** his God, who's stature he'll defend at any cost. Imagine a little tadpole so important!

Well, look. We just have to be patient with them. I was taught. *You know how they are. They've got this thing, and it **really** can kill them if it's not taken care of.* That's what we were told. So, let's be nice and help him out. Just oow and aah and agree it's God and then they'll love you and care for you and protect you from the rest of their own kind. Give it a name, like he does, Harry, for example, or Big Ben. That'll let him know you take it as seriously as he. It's a separate person, for Christ's sake, entitled to all the rights and privileges of this great nation.

So you have this guy, Alfredo, let's say, and his little dingy, I mean *big* dingy, Big Ben. Now it's two against one. Like *good cop, bad cop*. Alfredo doesn't **want** you to have to surrender to Ben, but if you don't, he can't be responsible for what Ben might do, like rape you or fuck your sister. He can't control Ben. Ben's a live wire. He's not like Alfredo, cerebral, thoughtful, poetic. Ben doesn't give a damn what he does. He just wants to *get his rocks off*, I mean, have an **organism**. It's something Ben needs to do or Alfredo might die.

Like some guy at a Sunday mass. All of a sudden Ben is banging inside his pants, trying to stick his head out of his fly. He doesn't give a damn who can see him or who gets poked if they come too close. He just wants to blow his lid. And nothing the guy does can shut him up. Not the scriptures, not the hymns, not the threat of damnation or Hell. So the poor guy, ready to receive the wafer, has to detour to the men's room and let Ben have his way.

This is serious stuff. If the church can't stop it, nothing can! You better not mess with it. If you say "no" or don't do your job right, it could mean death. You better learn to take care of Ben, for Alfredo's sake and your own.

It's tiring just to think about it. But, of course, in those days, the harder you worked, the greater your rewards -- not in direct sexual pleasure, of course, for in those days little was known about female sexual pleasure, but in your worth, in how sexy you were in **his** eyes. Any woman who can handle Ben must be A.O.K.

Now, on this particular night, I was at a disadvantage. I hadn't a clue what it took to please Ben, so I just lay there, rigid, scared to move. I figured Ben knew what he needed more than I, so I'd better just lay low and not interfere.

I *did* know I should moan, though. Every girl knows that. I'd seen it in the movies a dozen times. Rita Hayworth was a great moaner, Betty Grable, too. I learned from watching them. I lay frozen in place, my long hair draped perfectly across the pillow, very sultry like Rita used to do, and turned my torso slightly to the side to create the appearance of a cleavage. Ben loves cleavage. I knew that. So when I had it just right, I wasn't about to move. My knees were locked, my toes pointed to the heavens (because legs, we'd been taught, look better when your toes are pointed and your calves are tight as a drum. That's why women wear stilettos, to allow men sexual gratification even when they're walking through the mall). And Ben is no different. He likes good legs, too. No matter what the cost to the woman's arches or spine. Just try and point your toes with a 200 pound body thrashing all over you. Just try and keep up with Fred Astaire in four inch heels. Ginger Rogers did!

Damn! I thought. Everything's for Ben! Fuck him! Hmmmm.! Oh! Well. So maybe I didn't master the graceful legs the way I should have, but the moan, that I had down pat. Not a loud, gruff moan, like a girl who had no breeding, like a girl from the Bronx, but a soft, timid whimper, almost apologetic, illicit, reluctant, a moan that's clear it's in spite of itself.

Anyway, I was proud as a peacock, (no pun intended). But back to the question at hand. Did we go *all the way*? Maybe you don't think it's such an important question to warrant all this time. But for a Jewish girl from the Ukraine, it's critical. Like, *"Are you pregnant or are you not?" Don't tell me you're a little bloated. Your breasts are sore. Your period's late. Are you pregnant or are you not?* Let's put our cards on the table. *"ARE YOU A VIRGIN OR ARE YOU NOT?"* It's the only question worth pondering. *Don't give me a song and dance. I don't care what the hell he did with his mouth or his fingers or his feet, for that matter. Did he stick his dick in your cunt? It's as simple as that. Yes or no? Just answer the question. YES OR NO!!* How do you ask a guy something like that? *What, are you retarded?* He'd think. *Where were you when the lights were out? Napping?* But stupid or not, I didn't have the answer and I needed to get it.

I knew I was wet down there and I knew I hadn't peed, at least I didn't *think* I had -- and I assumed Alfredo hadn't either. He *did* get all hot and bothered, flailing his body up and down, fast as a motor in overdrive, grunting and carrying on like he was possessed -- and then he just stopped, like he was exorcised and then he went limp, panting, and catching his breath. I knew that was part of *going all the way*. But did he do it *inside* of me?

I wanted to ask: *Excuse me, but where was your dick when that was going on? No. I'm not making fun of you, Alfredo. I have this rare condition. You know, vaginismus, that's a women's disorder where the vagina contracts and prevents penetration? Well this is vagin*

ISN'Tmus. Only Jewish girls get it. We kind of go numb between the legs. But don't worry, we just L-O-V-E having sex. It doesn't interfere in the least. It just means we weren't sure if we were fucked or fucked up! We just need a little clarification.

Alfredo said I was so cute, asking if we'd gone all the way. Cute? I thought. Is he kidding?

He reached over and kissed me -- then held me tight as he could, like a good daddy who'd never leave. He stared into my eyes and let me know that he saw everything, that he knew me inside and out, that he could see me to the core and that he loved me, that he could see the rascal in me and he loved her, too, that he could see the wild child pretending she was a woman, pretending she was innocent and he loved her even more --because he was a big guy and this wild child was really no match for him.

He toyed with the wild child, like Mohammed Ali toyed with his opponents. Her bravado endeared her to him. He thought she was so "cute" and mischievous.

"How could you **not** know?" He asked me in all earnestness.

"Vell, I loved it. I really did, but it just never happened before and I......"

"Come, on, Beatricia," he interrupted, like There you go again being naughty. *It never happened before? Come on. You've been with a lot of boys."*

Damn! How could he think THAT? Well, I protested and swore and cajoled and carried on. You'd have thought he said I was a mass murderer. But nothing I did changed his mind. He was convinced I'd slept with many boys, and you know what? He didn't seem to mind in the least. To the contrary, he seemed to think I was adorable, what with all this sexual experience and yet, such a child. But I MINDED! You bet I did. I can't have him thinking I'm one of those girls who let's boys *take liberties* with her, one of those girls who boys don't respect in the morning! Better he should think I've got an I.Q. of 6 or that I'm even from BROOKLYN! Better he should think I've got a urinary tract infection! Anything but a *LOOSE* girl, *FAST, EASY,* a *SLUT,* a *WHORE,* a *TART*, a *TRAMP*, a girl who let's boys *TAKE LIBERTIES!!* Bite your tongue! I couldn't live with that.

I began to cry. These were no crocodile tears. I was hurt ...to the core. He tried his best to comfort me. Nothing he did would work. And the more he kept saying it was O.K. that I'd "been" with other boys, the more I cried and cried. He had to believe me that he was the first. Nothing else would do.

"*O.K, I believe you,*" he finally said to shut me up. But I wouldn't have any of it. What was said was said and there was no way to undo it. He could swear on a stack of bibles that he was only kidding and I wouldn't be convinced. He could swear on his mother's life and I wouldn't believe him. He told me his mother was dead.

"*Swear she'll live in hell if you don't believe me.*"

He swore. He swore. And that's what it took to calm me down and that's what it took for me to finally sleep. When I awoke, Bea from Brooklyn had a whole new slant on things.

SINAI

IT'S NOT EASY waking up next to a guy! Especially for the very first time! It's not so bad if **you** wake up first. Then you can brush your teeth, redo your face and get back into bed as if you'd never left. Then he wakes up, sees you next to him, your graceful, natural beauty and the ease with which you seem to fit. You're not one of those tarts his mother warned him about, a painted woman, a hussy in disguise who'll twist him round her little finger and turn him into mush. You're genuine and uncomplicated. You enjoy sex without having to draw a road map. You're beautiful without having to construct a face. You're pleasant and agreeable and you *never* rock the boat. Things just come easy to you because you're comfortable being you.

But if **HE** wakes up first! Damn! That's a different thing! *No way that'll happen to me*. True, I slept that night, but the kind of sleep an Israeli soldier gets on the Lebanese border. It was the night watch. Nothing would get past me. One stir from his side of the bed and I was up and alert, poised to bolt for the bathroom, ready for inspection. Fortunately, Alfredo was a heavy sleeper. By the time he awoke, I was in full combat gear.

It was Monday morning. I wanted to hang out the sheet like they do in Italy, but it was late and I had to get to school. Now that I was a *woman*, **maybe** I could get there. It had been impossible before. In all the months I'd been at Judson, I barely made it to school. Not that I didn't try. I did. I just couldn't pull it off. I was up against a brick wall of impregnable resistance. I suppose you could say I was *school* *phobic*, though, of course, at the time, I had no such way to identify this or any other behavior that troubled me. It just felt impossible, a task beyond the scope of my emotional repertoire.

No matter when my classes were held, first thing in the morning or late in the afternoon, I couldn't seem to get there in time. I'd get the "F" train to Queens Boulevard and wait on the platform for the train to Flushing. Sometimes, as I waited, a feeling of utter pointlessness would overwhelm me and I'd cross the platform and take the first train back to the Village. Sometimes, the resistance was bearable. I'd get to Flushing then make the long walk to the bus that would take me to Queens College. At other times, no sooner would I leave the train station, I'd turn around and head back. Sometimes I'd make it to the bus. Sometimes even to school. Sometimes even through the sprawling campus to my building, to my classroom, to the doorway, where I'd stand paralyzed, pointless -- then turn around and leave, but why?

Why, having managed to make the trip -- in the dead of winter, waiting on platforms and bus stops in snow and freezing rain would I then walk away, all for naught? I couldn't make sense of it, the waste, the sheer waste. And no one reproached me more than I.

But despite all logic and reasonable discourse, *I could not get to school.* At least not to THAT school in THAT place at THAT time in my life -- the waiting at each choice point in a foreign land, the distance, the vast open spaces of the bus route and the campus, the indifference of the buildings, the people who were as alien to me as I to them. This wasn't Judson, after all, my little red tenement, small, knowable, familial. I belonged at Judson. Never for a moment was I *foreign* there, despite my being so. But at Queens College, amongst my *own*, I couldn't have been more remote, an indefinable mutation from an indefinable place that bore no resemblance, whatsoever, to the culture at hand.

I was back in my coffin, screaming to be heard, alone, orphaned, separated from the *mother ship*, adrift in cosmic darkness forever. I HAD to get home! I wasn't being bad, skipping school, wasting time, hanging out. I HAD to get home! I HAD to hold on to something to stop me from my free-fall. *I wasn't a bad girl. I wasn't.* And the minute I turned around to go back, I knew I'd be O.K.

I could leave Brooklyn, all by myself, forever, and make my way in a strange, new place without a moment of fear, yet I couldn't leave the Village for an afternoon in Queens. Semester after semester, "F's," "Incompletes," "Withdrawals." I was put on "Academic Probation" that first year. The following September, they told me not to register. No matter. I registered anyway. These were the days before computers. I registered *EVERY* semester and *EVERY* semester I got the same grades: "F's," "Incompletes," and "Withdrawals." Occasionally, I'd get a "C," a "B" or even an "A" in a class I didn't attend, where a teacher understood the plight of a Russian student, a survivor of the Great War, a Displaced Person. But, for the most part, it was a sorry record, indeed. Yet, I kept trying, day after day, to get to class. You'd have thought this was a girl who'd never crossed the Atlantic.

Work was different, though. Not only did I leave the Village every Friday at noon, I'd travel three hours to The Concord Hotel in the middle of nowhere in the Catskill Mountains to work non-stop till Sunday afternoon. But it wasn't the same as Queens College. We all went up together, the *kids* who worked the weekends. We all bunked together. Real camaraderie, kids of every race and background. I didn't mind it in the least. I liked it. We worked for tips, non-stop, no benefits, no labor laws, nothing! The faster you worked, the more meals you could carry on your shoulder tray, the more tips you made. And we ate whatever we wanted. Not that it was offered. We just hoarded what we could get our hands on, leftovers, extras, steaks, brisket. Once you got the routine down, you had it made. Future doctors, lawyers and statesmen did their time in the Catskill kitchens. And then there was me.

I dropped the accent when I reached the bus at Port Authority, just another kid from Brooklyn making her way through school.

Sometimes Ellie went with me, but things weren't the same. Our lives had taken different paths. After High School she got a job and continued to live at home, the same dismal, lonely place she had once hoped to leave, the same dismal train ride back and forth to the city, every day with no exit in sight. Those trips together to Bernie Eisner's on Sunday afternoons were supposed to be rehearsals. One day we'd arrive in the Village and never return. That was the plan. But I guess she was too scared. And though she never said it, I think she was jealous that I left. Here I was, madly in love with Alfredo, traipsing around town wherever and whenever I pleased, to galleries, museums, cafes, adored and protected by Sinai, drinking with Franz Klein, chatting with James Dine, holding court at Judson, free as a bird, high as a kite.

Ellie was the one who always put on airs. But I was the one who was living them -- and I think it bothered her inside. To her, my odyssey was fun and games. She never really understood what made me run, what torment propelled my transformation. She saw my life as a lark, an adventure, pretending you're someone else, like playing dress-up when you're a child. She hadn't the vaguest idea how real it was, how deadly serious, how close disintegration loomed. But in those wonderful days of reverie and love, neither did I.

I had taken to wearing Indian saris. It was Sinai's idea, because I was his *"princess."* With my long, dark hair, he said. I'd do justice to his country's dress. He bought me my first Sari and I learned to wear it with pride and ease. It took a while to get the knack of it, yards of billowy fabric wrapped around your body, held in place by just the right number of pleats and tucks. But when I got the hang of it, I sauntered through the streets, Sinai on my arm and a red dot on my forehead. That was his idea, too. He said it was a symbol of the highest caste. And that was me, an aristocrat, just what my father had in mind.

"She's Russian" I heard someone, say as I passed, *" but she lived in India. That's why she wears saris."*

"What was she doing in India?"

"I don't know. There are a lot of stories. Someone said she was

adopted by an Indian family after the war and was raised in the Punjab. But then I also heard that she lived with an Indian family in the Ukraine. It's hard to know. She's very guarded. I guess because she's had such a hard life.

Whatever people may have thought or however difficult things may have been, Judson was kind to me. Yet, even so, the sense of wellbeing was only skin-deep. One night Sinai and I gave a party at the house. Actually, it was more than just a party. It was a *wedding* for his younger brother. Sinai asked me to help because he said I could do anything. And, of course, he was right. I got my training filling in for my mother when I was a child. I was the one who cooked and cleaned and ironed my brother's socks while my mother read. I was Cinderella because my mother had more important things to do. But it wasn't without rewards. She said I was a "good girl" - not like the other girls who never helped their mothers. I was special. It made me feel important. I polished the floor till I could see my reflection in it. Perfect. That's how I cleaned. I took pride in my work.

That's why Sinai asked for my help. At least that's what he *said*. Actually, I think it was that he wanted *US* to make the party, as if we were a couple. He wanted people to see us as a pair. Maybe he wanted Alfredo to see it that way. Maybe he wanted to show me off, his *princess* in her very own sari.

I worked hard to make the party a success. I cooked for days and cleaned Judson the way I'd cleaned my own house when I was my mother's helper. I gave it my *special girl* cleaning. And people noticed. I was Judson's favored daughter.

As the guests arrived, Sinai introduced them to me as if they were having an audience with the queen. I was noticed. Nobody said, *"Is this kid a fruitcake, or what?"* Maybe that's what they thought, but that's not what they said. To the contrary, they told Sinai he was so lucky! And he was beaming. I could see it.

The evening was going beautifully except for the heat. It was one of those 90-degree nights when the air is thick and immovable. And of course, we had no air conditioning in those days. That my place was in the kitchen made it all the more difficult. On the one hand I *wanted* to look sweaty and exhausted so people would know how hard I was working, especially the guys. But on the other hand I didn't want to sweat so much that the dot on my forehead ran down my cheek. That wouldn't be fitting an aristocrat.

People were piling in. It was hard to keep track of who knew my value and who just thought I was a lunatic. I wanted to make an announcement of my worth so everyone understood all at once, so then I could get out of the kitchen and sit down like a lady. This was a difficult problem that required a difficult remedy.

When there was a momentary lull in the traffic, I sat myself down, as if from exhaustion, my head carefully posed against the backrest, my eyes shut, an angel whose fatigue had overcome her, weightless, her body fluid, graceful though depleted, her milk-white skin drenched in perspiration.

"She seems to have passed out from heat," someone commented with alarm. *"What a wonderful young woman," So devoted. So giving. She must be a saint like her mother!"* Someone yelled for Sinai. Alfredo raced to my side. Sinai pushed him away and picked up my head, disturbing my artful hair-do! He immersed a towel in a bucket of ice water then covered my face in it to cool me off.

"Princess, princess," he yelled, as I felt the water pour down my cheeks carrying the dot with it and rearranging my face!

Had I not been so otherworldly, I would have cursed him out from here to Coney Island, or Kiev, as it were. But those eruptions of rage, those spontaneous, authentic cataclysms, warranted or not, were still years to come. For the moment I was indulging in the calm that only a fantasy can provide, that only a momentary suspension of reality can allow, like a surgery patient undergoing the scalpel, while high as a kite.

ALFREDO'S VISIT

DESPITE MY ACCEPTANCE within the Judson community, any sense of wellbeing turned out to be as transient as my national origin. I had to stay alert. One slip and my value could plummet. With summer close by, I had to find full-time work. The Catskills were first on the list. That's where the money was best, I knew, where *everyone* worked when school was out. Six days a week, eight weeks to the season. I couldn't pass it up. To earn even more, I decided to work in the cocktail lounge when my shift in the dining room finished for the evening. The hours didn't intimidate me. I was young and strong and needed the money and, besides, however difficult it might be, Alfredo and I could see each other on my day off.

I wasn't the least bit worried about being away from him the rest of the week. I was utterly secure in our love. Alfredo was inside my skin. We were so much in love. The kind of love you only know once in the Garden of Eden before God casts you out of paradise, the first love, when there's absolute certainty and absolute trust.

Summer came. I waitressed in the dining room of The Stevensville Hotel from seven in the morning till nine at night. That was the first job. Then I'd race to the second job in the cocktail lounge from 9:30 till 2:00 AM. Of course I barely slept. I was on a mission. On my day off I took the bus back to Manhattan to be with Alfredo and on one occasion he made the trip up to see me.

In the City, I was Russian, tentative, coy, naïve, befitting a child who'd been through the war. In the mountains, I was *Bea from Brooklyn*, resourceful beyond my years. Without an accent! I hadn't thought about the fact that Alfredo had never heard me without the accent until he was well on his way up to visit. My disguise would be unmasked, I worried, and he'd never love me again. I decided to borrow a car and intercept him at the bus depot. I had no license but it didn't trouble me. I was a confident driver since Sinai had taught me – on a *shift* -- on the New Jersey Turnpike!

Imagine this old guy in a turban and his young *princess* chugging along in a beat-up jalopy, jerking, stalling, grinding the gears into chopped liver -- and Sinai, praising me every inch of the way, drivers cursing at us, giving us the finger, screaming obscenities out their windows. Sinai didn't hear a word. He thought I was terrific. Maybe that was a reflection of how he drove. But for me it was a vote of confidence that allowed me to master the challenge.

When Alfredo got off the bus, I was there to greet him -- and his face lit up.

"It is O.K. if ve don't go to hotel?" I asked. "I always there. Let's go some new place. Yes?" He didn't care. He was happy just to be with me.

We made the afternoon an adventure, back roads and covered bridges built in the 1800's. We made love in the woods and carved our names on a giant tree whose exact location we mapped for posterity. *One day,* I thought, *we'll bring our children to the spot.*

But as the afternoon slipped away, Alfredo seemed eager to see where I worked, not a long visit, he assured me, just a brief one out of curiosity. No excuse could dissuade him. He was very persistent. Maybe he wanted to see the boys at the hotel, to see if he had any competition. Maybe he wanted to see a *"Jewish hotel."* That's what I thought. I knew he was curious about *us*, about *my people*. He told me once that he didn't know any Jews before he came to New York and *we're nothing like he thought*. My skin crawled. I imagined him challenging his family in defense of our relationship. I have to understand,

I imagined his father saying, that the Jews who visit Puerto Rico give all Jews a bad name! I'd heard these comments often in childhood when we'd visited the Island, about the Jews in chartreuse shorts with their fat bellies and loud wives who boss their husbands around and control the purse strings. And about the Jews who *didn't* visit Puerto Rico, the Communists with their heads up their ass -- all related to the Rosenbergs, no doubt. *You know how Jews stick together!*

Alfredo didn't say any of this, but I was guarded, especially when he reminded me that **his** family was prominent in Puerto Rico -- *though they were really from Spain* and *"not like the **Puerto Rican** Puerto Ricans,"* he emphasized.

Despite my fears of condemnation from his family, I imagined they'd finally yield because I was an orphan, after all, and besides, *why make a big deal of it. Alfredo would never **marry** a Jew. He was just screwing her!*

Now, if I told you that these imaginings were not surprising to me, you'd probably say you understood. Anti-Semitism, after all, was real and widespread in 1958. But that isn't why they didn't surprise me. At least not in the way you might think. The things I imagined did hurt me. But they didn't make me angry. I was *hurt,* because again I assumed I fell short of the mark. I was from the wrong place, the wrong people, the outside trying to get in.

And somewhere in this contempt, I heard an echo of truth. It was my own father, after all, who denied *his* origins, who refused to be a *Polish* Jew, herded to pogroms, treated like swine, groveling to stay alive, hated by the rest of the human race, the *Polish* Jew, in a shabby black suit, hunched over with funny curls hanging down the sides of his head, praying as he walked, muttering to himself and to God. No. My father would be *British*, refined, educated, above the fray, a *Protestant* Jew, "Shmuel" from London. You'd never catch *him* in chartreuse shorts! It all seemed so familiar. What I imagined Alfredo to feel, I understood perfectly. And it came from all sides. Let me put it in context:

When I was born in 1942, the Japanese had just bombed Pearl

STUMBLING HOME

Harbor, catching America in a long, vehement self-imposed stupor. What we didn't know couldn't hurt us, or so it was thought. In fact, Americans hardly knew what was happening abroad. My earliest recollections of childhood were of a secular home where the only orthodoxy was the commitment to the moral principles of leftist dogma. (Of course, I also remember the importance of the stock market in our daily lives, but the contradiction was lost on me for years to come).

In my childhood I remember *The Party* meetings in our home. This was, of course, in the years when communism and socialism were the only decent shows in town, when any smart young intellectual worth his salt would embrace the party, the period before the world knew Stalin's true colors, before the horrors of all brands of totalitarianism were seen, when the tragedy Raoul Wallenberg was still unknown, before the Soviet's power grab insulted the morality of the young, the period before survivors told their tales of what had befallen them at the hands of the Red Army, before news of Siberian death camps reached the West, the period before the hopeful had lost hope, the period when Morality meant the Left.

Manny and I hid on the stairs watching Party members arrive, secretively, surreptitiously, retreating with great caution to the basement for the work they had come to do. It was all very exciting to us, I suppose, like the ritual events other children look forward to in their religious and cultural identifications. My parent's had none of these other, lesser allegiances. I say, "my *parents*," but I suspect it was my father who was the architect of these identifications. Certainly he was their spokesman. My mother's politics were less clear to me, what genuinely lay beneath her remoteness, beneath her moralizing, romanticizing façade though I knew in her youth she'd been as much a leftist as my father. Yet I know full well that she was aware of the events in Europe, perhaps not the full extent of the carnage but at least its existence. Nonetheless, I say, "my *parents*," because, during the period I'm referring to, there was little about her to suggest disagreement, at least in the eyes of a small child.

Before my brother and I were born they, in unison, were averse to religion and the cultural events of the community. They flaunted their refusal to join the fold, the group, the mainstream, the values and protocols of *the little people*, as my father so often referred to *the masses*. This was not a man about to surrender to religion, to a God, unless, of course, it was the god of Spinoza or Kant or some other abstruse philosopher whom the neighbors had never heard of. If he wouldn't surrender to God, he certainly wouldn't surrender to a Rabbi or *the good* congregants of the local Shul. As a matter of fact, my parent's unwillingness to embrace *their* religion was a source of great dissension in my mother's family, which was, after all, the family of a Talmud scholar. Nonetheless, they remained outsiders. *Yiddishkite*, like all religious referents, was the opiate of the *little people*.

But I do know there was a period in the midst of their atheism when things began to change, at least for my mother, a period whose impact on me was as potent as a heart-lung transplant that resonated from the depths when I thought of Alfredo and *Jews*.

I'm not certain of the year but I suspect it was 1948. Now, mind you, I would have been only six, but the images, while vague, still thunder in my consciousness. I remember a big to-do, a lot of activity and pressured talk of death and "Zionism." I remember people coming to our home, not the communists, now, but others, coming for meetings not held in secret. I remember an urgency that existed, as if born over-night, from one day to the next.

My mother, detached and otherworldly as she'd always been, was now alive with anxiety and purpose. I rarely ever saw her cry, but the first time, if my recollections serve me, was at one of these meetings. I think it had to do with the *"underground."* I remember *that* word and its use in the context of great tumult and anger. I couldn't have understood what it meant but the word has always evoked fear in me. Now, it's possible I heard it in another context, the slave underground, the "Party" underground, both of which were sanctified in our home. But its connection in my memory to Jewish evacuation seems fixed. I remember my mother cupping my face in her hands, staring, with great alarm, into my eyes, like a deer in the headlights, demanding, as if I were in her mirror, that we must get these people out of Europe!

"What people, mommy? I don't understand."

"The Jews, like ourselves. They're dying," she cried. "We have to get them out!"

The woman who never spoke to me, spoke to her little girl of this! It scared me. And she repeated it over and over again, maybe so I'd never forget, maybe so I'd be prepared for the world as she was coming to see it. Maybe she was even right to do so. Maybe she was arming me, alerting me, fortifying me, preparing me for danger ahead... But the look in her eyes! I stuck my fingers in my ears. She pulled them out. I stuck them in again. She pulled them out again.

It was frightening what she told this little child. It was the new poetry on her tongue, not the poetry of 19th century romanticism that could sustain her alienation from her family, but the poetry of 20th century activism, of gas chambers, of cadavers walking from nowhere to nowhere, of little children, like me, torn from their mommies and their daddies whom they'd never see again.

"Remember the first day I took you to kindergarten?" she reminded me several years later. It had seemed so recent, the dread still lingered in me. I couldn't stop crying that first day of school. I darted from the classroom, running in abject terror through the streets like Richard Pryor -- and my mother had to run after me all the way home -- just because I was too scared to go to school.

"Imagine if your mommy and daddy are killed. Then you'll have to be alone forever! That's what happened to the little Jewish children in Europe. We have to get them out!" She scared me when she *didn't* talk to me and she scared me when she *did*.

I'm sure the year was 1948 when my mother shifted into high gear. What else could have created this passion and frenzied activity but the creation of the state of Israel? And along with her awakening, I remember my father's disdain. It wasn't the causes of salvation and liberation he objected to, not at all. He was a great believer in them. *But did they have to involve **people**? You know, the imperfect, little people. Can't we just save the **ideas** of them, like the people in Plato's cave? And why, if we have to save them at all, can't they be heroic people. Do we have to get involved with all these black suits and side curls?*

Actually, to be fair, my father's disdain was not for *Jews*. It was for *orthodoxy,* in whatever its form, Jewish, Christian, Taoist, it didn't matter. He just couldn't abide reverence or submission to a god. *They* were the *little people*, the hypocrites and self-righteous fools, the unquestioning believers in magic and hocus pocus who slaughtered and ripped off their brethren in the name of their lord. He abhorred religion, whatever its name and he abhorred the *pious* who surrendered.

So when my mother began to light Shabbos candles on the Sabbath, he rolled his eyes. What was interesting (though, of course, it eluded me at the time) was that my mother's growing kinship with Judaism had nothing to do with "God". Until her death she, like my father, remained an atheist. What emerged, rather, was a powerful connection to the culture from which she'd come. She submerged herself in Jewish history, culture, practice. Unlike my father, the pushcart and the struggles of emigrant Jews were not distasteful to her but rather, noble. I suppose of the two of them, it was she who embraced the stature of the "working man". Nothing about the "working man" repelled her. She, in fact, contrary to my father, ennobled him.

So in that sense, it was she who was the true adherent of the Left. The problem of her burgeoning Jewishness was not religion but the context in which the Jew, in every age, in every civilization was forced to live, the impoverishment, the squalor, the pushcart, the street vendors, the "merchant" as opposed to the thinker, the worker as opposed to the aristocrat. She knew that Jews, whatever their station, valued education, that even though she was born into the

Russian "peasantry", it was these very people who demanded that their children learn to read and write, speak several languages, play musical instruments, contrary to the town's non-Jewish families who, for the most part, remained illiterate. Whereas children of non-Jewish peasants were removed from school when they became old enough to work in the fields, or in the mills, children of Jews had to continue their education in addition to engaging in work.

The few Jews who were able to survive the Nazis were often able to do so because they spoke and read not only Yiddish, but German if they were German Jews, Polish if they were Polish Jews, Italian if they were Italian Jews and so forth. Many, who saw the handwriting on the walls, insisted that their children also learn Hebrew in the hopes that if they survived, could one day live in *Palestine* where they would be safe.

Zionism became my mother's religion. It was a religion of hard work, plowing the field, irrigating the dessert, growing fruit trees, the work of sweat and dirty fingernails, not the work for an aristocrat like my father. So while his distaste for Jewish orthodoxy was clear, it was in actuality a distaste for the working class that he, as a good Leftist supposedly revered.

Maybe her Zionism hadn't been a *good-enough* voice, but it was her own voice --- and seemed to embody some Herculean rage against injustice that perhaps had always lived just beneath the surface of her gentility. And it infuriated my father! Had it been a *nobler* voice, **his** voice, maybe he would have felt differently. Maybe he needed to squelch *anything* she embraced that wasn't centered around him, but the fact remains he put her down and mocked her growing allegiance to Jewishness. I liked it when he did that (though I must tell you, as I'm recounting it now, my heart is hurting. Yes, I *also* loved her. But not then, not in the years I'm talking about, not for years to come.).

At the time, I welcomed his mocking, his impersonations and dialects. My mother would light her Shabbos candles and he'd disappear from the room. Moments later he'd return wearing *a* dress, tripping in her high-heeled shoes and staggering under the weight of huge, padded breasts. Dripping with saccharin sweetness, he'd extoll the virtues of God and obedience. He'd shake his finger in my face and remind me of the punishments for sin -- all in a heavy Yiddish accent! The sarcasm eluded me, but not the fact that his skits were incompatible with violence, his own violence and the *other* violence my mother had warned me of. For as long as his show lasted, the threats from inside and out ceased to exists, but only for the life of the performance. At its end, as my father left, my mother would remind me of peril.

"You think Daddy is funny"? She'd ask in a pained voice. She was offended by his mockery. There were people in the world hurting and dying and nothing about his antics were humorous. At the time I thought she was referring only to Jews, but I was wrong. I came to understand that beneath all her layers of illusion was a woman who was genuinely offended by injustice, who genuinely cared about the underdog, at least to the extent she was able to identify that person as an underdog. Of course I doubt she'd ever seen me as an underdog. I was the one who could *wrap my father around my little finger,* as she often said. And this, from the woman who stood by as my father beat me -- then pretended it never happened! *"Daddy didn't hurt you, "* she'd say. *"It was just a tap."*

How could you stand by, Mommy, and pretend nothing happened? Isn't that what you said about the war? How can I trust what you say? How can I love what you love when it's tainted by your lies?

So that's what I heard when Alfredo said he wanted to visit the hotel at which I worked, my own overpowering confusion, the safety-danger dichotomy that infused everything and everyone, the echoes of anti-Semitism, the voices of danger, of Jews in danger, the pretense of friendship as *they* stare at your forehead to find the telltale signs of the horns that are merely hidden but are there nonetheless, the evidence the whole world knows exist, of your treachery, your satanic allegiances, your blood-libel. This is the subtext of anti-Semitism and my mother knew every word of it, of death and persecution, all the while beseeching me with one hand to listen and shutting me out with the other hand. Why is it surprising that I came to resist what she loved and run from what she revered. Maybe it's easier to accept the person who beats you than the person who pretends it didn't happen. And he, who beat the daylight out of us, but whom I could read like an opened book, (or so I thought) was my hero.

THE VISIT (CONTINUED)

I AGREED TO show Alfredo The Stevensville Hotel despite my fear of exposure. It would be a brief visit, very brief, we said, then I'd drive him back to the bus station. *How many people can we possibly meet in a few minutes who'll throw my nationality into doubt?* I assured myself everything would be just fine until a guy called out my name as I pulled into the parking lot of the hotel. Damn! He knew I was from Brooklyn. I had to divert him, then divert her, then divert someone else, all bizarre one act plays that would make anyone doubt my mental health. But to my astonishment Alfredo interpreted my coldness to these people as my reluctant to introduce THEM TO HIM!

That statement completely confused me. I had no idea what he was referring to. "*Maybe you don't want your friends to meet me,*" he suggested with obvious discomfort.

I was even more confused.

"*Maybe because I'm Puerto Rican?*"

I wrapped my arms around him, baffled that **he**, above all, would feel unworthy of **me!** I had to protect him from these terrible feelings I knew so well.

I saw an old Polish woman rocking in a lawn chair as if she were in a nursing home, a woman in her 80's whom I'd served in the dining room, who barely spoke English and could hear even less. I think she had Alzheimer's, or would have -- on Tuesday! It would be an improvement, I thought. *The cantankerous old bitty!* I grabbed Alfredo and approached her.

STUMBLING HOME

"Mrs. Kleinman," I said, "*Vus haben zee? Vhat's happening?* Have you eaten your dinner yet?" I yelled in her ear.

She looked up at me as if it were her last movement before death. I imagined she'd complain as she always did and I was prepared for it in my mind:

Yes, Mrs. Kleinman. This is Chow Mein. Yes, Mrs. Kleinman. It is Kosher. How do I know? Because the hotel says it's Kosher. No, Mrs. Kleinman, I'm not a Rabbi. Yes, Mrs. Kleinman, I believe what the hotel says. No, Mrs. Kleinman, they're not trying to trick you. No, I didn't watch them make it. Yes, I care if you get poisoned. No, I'm not a nasty girl. Yes, Mrs. Kleinman. This IS a whole order of prunes. No, we're not trying to starve you, (but the chef isn't a proctologist, either!). Yes, This IS chicken. Yes, I DO think it looks like chicken. (In this country, Mrs. Kleinman, we cook our chickens before we eat them. You're not in Poland now). Yes, Mrs. Kleinman, this IS chopped liver. Yes, Mrs. Kleinman. I do know how they made it. (First they ground up your dead husband, Murray.................)

"It's nice to see you, Mrs. Kleinman," I hollered in her ear. "I'd like you to meet my boyfriend, Alfredo." Silence. "This is Alfredo," I said again, raising my voice even louder. What does it mean when an old person closes her eyes and starts to drool? She either died or fell asleep. That's what I thought. But then she raised her head, looked him straight in the eyes and smiled from ear to ear.

"Oy," she said, reaching towards him, like stretching wood, and pinching him on the cheek. "*Dis is a boychick.*" She cooed with pleasure.

"He's my boyfriend, Mrs. Kleinman. He's from Puerto Rico."

"*Oy, vat a boychick,*" she repeated, slapping him coquettishly on the same cheek.

"He's wonderful," I said, kissing him lovingly.

Mrs. Kleinman laughed and clapped her hands, dancing in her lawn chair, as if she were watching Fiddler on The Roof. I smiled at

THE VISIT (CONTINUED)

Alfredo. He was ten feet tall, a man who felt loved, indeed. I kissed him again, then waved good-bye to my old dinner guest, as she continued laughing and clapping, like a brain-damaged child at the circus.

As we walked away, pleased and reaffirmed, we could hear Mrs. Kleinman scream, *"Mine glasses, mine glasses. He stole mine glasses!"*

BECKY

WAITRESSING IN THE Catskills wasn't exactly rocket science. So long as you had no major defects, like a foot growing out of your neck, and could accept the simple premise that the guest is always right, you should have done quite well. Which is why, when I heard that a twenty-two year-old girl in *medical school* had been fired after just one meal, my ears perked up. She'd caused quite a stir, I was told, right in the middle of lunch. I hadn't met her during that one-meal stint but the story was she was *quite unusual*. That was the word around the hotel.

It wasn't just her peculiar behavior that drew attention. It was the strange look about her, certainly not homely as you might think of *homely*, but odd looking. She was actually quite petty if she's leaned some basic rules of behavior Her lovely blue eyes dominated her face but her lips were always a bit too wet as if the saliva collected in her mouth and eventually trickled out because she just didn't know when to swallow. Especially when she got excited. It didn't make for a lovely impression, a young, female, Mick Jagger, spitting in your soup as she's serving you dinner. But God was merciful and gave her a gorgeous body and thick blonde hair that hung seductively down her back by the time we met. That was Becky, too.

What's most interesting, though, is that Becky didn't have to look as strange as she did. With a little care and preparation, she could have looked like Jeanne Moreau. She could be beautiful, but she was utterly unsocialized. And that's what happened, once or twice, when

I made her up and picked out her clothes and gave her pointers on how to behave. On those occasions, you'd probably have described her as *really sexy*. So it wasn't her face, particularly, that reminded one of a shopping bag lady! It was the whole persona.

Becky was a young woman who had no socialization. When other girls were learning to flirt, she was battling to survive with a schizophrenic mother on the lower East Side. Her mother was a *REAL* shopping bag lady! If she didn't have an apartment that was subsidized by the city, she'd have lived on the streets, screaming obscenities at little kids. No husband, no money, no psychological resources, always yelling at the voices in her head. The poor woman barely existed. And because of her incapacities, her daughter, Becky, was placed in foster care for part of her childhood and never learned the subtleties of acceptable behavior. Polish! That's the word. She never learned polish! She was primitive, my friend Becky, but smart as a whip and a fighter, if need be ……..the very qualities it takes to make it out of hell, because she did. She couldn't be a waitress. That's for sure. But she was spotted, early on, for her soaring I.Q and taken under the wing of a foster parent who pushed her along and made sure she excelled in school. She was one of those whiz kids who becomes an astrophysicist but can't button her shirt.

At twenty-two, Becky was a scholarship student at Columbia School of Medicine! Medicine was her niche, or rather medical RESEARCH. No live people for *her*, medical data, ideas that can't speak back. The day after Becky was fired from The Stevensville, she called me for help. She'd heard I had access to a car, she said, and that if anyone would go out on a limb for a stranger it was me. She'd gotten a new job at The Nevele Hotel that very day and had already been fired again. Now she was in a real jam. She tried to get a third job, she told me, but the third time wasn't the charm, so she had to leave and get back to Westchester. Could I just pick her up with all her luggage and drive her home?

Excuse me? I thought. *Pick you up and drive you to Westchester?*

STUMBLING HOME

I don't even know you!

She persisted. She wouldn't take no for any answer. No matter what I said she had an apt retort. Eventually I put my foot down.

" I'd do it for you," she finally said in all seriousness. She didn't even know me yet she had me squirming. She was immovable, as determined as a hurricane. And because she was so smart she could come at an issue from a dozen directions. If one tract didn't work she'd move on to the next. I told her that if I didn't work in the evening I'd lose my job. She asked for my boss's name. I was taken aback. Why in the world would she need that? Yet I gave her the name. She hung up thanking me casually as if nothing of any import had occurred. A few moments later I got a call from my boss saying he had no idea my mother was so sick and that, of course, I could take the night off to visit her in the hospital. And if, in fact, I needed an extra day, I shouldn't be shy about taking it.

So Becky was nothing if not cunning. And yet, invariably, I'd wind up feeling like **I** was the shyster, like her wanting me to drive her to Westchester. ***"I'd do it for YOU,"*** she said. How could I refuse to help someone who'd help me? Then she'd know I was selfish. She'd think I was unkind, and that I couldn't tolerate. Ever!

As it turned out, I chauffeured her all over New York that night. And despite the hour and fatigue, I wound up loving her company. She had no inhibition, whatsoever, no guilt, no self-doubt, no self-reproach. She could justify anything she felt or did and somehow it all seemed to make perfect sense. When we finally reached this big, fancy house in Larchmont at one in the morning, I wondered why she had needed to work in the first place since her parents were obviously rich. I parked the car along the cobblestone driveway leading to what seemed to be an estate. But instead of walking up to the front door, Becky motioned for me to follow her around the back. The house was dark. No cars were visible, no lights to guide us through the wooded property surrounding her home. When we got to the back, I expected her to walk up the steps to the rear door. Instead, she walked over to a ground floor window, removed the screen from the outside and began to raise the pane. What the hell was she doing, I wondered, shocked and fearful of the anticipated consequences to both of us.

The event reminds me of going to a store in downtown Brooklyn as a preteen with my next-door neighbor, Barbara. I must have been ten or eleven because leaving the neighborhood without an adult was absolutely forbidden by my parents and I distinctly remember feeling great anxiety at disobeying them. Barbara, on the other hand, was far more adventurous than I and far less constrained. That summer I even remember her wearing shorts that were so skimpy that her public hairs were visible. The sight was both outrageous and tantalizingly seductive. I envied her freedom and wished that I could be as provocative as she but I also knew that even if my parents had allowed it, I was so over-weight that the sight would not have been an attractive one.

When we got to Gimbels, a store chain that was similar to Macy's in the 50's, we browsed through the jewelry section trying on whatever struck our fancy. Then, out of the corner of my eyes, I see Barbara slide a ring into her pocket. My heart rate escalated to panic levels. I wanted to run but instead I froze in place, afraid to move or make any gesture whatsoever. That's when I realized she was trying to force a piece of jewelry, a ring, into my clenched hand. A moment later she was headed out the door and I right behind her.

That night her parents, apparently having found her stolen ring, called my parents. Over hearing some of the conversation, I stood like a newly deceased child at the door of God waiting for the final verdict. To this day, that wait was the most terrifying time of my life. I mention this fact so that, in contrast to several events I have yet to discuss, the degree of my fear may become apparent. I can only equate it to the terror I felt outside of Becky's home, as I clearly believed that some unbearable punishment awaited us.

STUMBLING HOME

Seeing my dread, Becky casually told me, as if annoyed by my discomfort, that the house we had just walked around belonged to her and her husband (whom she said she had only recently left, hence her job up in the Catskills). Now that she was on her own, she had to get some of her belongings and drop them off at her mother's apartment in lower Manhattan, with me as her conduit.

So there we were, "breaking and entering" in the middle of the night. And, of course, I wound up doing all the heavy lifting, the chairs, the tables, the TV, all HER own stuff, she swore -- stuff her rich, young doctor husband wouldn't let her take when she decided enough was enough. If it hadn't been for the photos of the two of them on the mantel, I never would have believed it was her house. The guy was a maniac, Becky said. But his family had money and she, a nobody from nowhere, thought her self lucky to be his pick -- at least at first. Boy was she in for a surprise.

So if she snuck in in the middle of the night to retrieve a few belongings, like the living room, who could blame her? Not me. I was ready to take the wallpaper by the time we left! Despite what people said about her, I was a true believer, brilliant but larcenous to the core.

ELLIE'S PATH

IT WASN'T UNTIL the summer was over that I saw Becky again, but I thought about her often, especially when I thought of Ellie. Ellie was like me, no better, no worse, not that she wasn't prettier and funnier and smarter than me, because she was -- but we were from the same place with the same points of reference. Becky, on the other hand, was like no one I'd ever met. She was only five years older, but tough as titanium. She had seen and done things I'd only heard about. Nothing scared her. She was a weapon -- not a gentleman's sword, but a missile you could trust in mortal combat. In comparison, Ellie was a lightweight, naive and frightened underneath -- like me. We tried to look tough but it didn't take an Einstein to realize it was only skin deep. Becky could talk her way out of Alcatraz, but when I finally spoke to Ellie at the end of the summer, she seemed, in contrast, to be linguistically challenged.

I'd gotten a message at Judson that she'd called and I was excited... but uncomfortable, too. We'd hardly spoken since I left home and I sensed she resented me for leaving her behind. Whenever we talked the conversation crackled with thunder that took the form of silence. There was so much happening in my life. I could barely contain my enthusiasm. But when I spoke to Ellie, I withheld excitement, as if I were being asked by Christopher Reeve how my life was going. Ellie, who'd once been filled with laughter, now seemed melancholy and inert. And I assumed I was to blame.

I called her back immediately, despite my ambivalence. What I heard was an Ellie I'd never heard before. She was sobbing, bereft, as if she'd lost everything. I'd never heard her voice shake as it did on the phone. I'd never heard her sound like a child, stammering for help. She'd always been so confident, so self-composed. The sounds echoed through my head as I sat on the stoop outside of Judson, sari and all, waiting to patch her up. Waiting and waiting.

The noon sun baked the cement beneath my thighs. I pulled my knees to my chest and wrapped my arms around them, a kid with a dot on her forehead waiting to take care of another kid in distress. The afternoon tourists paraded in front of the stoop, glancing down at the *Indian girl* with her chin resting on her knees. Maybe they'd never seen a sari before or an Indian princess sitting on dirty steps. One woman even stopped with her family to take a picture. You'd think I'd have been pleased to be the object of her attentions. But I wasn't. Maybe they saw an *interesting* young girl, a *special* girl from a far-off continent. But I knew better. I knew what the camera saw --- a girl with her panties showing! I lowered my head into my knees and then was safe from their ridicule.

God! I loathed *normal* people. How I wanted to be one of them, but couldn't. The dilemma tainted everything. Why else would a *nice* Jewish girl from Brooklyn who wants to be *normal* sit on a stoop on Thompson Street wearing a sari with her bloomers sticking out? Still, I thought, Ellie was counting on **me**. So how much of a freak could I be? I was a real logician, even then.

It was almost one o'clock when I saw a vaguely pretty but overweight girl walking towards me. *This can't be Ellie*, I thought for a moment, knowing, full well, it was. Her once lovely features had begun to bloat, as if filling, indifferently, with air. And the radiance that once drew you to her had dimmed - while some deep uneasiness took its place. Sadness and worry engulfed her. Her body, once slender, had swelled to carry the weight of her burden.

Our eyes locked as she approached me. I could see her tears and I knew she could see mine. The distance of our travels hadn't torn us apart. It was obvious from the first moment we saw each other. We both seemed to sigh with relief. But what was so new and disturbing to me was not the change in her appearance. But rather, that despite the excess weight and bloat, she seemed to be *deflated* to the bone, heavy, but insubstantial, puffed out, yet punctured at the same time. She was smaller than I'd ever seen her.

"Come, let's sit in the park like we used to -- when we were young," I said, poking her playfully with my elbow. She saw no humor in my gesture and walked silently toward the benches surrounding the fountain where we'd come so many times before, taking stock after Bernie's place, assessing the day's profits and losses. I was reminded of all that *girl talk* and was immediately nostalgic for what had once been. Invariably we'd assess the guys we saw that day, some sexy, some studious, some reading Walt Whitman, some reading about the war in Algeria, some about civil rights struggles in the South. Regardless, we always tried to guess who was *queer* and who was not. The word "lesbian" hadn't crept into our vocabulary yet, at least comfortably. So many words and concepts hadn't yet surfaced though clearly what underlay the language was known well, just unmentioned. Especially between Ellie and I, words were always inadequate.

We could sit in Washington Square Park for hours and never say everything we wanted to say. We hung on each other's words, eyes widened in awe at every revelation, every detail, every observation. And there was always more to say, even as we ran in the darkness to the Brooklyn-bound train because we were late again, racing, out of breath. There was always more to say, dissecting every guy, every gesture of his, every word, running to catch that train yet wishing, of course, that it never came.

But this time it was obviously different. We weren't headed to the park to talk frivolously about boys. You didn't have to be a mind reader to know that. A world had intervened. This was a funeral procession

-- but I had no idea whom we'd come to bury. Ellie walked, stone-faced, wearily, without saying a word and though I periodically made some awkward attempt at humor, I knew it was pointless and I felt embarrassed.

"*Let's sit here, Ellie,*" I suggested as we entered the Square.
"*No. I want to go where it's private.*"

I'd never heard her say she wanted privacy. There was dead silence. We kept walking. Something dreadful had clearly occurred yet I had no idea what it might have been. I thought perhaps one of her parents had died. But as terribly as that might have been, I doubted that was what was going on. Whatever was going on was even more catastrophic and life altering than that.

"*I'm pregnant,*" she finally muttered in a whisper, fixing the conversation in granite like a headstone.

I rubbed my forehead pointlessly. She didn't move a muscle, not even to wipe the tears that were running like wild fire down her cheeks. I reached in my pocket for a tissue that I knew full well I didn't have -- a gesture, just a gesture to make things right. I patted her cheeks with my shirt sleeve then moved as close to her as I could.

"*What are we going to do, Ellie?*" I thought out loud. She stared back vacantly, shrugging her shoulders. It was all too much to bear, the look implied. A look of horror and disbelief. How could it have happened? She used her diaphragm. She swore it. And I believed her. She was so fastidious about the care of her body, so unlike myself. Always prepared with the little accessories one might need in the course of a day, like the tissues I knew I didn't have. Ellie always had tissues.

I envied her, that she had the money to splurge on a pack of tissues. I could never have done that. Toilet paper would have to do. Of course our circumstances were different, she working and living at home, and I.... But still, these little differences struck me as emblematic of larger ones, that she was somehow prepared for life and I was just scraping by by the skin of my teeth.

So it wasn't merely the logistics of her predicament that baffled me, like what we were going to do about the pregnancy. It was that the predicament itself upset the balance of power. *God,* I thought, as I looked at her, so lost and forlorn. *How could she get herself pregnant?* I asked her if she could merely be late but it had been five months since her last period. *How could she have waited for five months? What was she thinking?* She wasn't thinking. That was the point. She didn't want to think. She had just tuned it out. I was awed by how she could do that, how she could just "tune it out," like my mother had been able to tune me out. For better or worse, I didn't have that capacity. Unfinished business barked in my ear until I focused on finishing it. Of course, I wasn't always successful, like trying to attend Queens College, but I was never free from the barking. Resolved or not, the matter would haunt me like a stutter, like Tourette's of the mind.

I slipped into my "helpful" mode, my gynecological mode, me who never used protection, and reminded Ellie that lateness didn't necessarily mean pregnancy. She wanted no part of the conversation. I persisted.

"Stop it, Bea! " She screamed, pulling up her blouse exposing her bloated, distended stomach. *"What's that, Bea? What's that?"* she sobbed, jumping to her feet, pacing back and forth, pounding her belly. *"Get it out of me,"* she begged, punching her self over and over and over. *"G-E-T I-T O-U-T O-F M-E!!!! **PLEASE!!!"***

I scraped the bottom of the barrel of "helpful" interventions, knowing full well all were merely reflective of my own impotence, my own need to deflect responsibility, to deflect the burden. There was indeed a major problem. I knew it and, above all, she knew it. The newly evident spots of baldness on her scalp were testament to her awareness of a major predicament.

I reminded her of a doctor we'd all heard of surreptitiously. But where was he? Was it Mexico, or maybe Connecticut? I wasn't sure. I wasn't even sure of his name. Girls talked about him in whispers. Someone had always heard of someone who'd been to see him. But his identity was shrouded. I knew he was far away. And it was difficult to get there, lots of secrecy, phony names. And it wasn't cheap. But even if it were, how would we find him? We had no idea where to begin. Neither of us had ever spoken to anyone who'd actually been there. He was like a phantom. Maybe even the kind of phantom people make up just to give themselves hope. One person tells another who tells another and suddenly there's a way out of this dilemma that could claim your life or at least change it forever.

Where once you'd had a future, now there was none -- but shame and humiliation, fingers pointing at you, people whispering as you pass, mothers rolling their eyes and alerting their young daughters to keep their distance; this condition can be contagious. You're now a pariah, a model for adolescent stupidity, for immorality, for the absence of parental teaching. So it wasn't just Ellie who'd bear the brunt of her misdeed; her family would now be forever identified as the parents who were too permissive, not permissive enough, too attentive, not attentive enough, too remiss in teaching her morality, not Christian enough, not Christian at all.

This latter thought occurred to me years later when a very successful friend of mine, knowing I was from Brooklyn, asked me if I'd ever heard of "The Highway?" Of course I had, I told him, it's where so many high school kids hung out on the weekends. I was surprised that he, having grown up in, in fact Manhattan, in "Little Italy" knew of Kings Highway in the heart of one of Brooklyn's largest Jewish communities.

"Yeah," he said, laughing and inflating his chest. "We all used to go to The Highway to pick up Jewish girls."

"Really," I asked. "How come?"

"Because they're easy!"

Interestingly enough, I'd never heard that, though I came to know it was not an unusual view. Of course, to me, it was utterly anathema; Jewish girls were, in my view, the least likely to engage in sexual activity. Maybe it was the absolute prohibition against ANY contact with boys that my mother espoused; maybe it was the enormity of the guilt that loomed just overhead should one deny these prohibitions; or maybe it was that movie roles dealing with female adolescents were invariably cast to non-Semitic "types;" the Sandra Dees of my generation. Non-Jewish girls, it seemed to me at the time, had all the fun. Boys wanted the blue-eyed blonde, not the dark complected, dark haired girl unless, of course, she looked like Elizabeth Taylor, those brunettes with milk-white skin and a small, slightly upturned nose.

Yet, here we were, a very Semitic looking girl-child trying to make her way in unchartered seas and her dearest friend, in the process of dying and being resurrected. Getting pregnant in the 50's was like that; at least the dying part; like living in Salem, Mass, in 1692, engaged in heretical activities. There was no way out. Once having been tagged, it was just a question of time before the good people of Salem exposed irrefutable proof of your heresy. And Ellie's parents were as guilty as Ellie.

But regardless of guilt, we ultimately knew that the search for the venerable New York abortionist in 1959 had to be discarded. Yet, no sooner had we done so, another idea came to mind. There were dozens of doctors on 57th Street, I argued, racing with new purpose. We could go to each and every one of them, stay in their office till midnight if need be, refuse to leave, and ultimately someone would help. Finally, I could see an almost imperceptible relaxation of the tension on her face.

Expensive boutiques lined the elegant street along with posh restaurants and medical offices that only the privileged were accustomed to use. One doctor, just one, I thought, and the problem would be solved. How hard could that be?

We rang the bell at the first office on the south side of 57th. If necessary we'll ring every bell from west to east then circle back on the other side. But the south side would be sufficient. Neither of us had any doubt.

A return buzzer let us in. The office was small but richly appointed. Nineteenth century paintings hung above the Queen Anne chairs that were occupied by proper matrons waiting properly for their turn. An impressive bronze to the right of the reception desk reminded me of my parent's home and a rush of melancholy overcame me. I reached, unconsciously, into my purse and fingered six $1.00 bills, all that I had until the next week's pay. For the first moment in almost a year I was afraid.

I looked at Ellie mournfully, at the grotesqueness of her stomach and the helplessness in her eyes. I looked down at my sari, what had become my usually attire, with shame and revulsion. I had to leave, to run from the filth and longings that were suddenly filling me without preparation.

"Do you have an appointment with the doctor? the receptionist asked, her eyebrows raised in unabashed disdain.

"No," I answered, Ellie paralyzed at my side. *"But we need to see him. It's an emergency."*

*"I'm sorry but the doctor doesn't see **anyone** without an appointment."*

"He has to see us. It's an emergency, " I repeated.

"What sort of emergency?" she asked dismissively. I pointed to Ellie's stomach than raised her blouse to her chin as if she were a mannequin.

"Oh, I'm sorry," the woman laughed, shooing us off with a gesture of her hand. *"Dr. Boyle is an opthomologist."*

"A what?"

"An Op tho mol o gist," she repeated phonetically as one might to a child. *"You'll have to find an obstetrician...a baby doctor."*

*"She doesn't **want** to have a baby!,* I shot back as if **she** were the child. *She **wants** to have an abortion!"*

The woman squinted as the chorus of well-dressed patients rolled their eyes and shook their heads.

"I'm sorry. You'll have to go somewhere else. "

"Where? Where can she get an abortion?"

"I really don't know... But you'll have to leave."

"*Fine* !" I said imperiously with my nose in the air. *"That's just fine. We didn't want to see that stupid doctor anyway!"*

It was just a bad start, I reassured myself back out on the street. Just a bad start. Regaining my poise, I reached for Ellie's arm. *"It was just a bad start, Ellie. Don't get discouraged. There are a million doctors around here… That woman was an idiot."* I could tell from her silence that she didn't agree but I held tight anyway and led her on. I rang the next buzzer briskly then waited with feigned bravado till we were let in. A large waiting room, unlike the first, pulsating with activity greeted us, mothers and their assorted children, men, nurses scurrying about with papers and forms and stethoscopes. We followed the sign to "Reception," and approached the desk. A hurried woman in a sparking white uniform reached out reflexively and handed us each a questionnaire.

"I'm with her," I said, pointing to Ellie at my side.

"Please have a seat and fill this out." Her voice was gentle but efficient. The kind of voice you follow without question. We looked around for an empty seat. There was only one -- next to a kind-looking, elderly lady. I motioned to Ellie to sit down then kneeled beside her on the floor, indifferent to the glances of patients around the room.

"What a pretty sari you're wearing," the old woman commented sweetly.

"Thank you," I replied, hesitating for a moment, as I censored the accent that had almost emerged. Ellie had never heard the accent and there was no reason to start now.

"I had a sari once," she continued, as a slight blush crossed her good-natured face.

"This may seem odd, but when I was a young girl I wore it to my high-school prom."

"Really? You must have been a.......**non-conformist**." I said with great emphasis, loving the word and proud of myself for knowing it.

"I was," she laughed gently.

"Bea," Ellie interrupted, pointing to her questionnaire. "What do you think?"

I looked down at the form, at the fiction she'd spun.

"Name?"......."Susan Levy."

"Date of Birth?"........September something, 1938." The extra four years might help, I agreed.

"Marital Status?"........"Separated."

"It's fine," I whispered. "They'll never check. There's only one thing I'd change."

"What"?

"Marital Status. Maybe if you say you're separated," I reasoned, "they'll want to talk to your husband before they give you an abortion. If you say you're divorced, you don't have a husband for them to ask."

Ellie agreed and together we checked the form one last time before returning it to the woman behind the desk, to *"Jill Sweigler, R.N,"* as her name-tag read.

"Levy?" Nurse Sweigler called out a moment later. "L-E- V- Y?"

"Yes?" Ellie answered.

"I can't seem to find your name in the appointment book. Who is your doctor?"

"Um..." Ellie hesitated.

"Dr. Nicoli? The obstetrician?" she asked.

"Um."

"Yes." I interrupted. "That's his name."

"Gee. I don't have your name down here. When did you make the appointment?"

"I made it for her," I interrupted again. "My sister's been a mess lately. Her husband just got a divorce when he found out she was pregnant."

"Oh dear! You poor thing." She put her hand on Ellie's shoulder as Ellie began to cry.

"Now, now. Everything will be all right. I don't have your name down but I'm going to send you in to see Dr. Nicoli as soon as he's free. O.K.?"

"O.K.," Ellie nodded with relief as we returned to our seats and settled in for a long wait.

"Susan Levy?" a voice called out a few minutes later. No response.

"Susan Levy?" the voice repeated. Still no response.

"Miss Levy?" Nurse Sweigler asked standing over us.

"Oh, Yes," I answered with a jolt, *"Susan, wake up. Susan, you're in a daze.*

"Oh! I'm sorry," Ellie shot back, looking at me then turning to the nurse in confusion.

"It's O.K." Nurse Sweigler reassured. *"I understand."* I stared at her for a moment, wondering if she was on to us, waiting to see what she would do, waiting for her to show her colors.

"Come with me, honey," she beckoned Ellie in a voice reserved for angels. I'd never heard such a lovely voice -- certainly not from a woman. But it was more than a lovely voice. It was a mommy's voice and I began to cry. She turned to me and put her arms around ME and stroked the back of my head. A flood of tears gushed from some place inside ME that I made no effort to contain. I didn't want to move. I stood limp, sobbing and sobbing in the comfort of her arms.

"You're worried about your sister, aren't you?" she asked kindly. I couldn't answer.

"I wish you were my mother." That's what I finally said.

Ellie began to follow Nurse Sweigler out of the waiting room. I wanted to go with them but hesitated. Is it customary? Would the nurse think it odd? Would the doctor object? I decided not to call any further attention to ourselves when Ellie asked if her "sister" could join them.

"Of course," she said. "That's what sisters are for."

Dr. Nicoli. His Italian name belied his appearance. Fair-complexioned, light, thinning hair, Richard Chamberlain without the good looks. Not unattractive, mind you, but unobtrusive, non-descript, someone whose face you'd hardly recall, yet who engendered absolute trust. A man, perhaps, from a small mid-western town that had no need for a sheriff, where a man's promise was his word, where what you saw was what you got. A man who'd never known heart-ache, or if he had, stiffened his upper lip and endured, a man who couldn't conjure up malevolence even if you'd shot his dog. A young, Protestant, Albert Schweitzer who left the farm and his momma to become a good doctor so he could take care of me, I mean, take care of Ellie. And it was evident he'd done what he set out to do. He was a man you could put your money on, who'd fix what he said he could fix and not make a big to-do about it. That's how it seemed, at least to me.

His presence was stunning, what it must feel like to be in a mommy's arms, what trust one must be able to access to throw one's self on the mercy of the court, what it must feel like to get a burger with fries when you've ordered a burger with fries. I'd have said *"thank you"* to the waitress even if I'd ordered a grilled cheese. That's why I wanted to extend *my* arm when Dr. Nicoli asked Ellie for *hers*, why I had to fight back the impulse to remove *my* blouse when he asked *her* to remove *hers*, to tell him *"all about it,"* when he was obviously talking to *her*. And I did resist, despite every urge to the contrary. *I'll wait my turn in line*, I thought. I trusted he'd get to me.

I waited silently besides the gurney. Ellie undressed behind a curtain then reappeared in a green hospital gown opened, absurdly, at the rear. Ellie, I thought, once my hero! God! That hospital gown cut her down to size. There she stood, exploding in the middle, helpless and out of control. It scared me to look at her yet I couldn't turn away. Not if I wanted to help.

"I understand, Susan, you'd like your sister to remain?" Dr. Nicoli asked her.

"Yes, please."

"Well, O.K., but I'll need to do a pelvic exam." Ellie stared ignorantly then turned to me for help but I could offer her nothing but a shrug of my shoulders and a barely perceptible shake of my head. He caught her perplexity and adapted his pace to hers.

"Just lie down on the table," he said kindly, "and move your **buttocks** to the Edge." Another blank stare.

"Move your hips down and slip your feet in the stirrups." Our gazes locked again in confusion. Her brows arched and froze as she moved with dreaded obedience toward the end of the table and lifted her legs to meet the enemy. She turned to me again for help and again I had nothing to give. Not even a word. I looked away.

"When was your last period?" he asked.

"Four or five months ago."

"Are you sure?"

"Yes."

The room became silent like a theater where an important play is about to begin. Nurse Sweigler placed a white sheet over Ellie's lower body, a domed amphitheater beneath which a great drama would unfold out of view of the paupers like me, too destitute to come up with the price of admission. Dr. Nicoli submerged his gloved hand in the arena then withdrew it abruptly.

"Susan," he said, grimly. "I'm not going to do a full pelvic. You're too far along."

"What do you mean?"

"It's dangerous at this stage of the pregnancy."

"What does that mean?" she asked again, her voice rising in alarm.

"I gather you want an abortion but it's too late for that."

"It can't be!"

"I'm afraid it is. You're more than five months."

"But you have to give me an abortion!"

"I'm afraid I can't, Susan."

"Isn't there anything you can do, Dr. Nicoli?" I interjected. "I've heard of all kinds of things...like the saline thing and things like that."

"There's nothing I can do," he repeated, turning sympathetically to Susan. "You're too far along."

"What about that pill. The morning-after pill?" I persisted.

"What about those places you can get an abortion in Mexico or South America?" Susan pleaded.

"Susan, it's too late."

"It can't be. It can't be," she cried.

"I'm afraid it is. Have you told your hus...........the baby's father?" Silence. "Do you know who the father is?" Silence. "Have you told your mother?"

"What does she have to do with it?" Ellie cried.

"You'll need to tell her."

"No. I'll get an abortion somewhere! Someone will give me an abortion!"

Dr. Nicoli thought for a moment, seemingly at an impasse, then put his hand on her shoulder:

"If you'd like, Susan, I'll have my colleague, Dr. Rosen, take a look at you. What do you say?"

"Yes, please."

A minute later there was a knock at the door and a young doctor in a white jacket and silver-rimmed glasses entered the room. Like Dr. Nicoli, his appearance was pleasant though unremarkable, the same sobriety that engenders trusts, the kind of mediocrity that's akin to a clarity of purpose, a studiousness unfettered by ego. These were not flamboyant men, not men called in a dozen directions by a dozen internal needs. These were men who probably never went to Bernie Eisner's apartment on a Sunday afternoon. And that was good, for it was that very singleness of focus that fostered such deference and respect.

"Dr. Rosen, this is Susan Levy," Nurse Sweigler said.

"How are we doing today, young lady?"

"I have to get an abortion."

"I've just spoken with Miss Levy," Dr. Nicoli interjected. "We've talked about her condition but I thought it might be helpful for you to take a look at her as well."

"That's fine. Now why don't you try to relax so I can examine you." He reached under the ominous amphitheater of white cotton where Ellie's future was being evaluated and did what he was meant to do with his able, knowing hands.

"When was your last period?" he asked somberly.

Ellie hesitated, was about to respond then hesitated again. "Three or four months ago," she said tentatively.

"Maybe five or six?" Dr. Rosen asked.

"No! Three or four months ago!" she stammered on the verge of tears.

"Sometimes women stain a bit in the first few months of pregnancy and think it's their period -- so they may not even be aware they're pregnant. I suspect that may have happened to you. Is that possible?"

"No! I didn't stain! It **was** my period!"

"I've just told Miss Levy that it's too late for an abortion," Dr. Nicoli said to his colleague.

"I completely agree. It's much too late. Have you spoken with your mother?"

"No! And I'm not going to!" Ellie screamed, bolting from the gurney to the dressing area in the corner of the room.

"Your mother will have to know," Nurse Sweigler said sympathetically. "If you don't want anyone else to know, there are places where you can stay until the baby........."

"A HOME FOR UNWED MOTHERS? I've heard of those places. Never! Never!" she cried from behind the curtain.

"No one has to know," she repeated. "You can give the baby up *for adoption immediately."*

Oh! My God! I muttered to myself. "But I once heard of a girl who..."

"*Girls in this predicament have been known to try all sorts of things,*" Dr. Nicoli interrupted. "*But believe me, my dear, there is NOTHING that can be done now. I think your sister needs to discuss this with your mother.....*"

"*I won't. You can't make me,*" Ellie screamed, shooting out from behind the curtain, grabbing my arm and pulling me from the office with her.

"Wait, Susan," Nurse Sweigler implored. "Wait..."

Her voice trailed in the distance as we ran up the street from one office to the next, from one terrifying edict to another, deeper and deeper into hopelessness, from youth and possibility to resignation and fatigue.

As darkness set, we'd finally come to the end of our travels -- back to where we'd begun. Not a word passed between us. We stood at the entrance to the subway with nothing to show for our efforts but silence. I tried to avoid Ellie's eyes. There was nothing to see in them -- nothing that I could do anything about. She looked around, as if deciding from limitless options where to go next -- like a first-time tourist perplexed by the vastness of the city -- then slowly turned and walked down the stairs to the familiar train that would take her back to the dismal Brooklyn apartment she'd never left.

I reached into my pocket as I followed her into the bowels of the subway -- then ran ahead to the token booth -- to save the day -- and bought us each, from my hoarded and cherished dollar bills, a one-way ride back -- or forward - as the case may have been.

THE BETRAYAL

I KNEW I should have called Ellie that evening but for some reason I can't recall, I didn't. Nor did I call her the following day nor the day after that. I assumed she'd told her parents, and yet, as peculiar as this may sound, I have no recollection of feeling anything about it or even thinking much about it in the days to come. But when occasionally I was reminded, my heart ached -- like watching a child die of leukemia when there's nothing, nothing you can do to stop it. You just stand there at the foot of her bed -- a mere twitch in the vastness of the universe, as destiny does to her the unbearable -- and all you can offer is some absurd gesture like picking up the tab for a stuffed animal she's too sick to notice.

The few times I thought of Ellie it was accompanied by a deep, deep sigh of relief that it wasn't me, that I wasn't the child being ravaged by fate, that I was free in my blessed Judson and that the God's were inexplicably watching my back. Then I'd move on to more important things and Ellie's plight would recede from my consciousness and concerns.

Most of what I thought about that fall was Alfredo. We were madly in love the way you can only love once in your life, silent and intense. Our eyes clung to each other. In our glances was our speech, a language that was rich and euphoric. Now and then he'd read to me (in Spanish, of course) from the poets he loved the most or I'd captivate him with tales of my childhood in the Ukraine. This was an awesome love, indeed.

And even when I wasn't with Alfredo he filled my reveries. I took him with me in my consciousness wherever I went and he turned sadness into joy, mediocrity into magic. So it didn't seem odd when a visitor to Judson said she'd heard Alfredo had a girlfriend.

"Beatricia, isn't that your name?" I recall her asking.
"Yes, and yours?"
"Maria," I believe she said. *"I teach with Alfredo at N.Y.U."*
"Ah! Spanish Literature?"
"Yes. We're in the Doctoral Program together." She'd been gone for the summer, she added, only to be greeted, when she returned, by constant references to *"Beatricia, Beatricia."* She was pleased to finally meet the girl who'd captured Alfredo's attentions.

"It's nice to meet you, too," I said, delighted, yet surprised, at the same time. Despite how much Alfredo loved me, the notion that I was thought about when I was gone was unfamiliar. Out of sight, out of mind, the way a baby assumes the mother ceases to exist when she can't be seen.

"Actually, I vas away for za summer too," I added. *"I only back at Judson for za last few weeks.."*

"You have such an interesting accent, " She remarked. *"Where is it from?"*

"Russia," I said, lowering my eyes slightly from her gaze.
"Oh! That's fascinating. I didn't realize you were foreign."
"Yes," I barely whispered.
"I don't know why I thought you were from Michigan."
"Michigan?" I laughed.
"Yes. I thought Alfredo said you were from Michigan."
"No, no. I from za Ukraine. I am exchange student from Kiev."
"But doesn't your father teach at N.Y.U.?" She persisted with obvious confusion.

"No," I laughed again.

"That's so odd. I thought Alfredo said he'd met you through your father, Dr. Wilder. Isn't he your father?"

"Dr. Wilder? No. Ve met last year at Judson."

"Well, so much for linguistics!" she laughed. "I'm glad to meet you, anyway, even if your name isn't Bea Wilder. At least I got the first name right!"

People were always getting my lineage confused. So, I wasn't concerned when someone got a fact wrong here or there, like who I was or where I was from. I would have dismissed her error without a second thought had someone else not asked me the very same question only days before: *"Isn't Dr. Wilder your dad?"* The first woman asked.

"Alfredo, my dearest," I said playfully that evening, only mildly perplexed by the coincidence. "People think my name is Bea Wilder! Dese Americans are strange. My name is Starr. Yes?"

"What?"

"Starr. Vy dese people thought I vas the daughter of some teacher named Dr. Wilder?"

"That's ridiculous. I have no idea why."

"My darling Alfredo," I cooed, as a vague thought crossed my mind. I wrapped my arms around his torso and perched myself on his knees, empathetically. I understood, full well, feeling inadequate, feeling that the realities of one's life fall short of the mark. I understood full well, as my father had before me, the need to embellish the facts of my life. If I, after-all, was Bea Starr from the Ukraine and my father was Samuel Starr from London, England, couldn't Alfredo be the boyfriend of Bea Wilder, daughter of **the** Dr. Wilder from N.Y.U.?

"My dearest love on earth," I continued with caring and patience, as cute as I could possibly be;"

"What?"

"Dat you made up who my father vas to impress people? I von't mind if you did. Really I von't.

"I don't know. What's the big deal?" He sputtered back, annoyed.

"Oh! My angel face is mad. Now, now. Don't be mad." I tried to reassure him. I could understand the need to impress someone. But he didn't respond. He tensed and backed away. "Alfredo," I said, sitting up, unwrapping my body from his as another light went off in my head. "Is dis about **Jews?** Did you lie about me because you were embarrassed I'm a **JEW?**" My voice lost its charm and energy. My body began to withdraw and my head shook like a pendulum in disbelief. "Jesus! That's **really** bad..."

Alfredo sat motionless. I imagined he was feeling foolish and very guilty. I wanted to let him off the hook. But ashamed of my Jewishness? I thought. That's bad.

"It had nothing to do with being Jewish," he shot back nervously, as if his words were charting a dreaded and unfamiliar course.

"Then vhy?"

"It doesn't matter."

"It does to me!"

"It **doesn't matter**, Beatricia!!!"

"But it **does** to me, Alfredo!"

"It has nothing to do with YOU!"

"How could it have nothing to do with me if you give your girlfriend a different name?"

"Forget it! Please. Forget it. It means nothing, Beatricia. It means NOTHING!"

"But I can't forget it now. It must have meaning. Vhy else wouldn't you tell me?"

"Beatricia, Beatricia, I love you so much," he implored.

"I love you so much too, Alfredo. But when you love someone, you don't lie to them. Didn't I tell you everything about my life in the D.P. Camps? Things I've never told anyone else?"

"Yes, Beatricia, you did."

"Then, you MUST tell me. People who love each other don't keep secrets."

"I can't, my darling."

"You can if you love me."

"I DO love you -- more than anything in the world."
"Than tell me the truth.
"I don't want to lose you."
"Lose me? What are you talking about?" A chill came over my body.
"My darling Beatricia," he uttered slowly, head bowed, his voice tentative as if walking across glass. *"I never met anyone like you. You're so… so deep, so honest. I've never been in love like this before..."*
"I know, my darling," I interrupted, *"but vhy vould you change my name?"*
"It had nothing to do with you. It just happened. I don't know why. It makes no sense. I got all confused..."
"**IT** just happened?"
"**It** meant nothing. NOTHING!"
"A girl, Alfredo?" The weightless sound of my voice barely reached his body. "Another girl, Alfredo? No. Please tell me 'no.'"
"Don't cry, my little Beatricia. It was nothing. I swear it."
"**IT? IT?** Oh, no, Alfredo."
"Please, Beatricia. Please."
"Who is she? WHO? Tell me!"
"Bea Wilder. That's her name. I met her at NYU. But I don't care about her anymore..."
"**ANYMORE?**...Oh! my God."
"It's over. It's over."
"Over? VHAT'S OVER?" I labored, turning away from the dizziness in the space between us. Nothing was anchoring me. Everything became dislodged, hanging by a thread, a single thread that connected the pieces of my existence, one thread, flimsy and ephemeral. I gathered a purpose from somewhere out of sight and turned to him with my head raised and steady to do what had to be done.

"Did you sleep with her, Alfredo," I asked, stoically, poised for execution.

He nodded.

RESCUE

I COULDN'T GO back to Judson that night -- nor the nights afterwards. The simple act of breathing took all my energy. My chest expanded and deflated erratically. The air couldn't find its way. I tried to direct it. I fought to push it through an invisible impasse that was bent on opposing me. In and out. In and out. Gasping for air, moving my body this way and that to maximize the success of my labors. In and out. In and out, slowly, methodically. Keep your mind on the ball. *Breathe, Beatricia. Breathe.* My fingers tingled, as if frozen, while sweat washed my face. Sometimes I'd vomit without rhyme or reason and always my eyes were filled with tears.

Perhaps another girl might not have been as shattered. Perhaps a *normal* girl might merely have been stung, then picked herself up and moved on to the *other fish in the sea*. That notion, though, was anathema, that there were *"other fish in the sea,"* like a child who's many foster parents send her back to the agency when they discover she's defective. At first she's hurt and discouraged but maybe not despairing because she knows she's resourceful and has conquered adversity before. Now, in her final foster placement, she's learned to mask her defects because they'll be no other chances. But when they, too, send her back, it's to a new reality, the end of the road, and she knows it. That's why despair is so deadly. There are no other fish in the sea and there's no point trying to convince her there are.

Until the moment of Alfredo's betrayal, I somehow believed I could mask my worth and still be loved. Or maybe I just never thought about it, whether one can love an imposter? Whether an imposter can feel loved, regardless. Maybe I misread his love for the imposter as his love for **me**. And when he sought out another girl, I assumed it was because I, the exile from Brooklyn, wasn't good enough. Maybe my father was caught in the same catch-22. Samuel Starr from Poland was deficient, a priori – So he had to mask his identity. But in doing so, he insured that any love one felt for him would have to be dismissed -- because the man they loved didn't exist. Maybe that was the origin of his rage, of his rootlessness. Maybe he was a vessel that could never feel full no matter how the market did because there was a hole in the bottom of his make-up.

Becky pressed me to stay the night in her small apartment in the West Village. One night lead to a second and then to a third. It would be only temporary, we thought, till I got my bearings, till I was able to breathe, till I could find some reason to get out of bed. When Alfredo tracked me down, Becky turned him away and refused his calls. When his letters came, she tore them up. When he waited endlessly outside our door, she ignored him. I asked her to. He had died. Or perhaps it was me who had died. In either case, the jig was up.

I wasn't trying to punish him or make him regret what he'd done. In some very real way, what he did made sense to me, seemed fitting. Of course I wasn't worthy of his love. I had to make him disappear so I could carry on -- maybe the way my mother had done to me so **she** could carry on. Maybe a child took too much of **her** air. So, when Alfredo begged and pleaded for me to come back, I was deaf. I'd learned my lessons well. Occasionally, when I weakened, he'd suck the air out of my lungs again -- and again I'd gasp for breath. But sometimes when I weakened, it was different. Sometimes my body would inexplicably *fill* with air and engulf me as if I were caught in a violent wind, too much air, too fast. In and out. In and out, frenetically, like a sprinter on her final lap. And that would wake me up and turn my mind from the death of my *self* to the pain I could heap upon him. I'd kill him off in my mind as he'd done to me - recklessly and without mercy.

But they were short lived and unpredictable, these moments of triumph and power. Mostly, I just lay limp on the sofa, mindless, lost in a fog without purpose or destination while Becky and Sinai kept the world afloat. I'm not sure how long it lasted, this visit to oblivion -- maybe it was days but it could have been weeks.

All I remember of it is one afternoon in the late fall when the weather had turned cold and damp. Sinai urged me to accompany him to Macy's to buy a coat for his sister in India. She was just about my size, he said, and it would help if I came along.

Together, we scoured the racks. I must have tried on a dozen coats, but one, in particular, stood out. Actually, it wasn't a coat at all but a hooded black velvet cape, floor-length and majestic -- not what a middle-aged woman needed to wash her clothes in the Ganges, I thought. But I was mesmerized by it, by my reflection in the mirror, a princess in her sari and regal cape -- a father's daughter, meant for special things.

Why in the world didn't everyone wear saris and a dot in the middle of their foreheads? I couldn't understand. *Why didn't everyone wear black velvet capes?* But when it was time to leave the store, despite my infatuation with the child in the mirror, we decided upon a sensible, brown wool coat that would, if nothing else, keep his sister warm. As Sinai walked to the cashier, he mentioned that she'd need a muffler as well and asked me if I'd pick one out while he waited in line. But when I returned with a matching scarf, he'd already paid and was ready to leave. The line was faster than expected, he said. It didn't matter. She'd do without it.

We got back to Becky's apartment as daylight fell and fatigue wore me down. I hurried up the stairs to the front door, eager for Sinai to leave, eager to avoid the discomfort that invariably accompanied my rejection of his advances. But on this night, to my pleasant surprise, my concerns were groundless. He kissed me on the cheek, smiled lovingly and handed me the large coat box that he'd awkwardly carried under his arm. I was confused for a moment.

"Sinai, what am I supposed to do with your sister's coat?" I asked as he turned to leave.

"Wear it, my princess."

"What?"

"Wear it, my Princess. It's for you."

And it was for me. Not the *sensible* brown coat that would merely do its job, but the black velvet cape that could do far more. I wore that cape everywhere, no matter how bitter the weather, no matter what my destination. Black velvet may not protect you from the elements but it protected me from something more lethal. And when the memory of Alfredo's betrayal hit me, I found, through the fantasy of my cape, a mechanism of flight, a way to stay, for the most part, out of the line of fire. And in time, I was able, once more, to do for myself what had to be done.

INTERNATIONAL HOUSE

(I'm on the bottom row, second form the left.)

THROUGH THE GRAPE-VINE I'd heard about Columbia University's *International House*, a foreign-student residence similar to Judson but infinitely larger. Though I hadn't yet seen it, when the time came to leave Becky's small apartment, I took the subway uptown to Riverside Drive and 120th Street to stake out my claim.

International House was a stately and imposing structure set on a large parcel of land facing Riverside Park and the Hudson River. The location was serene and almost bucolic compared to the Manhattan I knew best. Gone was the hubbub, the discourse of Lower Manhattan,

INTERNATIONAL HOUSE

Greenwich Village and the Lower East Side. International House was dignified and genteel and I needed to be cleansed.

Inside, the spacious lobby was filled with people in native attire reading, playing chess, sitting in small groups or mulling about. Off to the right of the lobby (which served as the residence lounge), music could be heard from rehearsal rooms where student violinists were preparing for a recital. To the left of the lobby was a large room with ping pong tables where Asian students was playing.

The mood of *"I"* House was strikingly wholesome and pleasant. There'd be no unfaithful Alfredo's here, no Ellie's in doomed and desperate races to rid themselves of their misdeeds, no lost children trying to find a home, no interlopers, no frauds and no outcasts. No. International House was Columbia University and with it came Columbia's stature and refinement. This was a place removed from life's struggles. This was a sanctuary, a cathedral, a place for solitude and renewal. It was a place for the Bea I wanted to become, a serious ea, refined and at peace.

I walked up to the registration area to the far left of the lounge and meekly asked the woman seated behind the desk how one becomes a resident. Noticing the sari and dot on my forehead, she didn't seem to reveal any doubts about my candidacy.

"*Are you a student?*" she asked.

"*Yes. I in da Art History Department. I study Indian cave paintings.*"

"*How interesting. Where in India are you from?*"

"*Vell, actually, I from Kiev. I'm an exchange student.*"

"*My goodness!*" she said with delight. "*I don't think we have **any** students from Kiev.*

Just take this application, fill it out and send it back to me as soon as possible. We'll need your school registration receipt and a personal letter of recommendation. That's the most important."

"*Danka,*" I said smiling. "*I vill send it to you soon.*"

"*Good. We'll look forward to hearing from you.*"

I nodded deferentially and walked out of her line of sight to a writing desk at the far end of the lobby where I sized up the application as a bank robber sizes up a bank on the first dry run. *It was manageable,* I thought. *It could be done.* The school receipt was simple but the letter of recommendation gave me pause, if only for a moment. Then, without hesitation, I sat down at the desk and proceeded to compose a testimonial in my behalf.

I don't recall the exact wording of the letter. It was something about a young Russian exchange student who was held in high esteem by the author of the letter. Something about the obstacles this young woman had overcome and the promise she exhibited. She would be a tribute to International House, of that the author was certain. And, if my memory serves me correctly, it was that very handwritten letter that I returned to the Registrar the very same day, signed, simply enough, *Mrs. Eleanor Roosevelt.*

Though my room at International House was very much like my room at Judson, it never felt the same. "I" *House* lacked the intimacy and *family* that characterized Judson with its mere 25 students. Had I lived at "I "*House* for a dozen years, I doubt I ever would have come to know everyone's name. I spent my time playing chess in the lobby and developed, I think, a reputation as a rather odd yet mysterious creature. Sometimes I played ping pong with the Asian students and occasionally even won. Regardless of the outcome, the challenge was always invigorating. With female players, it was a different story. Despite my invariably being the better player, the games with women were fraught with tension, as though something deeply significant were at stake, as though some subterranean power was being wrestled with. The same was true of chess with women where, there too, a win should have come easily. Instead, the games were filled with discomfort.

For a while I thought I was fortunate to be at International House, not as fortunate as being at Judson, of course, but more so than Brooklyn. The possibility of losing it drove that reality home. Like the day I was talking with an Indian girl, Sabaga, on the lawn outside, dressed in my sari and the usual dot on my forehead. In the distance, I thought I saw something that scared me. Far down the hill were two people whom I could have sworn were my parents. Now, I'd seen them on occasion when I went back to Brooklyn for some obligatory event, without the costume or accent, with my head between my legs. But they didn't know I was at *"I" HOUSE. It couldn't be them.* I reassured myself. I strained to make out who the people were as they walked closer and closer -- till finally, I recognized my mother and my father walking straight toward me smiling from ear to ear. A flood of dread swept over me, that they'll expose me and I'll be asked to leave. But there was no time to run. They'd seen me already and were calling out my name.

"Sissy, Sissy," my mother called to me, waving her hand in the air. Damn! I thought, 'Sissy,' no less. Not even 'Beatricia'!

"I think those people are calling you," Sabaga said, pointing to my parents as I pretended I didn't notice. *"Beatricia, those people are trying to get your attention."*

I turned around nonchalantly as my mother approached me and kissed me on the cheek.

"Sissy, you look BEAUTIFUL...," she said to my father. "Doesn't she look beautiful, Sam?"

"A chip off the old block," he toyed, lifting me off the ground in a spin. *"How you doing, kid?"*

"Good, good," I mouthed, as inaudibly as possible.

"Sam, look at this beautiful sari," my mother continued, "and what a beautiful girl," she said, pointing to Sabaga.

"Thank you," Sabaga nodded, seemingly perplexed by the encounter.

"Sabaga," I said in a whisper. " This is Sam and Etta."

"Nice to meet you," she responded, bowing her head ritualistically.

"Oh! How nice, how nice," my mother delighted. "Sam, isn't that lovely?"

"*To you, too,*" my father clowned, holding his hands in prayer position and bowing in kind.

"*Excuse me, excuse me,*" I said, grabbing Sabaga's arm and leading her a few feet away. "*Dese people are strange,*" I whispered, my accent in tact. "*I stayed vid dem vhen I first came to America. They are very strange but I must say hello for a few minutes. Vould you save me a seat in the dining room? I'll come right in.*"

"*Of course,*" she answered, turning to my parents. "*If you please excuse me, I must go now. It was so nice to meet you.*"

"*Oh! It was lovely, lovely,*" my mother gushed as if she'd met Indira Ghandi. My father bowed again, circling his index finger and lowering his head ceremonially. I took their arms and led them off in the other direction as Sabaga returned inside.

"*What a lovely girl,*" my mother beamed. "*And so pretty.*"

Little else was said except how they ADORED my sari and how BEAUTIFUL I looked with a dot on my forehead and how INTERESTING it was and what did it represent. Not a single question such as, "*Gee, kid, are you all right?*" or "*How you fixed for money?*" or "*Do you need anything?*" or "*What's wrong, honey. How can we help?*" Not a word such as, "*Oh, my God! My child is in trouble! What's she doing with a dot on her forehead!*"

Omissions like this were nothing new yet it was the first time it occurred to me that they were, indeed, omissions.... that my parents had left something very important out. I couldn't come to terms with the insight. Despite relief that the encounter hadn't exposed me, I was left feeling utterly exposed, naked and insubstantial. *How could they **not** have been alarmed,* I kept asking myself? How could they ask about the caste mark and not about **me**? How could they not see my pain? How could parents not get *personal*? Maybe if I'd read them Indian poetry or told them of the fascinating people I'd met, maybe then they would have been curious. But. It was only me, in my little sari.......with my little dot on my forehead. And so, eager to get away, I told them I had to return to my studies. We kissed good-bye and went our separate ways (after my father slipped me a ten dollar bill) – they, back to the safety of their illusions and I, back to the safety of mine.

I remember crying in my room after they'd left and I remember having difficulty falling asleep that night. A coffin underground was reaching for a child and she was almost caught in its clutches. Almost. But, not quite. What was more evident that day than any days before was the vast distance between us, how utterly strange it was that two parents could not have had a moment of concern for their child, dressed in costume pretending she was someone other than who she was, not a hint of doubt that perhaps something was wrong, perhaps something was terribly wrong. To the contrary what seemed most evident was the pleasure they felt in seeing their child adopt a romantic persona, become an *interesting* character in what might have been one of her father's *interesting* plays, as if she indeed was the character she inhabited. How could they not ask the most elemental questions of this peculiar girl: why was she wearing a sari? Was she all right? Did she need anything? Was she happy? Of course none of these concerns was expressed because they saw nothing peculiar about her and secondly all people to them were characters in literary fiction. It was all a play. The only meaningful questions were whether or not the characters were constructed well enough, whether they were heroic enough and what they reflected about the author.

I was thinking of Ellie the next day more than I had in months. In the turmoil of our lives, we'd gotten separated, though I knew, full well, it was I who had left. Whenever I had wanted to call, something always seemed to intervene, maybe my dread of hearing what I expected I'd hear, maybe my guilt at having been spared the horror of what I knew was before her that day on 57th Street, maybe my preoccupation with the chaos of my own life. Maybe I was just running too far and too fast to look back. Whatever it was, I missed her terribly and knew it was time to call. When I finally reached her on the phone she seemed a thousand miles away. Her once cheerful voice was subdued and staccato as if it were coming from a body suspended in cement and resigned to be there:

"*I had the baby,*" she told me almost matter-of-factly. "*My mother sent me to Staten Island to a home for unwed mothers.*"

"*Oh! My God! What did you have?*" I asked with excitement, as though it were a blessed event.

"*A girl............But I don't want to talk about it.*"

"*O.K. Just tell me her name.*"

"*I don't know........*"

"*You don't know?*" I asked naively.

"*No.................and I don't want to talk about it.*"

"*But Ellie,*" I persisted till, finally, I understood.

"*I'm going out with someone,*" she continued, changing the subject.

"*Great!*" I said, artificially, spinning from the reality of what she'd been through. I wanted to ask her a million questions. I wanted to know everything that had happened, the baby, the home, the delivery, the adoption. Everything. "*How did it feel to have a baby?*" I was dying to ask her. "*Did it hurt? Did you cry?*" But I knew I couldn't ask. Even if she'd wanted to talk, she didn't seem to have the energy.

"*So who is he?*" I finally asked. "*Who's the lucky guy?*"

"*Nobody.*"

"*What do you mean, 'Nobody?'*"

"*He's just a lawyer.*"

"*That's great, a lawyer!*" I said, shifting inside from sadness to envy.

"*That's what my mother says.*"

"*Well it is! It's great! What's his name?*"

"*Steve.*"

"*What's he like?*"

"*................He's short.*"

"Jesus! You don't sound like you like him very much."

"My mother says I'm the luckiest girl in the world that somebody wants me after what happened, especially a Jewish LAWYER! She thinks it's incredible."

"What do you think?"

"She says I should be really happy, that I'll never get another chance."

"But what do you think? Do you like him?"

"I guess I'm lucky. He's a lawyer...... and he's ...."

And that was that! I tried to tell her about Alfredo and International House but she didn't seem interested. Maybe she was just preoccupied or maybe we had just moved too far apart. Our closeness felt ruptured. I hoped it wouldn't be for long.

Sabaga's room was down the hall from mine on the third floor. After the encounter with my parents, I'd been reticent to approach her. Yet, as time went on, it was clear she was unaware of their relationship to me, saying only that she thought they were peculiar. That I could maintain the charade, accent and all, in the presence of my parents was an irony that continued to plague me and invariably left me sad.

Despite it, I was grateful for Sabaga's friendship. Her seemingly cloistered experience and the differences in our cultures, she from India and I from the Ukraine, weren't impediments. We shared "girl stuff" and laughter, not the kind of cynical laughter I shared with Becky, but giggles, like Ellie and I had shared a lifetime ago.

"Beatricia," Sabaga whispered naughtily in the lobby, *"did you see HIM? He's so cute."*

"Nyet! He's too blonde. But vhat about that guy over there? He's gorgeous!"

"Oh, no," she said, shaking her head. *"He looks like all my cousins*

back home. But his name is Srinivasin if you want to know."
"Do you know him?"
"Not really. But I know he likes YOU."
"How you know dat?"
"He told me you have beautiful eyes."
"He did?"
"Yes," she nodded naughtily, her dark skin glowing. "He asked me if you are Indian."
"What did you tell him?"
"I told him the truth, that you are Russian but that you lived with an Indian family."
"Hmmmm," I schemed, raising my eyebrows.
"I'll introduce you to him if you'll show me how to paint my eyes like yours."
"You've got a deal."

Sabaga loved make-up the way twelve-year-olds do when it's prohibited. And I loved showing her how to use it. I'd missed that experience when I was a child, the little girl making up her mommy as if she were a precious doll and mommy delighted to be part of the game.

But of course, my mother never wore make-up! Now Sabaga was my doll, all painted up and smiling. We grew fond of each other during my months at *The House*. She was sweet and kind and seemed genuinely to like me though, of course, she couldn't know me at all. Or could she? Sometimes I wondered about that. Sometimes she'd look at me as if to wink, as if to say, *"I know."* It disarmed me when she did that. I'd turn away.

But whether she knew me or not, she lived up to her end of the deal and introduced me to *Srin* who was even more gorgeous up close than he was far away. Sabaga told me often that lots of guys look like him back home, but to me, he was Valentino and Tarzan rolled into one. It wasn't long before Srin and I became intimate. I don't recall what he was studying or why he said he didn't live in *"I"*

House anymore, but he didn't. He had an apartment on ll2th Street which I never visited because if he was there, he said, he'd be typing his dissertation and needing his time alone. I had no idea what a dissertation was, of course, but I knew it was serious. He worried about it, more and more, it seemed, the closer it got to completion.

We talked a lot about how life would change when he was done, how that moment would feel. I knew it would be the most important moment of his life. So on the day he was to have presented his dissertation, I showed up at his door to surprise him with a copy of Keats (that Sinai had given to **me**) and a bottle of Red Mountain wine to toast his success

I stood in the hall outside his apartment, poising myself for what I assumed would be his delight with my unexpected visit. I knocked on the door but there was no answer. I knocked again. Still no answer. He must be home, I thought. It was 6:00 o'clock. I knocked once again, this time calling to him through the door.

"Srin," I said flirtatiously. "It's me." No response. "Srin, it's me. Beatricia." Still no answer. I knocked harder.

"SLUT!" came a scream through the air.

"SLUT! GET OUT OF HERE! GET AWAY FROM MY HUSBAND!" screamed the voice behind the door as it flung open violently**.** *"HERE! YOU SLUT! TAKE YOUR PANTIES!"* the blonde woman railed, throwing a pair of underpants in my face. *"AND DON'T EVER COME BACK HERE AGAIN! YOU WHORE!"* she howled, as Srin stood speechless behind her, his mouth wide open and his eyes bulging with dismay.

The door slammed in my face. I bent down to pick the panties up from the floor when my knees gave way to the weight of my humiliation. On the cold floor, I cowered as voices revisited me, shaming me, this pitiful creature on a dirty floor groveling for a pair of dirty underwear I didn't even think were mine. I was mortified by a world I didn't belong to -- no one's wife, no one's daughter, no one's

STUMBLING HOME

American child -- no Jewish lawyer's girlfriend. His wife's face kept appearing though she'd long gone. Not Srin's face. That disappeared without effort or regret into an abyss of irretrievable memories. As I lay powerless on the cold floor, I kept thinking about *her* face, fair and nondescript, a face of loathing and contempt, engulfing me, ready to spit in my eyes, pointing it's finger of guilt, despising me, deafening me, killing me off -- the wayward, evil daughter.

68 PERRY STREET

BECKY OFFERED ME safety once again. She, too, was racing and longing for solid ground. For some inexplicable reason she seemed to think she could find it in me. Maybe it was my resourcefulness that she misinterpreted as strength, maybe my impulsivity that she saw as decisiveness. Maybe she liked my humor because she had none. Or maybe she knew I'd never reject her as so many others did -- for her lashing tongue, her larcenous ways, or the spectacle she made of herself. Maybe she knew I was on to her, to the ways she could cut people to shreds in one breath then save their lives in another. Maybe she knew that, in her, I witnessed the most striking acts of cruelty and the most exquisite acts of kindness -- and saw pieces of them both in myself. Whatever it was, Becky looked to me, as I to her, for rescue.

Though most people were wary of her, Becky was a magnet for others, people who were passive or depleted, unable or unwilling to take action in the world, people who were eager for Becky to take action for them. And she was ready to take up their cause. I was one of those people, or so I felt, though I doubt anyone else would have seen it that way, and certainly not Becky. Whatever it was that drew us to each other, when *INTERNATIONAL HOUSE* lost its glow, I came knocking on her door and together we decided to look for a place to live.

Divorce had left Becky wanting for little. Despite her money, though, she would have been happy with a tenement like Bernie Eisner's on the Lower East Side. But that wasn't for me. It was the West Village of Henry James, Poe and Edna St. Vincent Millay that I held out for. To understand the choices, you'd have to know the neighborhoods. Bernie's place on 6th Street and Second Avenue was the *East Side*, though landlords had begun referring to it as the *"East Village"* so they could jack up the rents. But whatever you called it, the East Side was still the remnant of a ghetto once inhabited by Eastern European immigrants who had arrived at the turn of the century, too poor to live anywhere else. When they could finally afford to move, they moved uptown and were replaced by new, disparate groups who were bound together by their poverty. By the early 60's, the Lower East Side, or the emerging "East Village" was populated by new immigrants from Spanish-speaking countries, by young runaways, throwaways, would-be poets, anarchists, elderly Europeans who hadn't achieved the great American dream and anyone else who could only afford an apartment with a bath-tub in the hall. Oftentimes, several apartments shared a common bathroom in the hall. "Railroad" flats were typical of the area where you'd have to walk through tiny adjacent rooms to get to the next. It's where you lived if you couldn't afford not to and I'd have none of it. Becky and I were privileged. She was a genius and I was a Princess. Though we could have afforded *two* bedrooms on the East Side, we chose not to go that route. No matter how large the apartment, the location just wouldn't do.

The West Village, on the other hand, is marked by four-story brick row houses set back from the sidewalks and cobblestone streets, by low iron gates reminiscent of Europe. Wide, palatial steps lead to parlor floors with quaint gardens in the rear, accessible through the parlor or ground floor below. Marble fireplaces and high ceilings distinguish the rooms. Rich mahogany double doors slide outward to libraries or formal dining rooms. Deep tones of velvets and wood cover the walls. Old dumb-waiters that once served as a lift for dinners and afternoon teas can still be found in the brownstones and grand townhouses on streets walked by giants. That's where we belonged, my larcenous friend and I.

To our great surprise we managed to find a newly renovated *one-bedroom* apartment on the second floor of a beautiful brownstone at sixty-eight Perry Street in the heart of the West Village. The apartment was spacious and crisp but had lost, through modernization, much of the original embellishment. But it was light-flooded and elegant and directly above the parlor apartment occupied by a European author whose comings and goings were the envy of my young life.

Tanya De Ramma was a *grand dame*, 40ish, Garboesque and recently published. What few reservations I had about spending the colossal rent for the apartment above hers was dispelled when I met her. Sophisticated, elegant and seductive, she was the quintessential figure whom a 17 year/old in transition could idolize. She was everything I'd pretended to be at Bernie Eisner's -- with my black, crepe dress and cigarette holder and air of decedent sophistication. She was Gertrude Stein in the body of Lana Turner while I was Alice B. Toklas posing as Morticia.

As it happened, I found myself running into Tanya De Ramma almost daily. Sometimes when I left my apartment I'd pass her opened door and see her walking about in silk lingerie, nymph-like and graceful, without shame or the slightest bit of embarrassment. She was an author, after all. Author's were above the fray. She was a WOMAN, the first WOMAN I'd ever met. My mother, short, gray-haired and bespectacled, with a radar device on her head, confused me and confused my sexuality. Until I'd met Tanya De Ramma, there were no females I wanted to be, except, of course, Ellie, before she lost her status to the helplessness and vulnerability lodged in her womb. Tanya De Ramma was never vulnerable and certainly never helpless. She was a woman of eminent strength and power.

Even though I was *just a kid*, Tanya De Ramma never struck me as patronizing or dismissive. She never failed to greet me warmly as though she were genuinely pleased to see me and it reaffirmed my decision to forfeit the second bedroom we easily could have had had we moved to the Lower East Side.

As it turned out, though, it was **my** bedroom that was forfeited since, on the very first day of our occupancy, Becky walked straight into the bedroom and claimed it as her own.

"*Bring my things in here,*" she yelled to me from *her* bedroom.

"*O.K. I'll be right there...*" And I complied as any good friend would....though it bothered me that I wasn't even worth a negotiation. She clearly had the money, the chutzpah, the knowledge to make her way in the cold world but at least she should pay more since I don't even have a bedroom for myself.

But the possibility of having my own bedroom in a one-bedroom apartment never occurred to me, so I was quite content to sleep on the couch in the living room. I was still my mother's daughter without a room of her own.

But it was, after all, **sixty-eight Perry Street** and a small price to pay for such luxury. Though the bedroom wasn't mine, the apartment's decor was. Not the *incense-and-bean-bag* décor of Bernie Eisner's or the *mattress-on-the-floor* motif. Our renovated brownstone apartment, with its hard-wood floors and fireplace, its raised ceilings and high windows that accessed the light from all of New York was filled with thrift shop art and touches of India that Becky's money and memories of Ellie's Brooklyn bedroom provided. The apartment was more than we ever could have hoped for and I lived in it with great pride and joy.

Of all the pleasures I experienced at the time, entertaining in *my* home was top of the list. It didn't take long for me to find my guests. Sitting in the cafeteria of The New School as I always did (with a copy of Plato in my hand and a cigarette between my crimson lips), I attracted other Indian students. And while female students in saris were not unusual at The New School, (which tended to attract an international student body), saris, cigarettes and false eyelashes were. In no time I made a group of friends, all Indian and all male, Rohini, Chondra, Amir and a host of others. I tried to see myself as a queen *bee* although it often felt far from the truth. Yet in the few times it felt authentic I knew the wounds were beginning to heal.

When I wasn't going and coming from Queens College without ever setting foot in a classroom, I was in the cafeteria of The New

School, charming my handsome young compatriots who couldn't figure out where I was from or what I was suffering from. The day I met Chondra, he approached me as I was reading Plato and awkwardly turned my book right-side up! When you're Slavic, the English alphabet is difficult to master!

Sometimes I was adopted from the D.P. camp by an Indian family, hence the sari and peculiar verbal style. Sometimes I was merely a devotee with a yen for Indian cave paintings and a fascination with handsome young Brahmins. Though I rarely said "no" to any one of them in particular, I didn't consider myself promiscuous. My *soul* remained a virgin. I was Indian -- or Ukrainian and we foreign intellectuals were all, at our core, asexual (at least the one's from Brooklyn). Men came and went but it was always the same. If you were turbaned and dark you slept on the sofa with me. If you were fair-haired and fragile, you slept in the bedroom with Becky. Eventually, though, the arrangement became troublesome when Becky's boyfriend, blonde and aesthete, couldn't find a reason to leave. In a matter of months I had *two* roommates, one with a loud and lacerating mouth and the other mute from birth.

I'm sure Tanya De Ramma knew about the goings-on just above her ceiling, but she never said a word. She was far too discrete to pay it any mind. And besides, what was really going on up there? A teen-ager in a sari who sang Russian dirges, who strummed her guitar and entertained the Pakistani army and a blonde with an effete poet in tow? Other than our evening soirees, we were quite reasonable tenants.

Fresh from serenading my public in Washington Square Park, Tanya De Ramma stopped me in the hall.

"I see you have your guitar," she said in a husky, dramatic voice. "Sometimes I hear you sing at night. Such a voice from such a little thing. What language are your songs?"

"Russian," I said. "They're songs from The Red Army Chorus.

'Songs of Free Men.'"

"Oh! How exciting. I'd love you to sing for me."

"I'd like that," I quivered in disbelief.

"What about this evening? I'm having a few friends over. I'm sure they'd be delighted."

"Well," I stammered, "I guess that would be O.K."

"We'll see you about eight?"

"Da, I mean, yes. Eight vould be fine." And off I scrambled up the stairs, star-struck and brimming with excitement.

"Becky, Becky," I gushed, barely closing the door behind me. "You won't believe what just happened!"

"Tell me in Hindi."

"Don't joke. This is serious. Tanya De Ramma just asked me to sing at her house tonight."

"With your sitar, I mean guitar?"

"Becky. Stop it. I'm not kidding."

"O.K. O.K. That's nice."

But It was more than nice, I thought. Tanya De Ramma was the *heppist* woman I'd ever met. I imagined all kinds of famous people at her party, writers, poets, Ginsberg and Ferlinghetti. I fluttered my lashes and sauntering across the room like a short Tallulah Bankhead, anticipating my debut, anticipating my rise to glory.

Making my descent down the one flight of stairs, I was conscious of the fact that under my black velvet cape a sari hid a body still plump with adolescence. It was not yet the body of a *real* woman, I thought. Maybe it never would be. In the meantime, the less seen of it, the better. Instead, I relied on my face, theatrical and heavily made-up to gain me the attention I craved.

"Why do you wear all that stuff on your face?" people would ask. "It makes you look like a clown!" But what did they know? I thought. They're just bourgeois fools. What did they know about people like me? They 're probably jealous. The face in the mirror was gorgeous, I decided – **IF** caught at *just the right angle, just the right light, just the right expression*. And once caught, it would obviously have to remain frozen in place, limiting my movements and the kinds of interactions I could enjoy. Showing my profile or walking into the wind was prohibited. Nor could I meet friends in daylight. That was the task as I prepared to visit Tanya, finding the perfect face. After hours of failed effort I finally captured one I could live with and framed it in the hood of my black velvet cape.

"You look ridiculous," Becky said, as I was preparing to leave. *No matter*, I thought. *Look at the source!*

My guitar in tow, I descended the stairs slowly and deliberately. As I approached Tanya De Gamma's door, I stood for a moment and held my stomach in tight, then knocked gently and waited. An old man, 40ish and balding, opened the door and motioned for me to come in.

"Sweetie, your neighbor's here," he called to Tanya in another room.

"Oh! Lovely, lovely," she responded effusively as she made her grand entrance. Scantily dressed in a gauzy red kimono, I could see her silhouette through the sheerness of her robe. Her immodesty stunned me though I tried to tell myself she was an artist and this is what artists do. It intrigued me. I could almost make out the contours of her breasts. This was so new to me, so embarrassing yet so sophisticated. Suddenly, I knew Brooklyn was very far away.

"Darling, come in. Come in," she gushed. "How lovely to see you. Take off your beautiful cape and sit down. Make yourself comfortable. I'll be back in just a jiffy. Henri, Henri, darling. Get our guest a drink.."

"What would you like?" the elderly gentleman asked me dutifully.

"Um...Nothing. Thank you," I declined.

"Nothing?" he repeated. "But you MUST have a drink. What would you like?"

"Well," I paused, trying to think of something impressive.

"How about a scotch?" he asked.

"Scotch? Um..."
"Or something else?"
"Wodka? Do you have wodka?"
"Sure. One vodka coming up. Straight or on the rocks?"
"On vhat?"
"On the rocks... or straight?"
"Do you have a little glass?" I asked meekly, hurt that he'd even suggest I would drink from the bottle.
"A glass?"
"Just a little one, maybe?"
"She's got a sense of humor, your neighbor," he yelled to Tanya.

I laughed awkwardly. *This guy is mean*, I thought. *What nerve! Doesn't he realize who I am? I'm not some little beatnik at Bernie Eisner's place who guzzles cheap wine from a jug.* I shifted my body on the couch till I found just the right position, legs crossed, spine straight, head tossed back with abandon. By the time he returned with my drink, I was well posed. Aristocratic, blasé!

"*Wodka* in a little glass," he said mockingly, handing me enough vodka for a dozen Cossacks. "*Skol!*"
"Excuse me?" I asked.
"Cheers, kid."
"*Shukrir.*"
"What?" he asked.
"Thank you." I translated.
"Is that Russian?"
"No. It's Hindi."
"Hindi? You speak Hindi?"

I was just about to share my history with him when, all of a sudden, my words froze in their tracks. Totally nude, Tanya pirouetted into the room straight for the old man who didn't bat an eye.

"Henri, you're so sexy," she cooed, wrapping her white body around him and rubbing her large, firm breasts across his chest while he laughed matter-of-factly. "Come on, Henri. Fuck me."

Oh my God! I thought. *What am I doing here? How do I get out of this place?* I turned my head away as fast as I could, as though something incredibly interesting had just caught my eye in the other direction. *How do I leave? I can't just walk out! What would they think of me? A whining little baby from Brooklyn. An impostor! A fake trying to be so sophisticated. Just a kid from Sheepshead Bay.*

I squirmed deeper into the sofa and nonchalantly tried to remove a speck of dirt from the wall behind me when the doorbell rang and rescued me. Tanya waltzed to the door on her tip-toes, her breasts dancing up and down, and flung open the door with laughter and reckless elan.

"Danny, Danny, you beautiful boy. I've been waiting for you. Henri won't fuck me," she pouted coquettishly to the young sailor in the doorway.

He smiled, grabbed her breasts in his hands and pulled her toward him. He couldn't have been more than twenty, this blond boy with his crew cut and clean-pressed sailor suit. *Right out of the Kansas Plains. What could he possibly be doing here,* I wondered in awe. *Such a clean young lad?* He kissed Tanya's nipples with the front door still ajar as I sat near-by on the couch.

"This is my darling neighbor," she said to the young sailor. "Isn't she just a dear?"

He nodded disinterestedly as she whisked him inside the apartment, closed the door behind him and began to unbutton his trousers.

"Hey, Henri," Danny called to the old man without skipping a beat. "How's it going?"

Henri smiled knowingly and walked toward the sailor as Tanya pulled his trousers to the floor. Nonchalantly, Danny removed his sailor shirt. Henri stripped from the waist while Tanya cackled and danced erotically around them both. I was sitting directly to the right of the door, directly to the right of them. To leave, I would have had to ask them to step aside or push my way through. Even if I had been able to stand up at the time, which was doubtful, I couldn't draw such attention to myself. I couldn't leave and have them think I was afraid or shy or childish. No. That was simply unacceptable. *But how long can you get away with staring at a speck of dirt on the wall,* I thought. *How fascinating can it possibly be?* I tried to fixate on the floor, the ceiling, my feet. *This is all so hum-drum, so tedious,* I implied with my eyes. I flinched, as they began groping each other's nude bodies in the middle of the living room, not three feet away. Henri, his starched shirt hanging over his belly, reached for my hand. I had to fight back a burst of anxious laughter as I tried to avoid eye contact with this fat old man whose hard, horizontal penis stuck out like a shelf. I'd never seen a penis before. Not really. Sure I'd *met* several of them, even shaken their *hands*, but I never actually LOOKED at one. And besides, even if it were daylight, which it rarely ever was when a penis and I met, I could never get myself to greet it, head on, so to speak. Hence, a penis was, to me, what I'd imagine it was to a blind woman. I knew how it felt but couldn't pick it out of a line up. But here was Henri, a great man, I assumed, with this peculiar, unfamiliar object pointing straight at me, beckoning me.

"No.... really.... no," I uttered, turning my eyes away.

"Come on, sweetie," he urged, pulling on my hand.

"Come, darling," Tanya coaxed from the floor as the sailor positioned himself on top of her.

"Oh, no, no," I laughed nervously. "No thank you....."

"You'll like it," Henri said.

"No.......no.....thank you very much but..."

"Darling," Tanya interrupted, "It's so much fun. Don't be shy."

"I'm not shy...I'm just not ...how you say...in the mood."

"I'll get you in the mood," Henri struck back.

"Yes, my darling, he's very good at that," Tanya said as the sailor's body overcome her.

"Come on," Henri urged, reaching his hand under my sari.

"No, please. I really...not in the mood."

"Come over here," Danny told Henri, his nude body heaving up and down on top of Tanya's.

"O.K.," said the old man, gliding toward his friends. "Oh Danny *boy, the fife's, the fife's are calling......"* he sang, lifting his leg over Danny's back and mounting him from the rear.

What in the world is he doing? I thought. I followed him surreptitiously with squinted eyes. *They're playing giddy-up! He's on top of her and the other one's on top of him!* I tried to understand what was happening, straining to see out of the very corner of my eye. Henri grabbed his large penis in his hand, guiding it towards Danny's anus. *Damn!* I jolted silently. *They're fruits, But they can't be. Danny's sleeping with Tanya!*

"Henri, baby...," moaned Danny as Henri pounded his body into Danny's and Danny into Tanya beneath him. Up and down, up and down, convulsively, the three of them, panting, grunting, groaning.

Oh! My God! What am I doing here? I couldn't tear my eyes away. I didn't want to miss a thing. I wished I could have been closer, an inch away -- with a magnifying glass -- so I could see every movement, every anatomical frame, every limb and muscle and skin and hair, every juxtaposition of sin and awe.

I couldn't just sit and stare so I grabbed my guitar and posed it on my lap. *A little music.* I thought. *That'll divert me. But The Red Army Chorus?* My mind was a blank.

> "On top of old Smoky, I sang,
> All covered with snow,
> I lost my true lover
> For a courtin' too slow....."

Up, down, up down..."*Yes Danny, Yes,*" Tanya moaned. In, out, in, out...."*Fuck me, Henry,*" Danny wailed. In, out, in out....
    "Oh, courtin's a pleasure And partin is grief..."

"Danny, don't stop..." In, out, in out....
    "A false-hearted lover Is worse than a thief....."

"Yes, Danny. Oh-h-h-h....." In out, in out, in out, in out........Then silence except for the thunder of bodies detonating amongst themselves. Silence.........

"I came! I came!" Tanya screamed, severing the rhythm of the moment.
What? What's she yelling about? I asked myself.
"I came! I came!" she cried as Henri rammed Danny one last time before sinking to the floor in a sea of sweat and depletion.
"Did you hear me darling?" she beseeched me. *" I came!"*
Silence. The room was still.
Henri lay on his back, his firm member now withered and limp. Tanya lay beside him, smiling with her eyes closed as Danny, stretched out like a wish-bone, tugged skillfully at his penis till his body pulsated, stiffened then weakened and collapsed.

I stared for a moment at the bodies on the floor, half waiting for what might come next, half dreading it and wishing to flee. Trembling with embarrassment, I prodded my paralyzed legs to do what the rest of me couldn't. And with opportunity slipping away, I finally managed to grab my guitar and silently escape out the door.
Where in the world had Tanya "come," I wondered with great bewilderment as I quietly climbed the stairs. *Where in the world had she "come?"*

LEE

AS THE MONTHS passed, Becky and Hans became inseparable. The little privacy that once existed disappeared when Hans moved in --- and watching him walk around in his Boxer's ceased to be cute. It was time, once again, to move on. I suspect there was also a bit of jealousy on my part, though I certainly never acknowledged it at the time. Here was Becky with her tall, blonde boyfriend...... and then there was me. Not that I found Hans particularly handsome or that I found my Indian friends less attractive. No. Rohini was much more attractive to me, but the fact was, men like Hans, *normal* men, seemed rarely attracted to me. Alfredo may have been *normal*, but I never saw him as that. His dark good looks and Spanish accent removed him from the class as did Rohini's dark good looks. *Normal* is Sandra Dee, blonde, blue-eyed, unremarkable. It's the absence of affect, of intensity or conflict. It's pleasant, peaceful and composed. It's not too smart, too special, too kind, too willful, too wanting. It's satisfied. It never makes a fuss or calls attention to itself.

I remember one afternoon walking across Broadway to International House. On the far side of the street was this *regular* guy I'd seen around who always made a point of trying to talk to me. I suppose I would have thought he was really handsome had he not seemed so unremarkable, so American, so white, so like the guys from Brooklyn. I never gave him the time of day. He wasn't bleeding all over the street or talking to God. That would have worked in his favor. Anyway, when he saw me, he came running across Broadway to make his pitch.

"Wait up, Bea," he called, as I hurried off.
"I'm sorry, but I must go. I'm in, how you say, such a ....hurry."
"Hold on....hold on. I want to talk to you."
"I must go."
"Why do you talk with that accent," he asked as he tried to keep pace with me.
"I don't know vat you talk about," I shot back defensively.
"It's O.K. I just want to know why you talk like that. I know you're from Brooklyn."
"You must be mistaken. I from Kiev."
"Come on, Bea. See, I even know your name."
"Please. Leave me alone."
> "I'm just trying to get to know you," he urged, as I quickened my steps. "You're really beautiful. I've seen you around and I wanted to ask you out."

"Go away, go away," I pleaded, as if he were the Gestapo trying to make it with a Jew who was trying to pass.

What was that? I asked myself. If I'd wanted so much to be *normal*, why wouldn't I have wanted a guy like that? And why would I dress the way I did, in saris and Indian garb. Even if I didn't *feel* normal, I could have LOOKED normal. I could have become invisible again, plain again, fat again, passed over in the allocation of all I had wished for as a child. *No!* I said to myself. *It didn't work then and it won't work now!* That's how I saw it. So I staked my fortune on a Ukrainian/Indian princess whom you couldn't miss in a fox hole -- and that gave me hope that one day I'd get my due. So much for logic!

Meanwhile, I was jealous of Becky. Not only did she have *Hans*, she had money to burn. Her husband, whom she'd left in Larchmont, paid her off handsomely! And she didn't even seem to appreciate it, not like Ellie who was willing to sell her soul to a Jewish lawyer so he'd keep her safe. I envied her, too! Someone willing to take care of you! How did these women do it? The route escaped me. It was time again to move.

I was getting weary. I'd begun to run out of paths. I called Lee whom I'd met in the mountains the summer before. At thirty-six, newly separated and the mother of a five year-old daughter, Lee was a teacher at a crossroads -- eager for the extra money that a summer job as the hotel's Day-Camp Director would provide.

My connection to her was the talk of the staff. What was a Socialist from Queens, old enough to be my mother, seemingly straight as an arrow, doing befriending an eighteen-year-old in a tailspin? She was probably in a tailspin too, but I didn't understand it then. Not that it wasn't apparent, I suppose. And "befriending" would have been an understatement. After work we'd cruise the mountains in her beat-up old Chevy making the rounds of hotel bars, drinking into oblivion and seducing every guy in sight. Reckless and hell-bent at the wheel, I got us where we needed to go -- along dark country roads till the sun rose in the morning because Lee, with all her radical politics, was afraid to drive.

Another truth whose meaning I failed to appreciate at the time. To me, we were just party girls without a care in the world, even when I drove us into a ditch because the road decided to disappear. We laughed till we were sick. Not once did she scold me that night, this woman who seemed to know everything, who had a way of zeroing in on people right to their core, who was smart, self-righteous and terribly critical.

But as time went on, it was **she** who seemed to think that **I** knew it all, that **I** was the one to lead! Me in a free-fall and she in my shadow! Maybe she thought I had it all together because she only knew *Bea*

Starr from Brooklyn -- and that was a real skewed sample! Not that she didn't know the rest -- like *International House* and Judson and the Ukraine, because she did. She just laughed it off like it was a charming adventure and never put me down. And that endeared her to me all the more, this wise woman whom I adored, who thought I was O.K., this Tanya De Ramma with a proper libido. I loved being around her but hadn't a clue why she felt the same, except to figure she was looking for a man and I was the best scout in town. I never imagined there was something eating at her the way there was at me. By the time the summer was over and it was time to say good-bye, the depths of our friendship was clear.

"Come to Queens and live with us," Lee asked suddenly, *"like another daughter. It'll give me company and you won't have to worry about rent."*

It didn't take long to decide. My bags had been packed since birth.

We walked through Jackson Heights from the subway to her modest pre-war building. The day was dreary and overcast, a day when nothing feels like it'll ever change. The neighborhood was dark, too, brick apartment houses indistinguishable from each other, sucking up the open spaces and changing the color of day. It was Sheepshead Bay without the single-family homes, without the sense of moving up, without evidence of the American dream.

Lee's apartment on the eighth floor could only be described as utilitarian. The tiny bedroom for her daughter, Danielle, was virtually hidden behind an even smaller kitchen that looked like it had never been used. *No cookies were baked in this place*, I thought, *no pancakes for the happy kids on Sunday mornings*. Near the bedroom that she and her husband once shared was a living room reminiscent of a rooming house for transients only -- except for the books. Had it not been for the books, I'd have thought I was in Ellie's apartment in the projects off Nostrand Avenue. But this wasn't simply a poor home. It was that, too, but that was incidental. It was a home whose mistress didn't care about appearances, for things or objects or tradition, for the stuff of an emotional life or the body that housed it. This was a home for the head only -- the Marxist literature and Communist periodicals scattered thoughtlessly where you might have welcomed a comfortable chair or a nice cup of hot tea. It was all so familiar, like my own home, yet without the polish of money. Even her little girl was familiar to me, isolated at the end of an apartment that seemed ill fitting for a small child who was hungry for *mommy*.

But that's not how it was for me. I was the *other* daughter. For me it was safe and comfortable, even having to share a bed with Lee. It was, for the two of us, just a base camp on a climb to completion.

No sooner had I moved in, I knew I was heading in the right direction. I'd relied on my accent only intermittently, of late, and never with Lee. But as time went on and I began to meet her friends, I found myself relying on it less and less -- till one day when a remarkable thing happened: It was a Friday morning, I recall, and I prepared, as usual, to spend the weekend working in the mountains. Lee was having friends over that night, her group of savvy, irreverent, sassy women friends and their husbands, or someone else's husbands, as the case may have been. These were old women by my standards, mid-thirties, for the most part, but they liked me and adopted me as a kind of mascot or kid sister. I liked them, too. They fascinated me, how they talked straight with each other and ran the show as their husbands took the back seats.

I resented having to leave for work. I wanted to stay and see how *the girls* were dressed, their make-up, listen to them bad-mouth someone's husband or wife, hear the gossip of who was sleeping with whom. I wanted to see their husbands again. I delighted in the attentions they paid me, how they seemed to enjoy my presence.

By the afternoon, as my resentment mounted, a thought occurred to me that had once been abhorrent but that now felt like a breath of fresh air. It was a simple thought but really quite remarkable: *I'll find a normal job,* I said to myself, *nine-to-five, like girls do who don't speak in tongues. I'll become a woman, one of the 'girls,' like Lee and her friends. I'll buy a skirt and a sweater and pumps and I'll go to work on the subway.... and complain about the heat and my boss. And one day I'll have a real apartment and be able to afford tissues instead of toilet paper to blow my nose. Yes! That's what I'll do!* The path opened and, like the Bermuda Triangle, sucked all evidence of saris or the Ukraine to the bottom of the sea. I knew things would never be the same again!

A friend of Lee's arranged an interview for me at *The American Jewish Committee* on 56th Street in Manhattan. The organization's name made me anxious at first until I found out it was also called *The Institute for Human Relations. That's better,* I thought! It was all the *normal* I could handle for one day. The Public Relations Department at The Institute for Human Relations needed a secretary. I tried it on for size. *"I work in The Public Relations Department at The Institute for Human Relations."* "Where?" the person might ask again. *"The Institute for Human Relations,"* I'd repeat with great clarity and pride. It was easy to get a fix on The Department of Public Relations, even for a neophyte. The department was small, two offices side-by-side, one for Harold Steinberg, Director, and the other for his second in charge, Marty Duchovny. Outside each office was a desk, typewriter and file cabinet for their respective secretaries and an extra *work station* for transient office help.

It was for Marty Ducovny that the position was available and it was he who interviewed me first. I tried my best: Kafka, witty anecdotes and appropriate cynicism. He seemed to like me. Maybe he saw through the young woman trying to be a wise guy but she had guts, more than met the eye, I hoped he thought.

Marty struck me as a kindly man, a bit beaten down, perhaps, by his overbearing boss, but gentle and decent. That's what I noticed most. He was also very handsome, but at least thirty-five and far too Ivy-league for my tastes. We had a good rapport. I was certain of that and grew more comfortable as I moved on to my next interview. I could hear **The Boss** screaming as I approached his office. I walked past his secretary, Sylvia, a still attractive woman in her forties who must have been a knockout twenty years before. I could hear **The Boss** continue to berate her from inside his office as she fumed to herself at her desk outside:

"I told you pastrami, pastrami," he yelled to Sylvia. "Not corned beef. When do I ever eat corned beef?"

"You always eat corned beef," she disagreed hesitantly.

"What? What are you yapping about now?"

"I said you always eat corned beef."

"That's bull shit! I never eat corned beef. Get me a pastrami sandwich."

"I can't, Harold. It's too late. I have to leave early tonight."

"What did you say?"

"I said I promised my husband I'd leave by six tonight."

"Let him wait."

"Harold, please."

"For twenty-two years you've been keeping him waiting."

"Fucker," she said under her breath."

"What? You said you want to fuck?"

"I said O.K. O.K. I'll get you pastrami."

I walked into The Boss's office with great trepidation. Not that I was afraid of him physically. Rather, it was a more amorphous anxiety, that I might end up like Sylvia twenty years down the road, at some dismal job day in and day out as the years passed, watching the clock, fucking the boss, withering away into oblivion, a fear of becoming invisible that I knew so well. But I kept walking.

Harold Steinberg was a tall, overpowering man in his forties who sputtered as he spoke. His gawky body moved impatiently as if he shouldn't have to tolerate what he has to tolerate, as if he was running out of patience or just plain fed up. He chain smoked with the same abrupt, staccato movements as he paced -- looking me over like a junkie needing to score.

"Sit down," he said without introduction. "Can you type?"

"A little."

"That's O.K. You'll learn. I like the way you look. That's more important."

"Thank you," I said, relieved I hadn't dressed more demurely.

"Has anyone ever told you look like Elizabeth Taylor? Of course they have. You look like an actress. Do you act?"

"No."

"I'll bet you have a lot of boyfriends, huh? .... Sylvia," he yelled, mid sentence, "Get me the pastrami..."

"I'm going. I'm going."

"So. Do you?"

"Do I what?" I asked in confusion as his phone rang. He picked up the receiver and placed his hand over the mouthpiece.

"O.K.," he said, shooing me away to leave. "You're hired. You're a great kid."

THE ATTACK

BETWEEN LIVING WITH Lee and working at The American Jewish Committee, my life was becoming more routinized and more stable. My willingness to leave *the Ukraine* behind was evidence of greater stability. But I didn't think of it in those terms. My only real barometer of wellbeing remained men. If I was loved by a man whom I loved back, I was O.K. If not, I fell into the abyss. Lee seemed to have a similar yardstick. And there were men in abundance, so everything was just fine -- until late one night when the earth shook.

It was well after midnight. Lee and I were asleep after having spent some time with Gene, Lee's ex-husband. It wasn't unusual for Gene to visit, despite their divorce. The two of them thought of themselves as sophisticated and rational adults. From the moment I met him I could see that, strained as their relationship was, it was far from over. They chatted, as if in code, ostensibly about their daughter but really about the status of each other's life, reading one another's imperceptible cues, power dancing in their minds. At the same time, particularly on that evening, I felt Gene's glances and a vague flirtation that made me both uncomfortable and flattered. It wasn't just that Gene was handsome and very, very smart. He was, but more importantly, he was part of that circle of friends that I so admired and wanted to join and its only male who seemed able to hold his own among the sharp, ascorbic women. Maybe the only way I could belong, I thought, was to sleep with one of the husbands, like Lee did - and others did as well, a kind of sardonic initiation or triumphant rite of passage. The thought certainly crossed my mind.

What I didn't understand in my youthful idolatry of this handsome, quick-witted, older man (who also happened to be a writer and socialist!) was that Gene was, first and foremost, a lush. The longer he visited that night, the more he drank till, finally, he sank into the living room sofa and passed out.

This was the pattern, Lee said. This was the story of their marriage. Despite all his charm and talent, he just couldn't hold on to himself for very long. At close to midnight, we left him in his oblivion on the sofa, shut out the lights and went into the bedroom to sleep.

It must have been two or three in the morning when a knock at the front door awakened me. I rose sleepily and walked past the living room where Gene was still out cold.

"Who's there?" I asked, my eyes barely opened.

"Jeff," the voice outside responded.

"Jeff?"

"Don't you remember? Jeff...Your boyfriend."

My boyfriend? I asked myself in bewilderment. *Jeff? Jeff from The New School? Jesus. I haven't seen him in forever. And why had he said he was my boyfriend? What the hell is he doing at my apartment at 3:00 o'clock in the morning? And how had he found me?*

I unlocked the door and opened it cautiously. There, almost unrecognizable, was the one American guy I'd seen a few times at the New School before my move to Queens but whom I'd I hadn't seen in a year or two. I didn't know quite what it was at the time but something about him scared me. Nothing I was able to put my finger on then, maybe the way he looked at me sometimes, the way he clung, maybe the way he seemed overly connected to his mother whom he was always talking about. It disarmed me and made me uncomfortable. I said good-bye and never thought of him again.

Now he stood in the doorway, two hundred pounds heavier, his head shaven and his eyes burning with fire. *"Jeff?"* I asked, barely recognizing him.

"Can I come in?" he pleaded.

"But it's the middle of the night. How did you get my address?"

"Please, I just want to talk to you for a few minutes."

I hesitated, stunned by his transformation.

"Please," he repeated. "Just for a minute."

I searched his eyes for reassurance. All I could see was someone defeated, someone bloated and misshapen. *Why did he shave his head? Why did he get so fat? The poor soul. There, but for the grace of God...* I thought, as I opened the door reluctantly. He walked into the foyer, heavily, as if drugged. I reflexively stepped back out of his way and turned to see if Gene was still unconscious on the sofa. The apartment was dark and dead quiet.

"Can't we go out again?" He pleaded. "We really loved each other."

"Jeff," I said gingerly. "Love?"

"Please. Can't we go out again?"

"It's the middle of the night. You must go home. Please."

"But I love you."

"Jeff. You hardly know me. Please. I must get to sleep."

"But can we go out again?"

"Let me call you in a few days, " I said hurriedly, reluctant to have our eyes meet. "I'm sure I can find your number. We'll talk about it then."

"O.K. O.K.," he pouted, head lowered yet obedient, like a child being sent to his room -- then turned timidly and walked out the door without another word.

I closed the door behind him, double-bolted the lock and sighed with relief. I made a mental note to tell Lee in the morning to **never, ever** open the door to anyone she doesn't know and if anyone named Jeff should call, tell him I've moved.

THE ATTACK

I was fast asleep when another knock on the front door awakened me two hours later. *Damn!* I thought. *This can't be him again. If it is, I won't let him in this time,* I promised myself, walking, half dazed, to the door.

"Who's there?" I asked, still in a fog.

"It's me, Jeff."

"Please. You must go home."

"I have to talk to you... just for a minute."

" I can't, Jeff. Please. Go home."

He'd have none of it. He persisted, his voice still beseeching and weak but clearly strained. I was afraid he'd wake up Lee and her daughter. I turned to see if Gene had awakened, hoping he'd help but he was SEEMINGLY still passed out.

I reached for the doorknob reluctantly then withdrew my hand. I hesitated -- then reached for it again. I unlocked the door, opening it by a hair to tell him to his face to leave...............when everything stopped, like death. The next thing I recalled I was laying on the floor reaching my hand to the side of my face as if to hold it together. My mouth, filled with blood, was oozing. I tried to scream but my jaw wouldn't move. My brains were screeching. My body, powerless as dead weight in cement, wouldn't budge -- but I could still hear him only a few feet away, his huge bulk compressing Lee's chest on the floor as he pinned her down and choked her round the neck:

"I'll kill you, Lisa. I'll kill you," he foamed, hitting the mother who apparently appeared at will in his head, as he banged Lee's head into the ground. I could see it from my bloody eyes. I could see Lee's terror and it liberated me and got me to my feet. Without a thought I lunged toward him and jumped on his back to pull his body off her.

"Please, Jeff. Please," I cried. " I made a mistake." I was asking for the impossible that still in my infancy seemed possible. How can the deaf hear what's not auditory, what's not a sound? How can you make sane a mind that sees what isn't there? There are no threats, no consequences I could muster that would have any impact on what he was set to do. "It was just a tap, Sissy. Just a tap." At least my perceptions were still in tact. I knew it wasn't just a tap! Of that I was certain. But what do you do about the fist? First don't say it was a flute. First you must know it's a fist. And I did. That far I had come. But now what? How do you protect yourself from its impact? That lesson I hadn't read yet, so, despite its power I resorted to wish fulfillment.

Somewhere in the cavernous depths of my history I resorted to what had never worked before! Why would I seize what I had no reason to believe would be productive? Yet I persisted as the good little Beastress tried repeatedly to quell her father's rage; became a sweet little girl doll who would be irresistibly lovable at least till her daddy regained his composure.

She would persist until Jeff finally, finally realized his error as he hovered on top of Lee. *"I was wrong. I know it. It'll be O.K."* I implored the deaf as he slowly began to release her neck from his murderous hands.

"Lee," I demanded, slowly, purposefully, signaling her with my eyes wide open in immutable determination. *"Get up! Get up **NOW!** Go inside! Do what I tell you,"* I ordered her, each word paced, emphasized, deliberate, as I wrapped my arms around Jeff and pulled him off her, holding him, restraining him, like you'd restrain a toddler who's attacking his baby sister.

*"Go into the bedroom, Lee, and lock the door. Do what I tell you! Do it **NOW!**"*

I reached for Jeff's face, gently turning it towards me. *"It's O.K., Jeff. It's O.K. You were right,"* I reassured him, staring into his crazed and violent eyes, quieting his rage, quieting his violence as I'd tried to do with my father so many times before, restraining the fury so we'd all survive. It was so familiar, this role, so terribly familiar.

" Lock the door, Lee. It'll be all right. Lock it!" I demanded, as she staggered to her feet and made her way into the bedroom, locking the door behind her.

"It's O.K., Jeff. It's O.K.," I said again, holding him tightly against me until I heard the lock of the bedroom door... when only then I released my arms....

And felt the impact of his fist against my broken jaw, knocking me to the ground once again.

"I'll kill you, you bitch!" he raged, grabbing my hair and pulling me to the bathroom behind us. *"I'll kill you, Lisa! You're dead!"* he chanted as he took off his clothes and demanding I remove mine, imprisoning me, behind the bathroom door.

"Do it or you're dead!" Lisa, Lisa, Lisa. Over and over and over again, with a razor to my throat, unable to make a sound, swallowing my screams liked I'd done when I was a child, sealing my eyes shut as I hid from my father and prayed he would disappear.

"You fucking bitch," he railed. *"You fucking bitch! Do it or you're dead!"*

The blood seeped through my clenched teeth, dripping down my nude body, dripping between my legs. Not a sound except for the thunder of his lunacy, except for the sound of a body bouncing off the walls.

"Do it or you're dead! Do it or you're dead!" Two hours. **Two whole hours!** My blood covered the white tiles and basin where he rammed my head, as if to mutilate his Lisa, whoever she was, and turn her into mush. When I could no longer bare the pain, when the wish to end the tyranny and all the tyrannies before were upon me, unthinking of the consequences, uncaring, welcoming the end, I screamed. At the top of my lungs, from the place of all indignities, I screamed so even the Gods could hear me..........and then.............. and only then..........he curled up his nude body in the corner of the shower........like a child, twisting to hide from **his** father's wrath.

I ran from the bathroom without a stitch of clothes, screaming for my life, marking a trail of blood through the apartment, out the front door, into the hall, pounding on my neighbors doors,

H-E-L-P M-E!!!!!!! H-E-L-P M-E!!!!!!!!!!" I screamed. No one responded. I ran from door to door -- seeing him from the corner of my eye dart out the apartment, nude and crazed, running through the hall, down the stairs and out of sight.

I remember Gene leading me from the hallway back inside and I remember Lee screaming into the phone to *"Come quick. Come quick."* And I remember the police questioning them. *Who was he? How did he get in? What did I do to provoke him?* Lee didn't know. All she knew was that she heard a commotion and went to see what was happening when someone threw her to the ground and tried to kill her -- and somehow she got free and ran into the bedroom and locked the door behind her. She stayed there *in shock*, she said, afraid to move a hair. And the next thing she knew I was screaming from the hallway and Gene was yelling to her to call the police.

Gene didn't know anything. Or so he said. He was out cold on the sofa. He hadn't seen anyone, he said -- till my screams woke him up and he saw me running through the hall, nude and hysterical. But I knew. And I told them, the police, as well as I could -- with my jaw shattered and my face swollen and contorted. No. I hadn't provoked him. No. We didn't have a date. No. I didn't invite him in. No. I wasn't flirting. No, he wasn't my boyfriend. No. No. No. How do I get them to see what happened, to see it through MY eyes; how do I get them to see how dangerous he was? to arrest him and put him away?

"Here's the story," one of the officer's said, succinctly, as if to shorten this meaningless waste of his time. *"We can arrest him but he'll be out by morning -- and then he'll come back and **really** finish the job. Is that what you want?"*

"No, no, please," Lee cried. *"I have a five-year old daughter here. You can't let him come back again."*

"Well, that's what's gonna happen, m'am.. If we arrest him, he'll be back. I've seen it happen a dozen times. You don't want to get these guys mad. They come back. You can bet on it."

"But why will he be out in the morning?" I sobbed through my clenched jaw.

"Because it's your word against his," the cop said, "and maybe you did **something** to set him off."

"I didn't do anything. I haven't seen him in over a year."

"I'm not saying you deserved it, kid. I'm just telling you he'd be out in the morning."

"But he tried to kill Lee too. It's **both** our words."

"I didn't see him, Bea. I didn't see him."

"You didn't **see** him?" I asked her incredulously. "He was on **top** of you!"

"I didn't see him. And even if I did, who says they won't let him out anyway?"

'How can you say that, Lee? How can you say you didn't see him?"

"I have to think about Danielle. I'm her mother."

"I'm thinking about her, too, Lee."

"She's right, kid." The officer injected. "If you didn't know him that's one thing, but he's your **boyfriend.** That's a whole different thing."

"He's **not** my boyfriend. That's just what **he** said."

"Why would he say that if it wasn't true? And if he wasn't your boyfriend, what was he doing in your apartment at four o'clock in the morning? You betta get to the hospital and get yourself taken care of. I know what I'm talking about. I didn't become a cop yesterday."

"But look at me," I cried. "Do you know what he did?"

There was no way to reach them, to have them understand, nor care, no way to have this event meaningful to them, no way to prevent them from hearing me through my mother's ears. It was late, after all. They wanted to finish their shift as uneventfully as possible. No big tadoos….no court appearances, affidavits, reports, no big magilla. Surely I could understand he's just a cop trying to get home as quickly as possible. He's got a family too. It's been a long day. The last thing he needed was to get involved in one of those "domestic" assault cases that can go on forever just so some bitch can get back at the bastard for screwing her friend. And the judge doesn't need this bullshit either. You're never gonna convince him you didn't do something to get the poor guy so mad. They see this kind of thing all the time.

How come you let him in? You're trying to tell me you just opened the door to some stranger at two in the morning? How did he know where to find you if you weren't his girlfriend? How come you didn't scream bloody murder when he first came in? How come Gene just played dead? They knew it was just a lover's spat. That's why they didn't get involved. They knew you were fucking taunting this poor guy and he finally snapped. He didn't kill you, after all. Some other guy might have... the way you chicks bust a guy's balls. Just leave it alone. You're lucky he didn't REALLY hurt you. If you were taunting my son the way you must have been taunting this poor slob I'd have told him to.

"He had a razor ... Look, look! And I knew he'd kill me if I screamed. Did I do **this** to myself?"

"Look, I have his name. If you want him arrested, you can come down to the precinct later. *But I think you'll regret it."*

"The officer's right Bea. Please, Lee implored. *"I have to think of Danielle.*

We went to the hospital, Gene and I, while Lee stayed at home with their daughter. I could barely make it back to the apartment. I walked slowly, leaning on Gene for support. We passed an excavation site where a building was planned for construction. Despite the darkness, I could see a massive trench behind the barrier and fought, within myself, the impulse to dive, head first, to its bottom. Had it not been for Gene, my wish for peace may have won out. I didn't tell him what I was thinking but I had the feeling he knew -- because as we passed the site, he tugged at me gently to quicken our pace.

THE ATTACK

When at last we got home, Lee was sitting motionless in the living room staring blankly at the floor.

"Bea," she called. *"Can I speak to you?"*

"Yes?" I asked, still hurt by her statements to the police.

"Please come over here. Sit down. We need to talk."

I walked towards the sofa with difficulty, wondering how best to sit myself down when Gene reached out for my elbow and helped me lower my body to the seat. I'd thought about this talk from the moment we'd left the hospital. I knew it would come and I was prepared to accept her apology. I knew she'd spoken hastily, my activist friend. I knew she'd spoken out of fear and with just a little time, she, my mentor and hero, would reconsider.

"Yes, Lee?, " I asked, forgivingly.

"Bea, this is so difficult…" she began. The strain was clear. Her speech was reluctant. Her face was somber and penitent as if she was about to do something shameful but necessary.

"But I have to think about Danielle…I know you'll understand…. Maybe it would be best if you move out for a while. Just for a while."

I could feel Gene staring at me as I tried to disappear. He put his arm on my shoulder. I pulled away, as if to hide and fought back the flood of tears that was threatening to expose me.

"It's only because he knows you're here," she faltered. *"If he knows you've moved out he won't come back."* She searched Gene's eyes for agreement. He said nothing.

"Aren't I right, Gene? If she's not here, he won't come back." Gene again was silent. *"Why don't you say anything? You know I'm right."*

He turned to me, reaching for my hand and stroked it as you would a widow's at her husband's wake.

"Why don't you stay with me in the city?" he finally said. *"There's room enough and it's near your job."*

My eyes were fixed on him -- or through him. I saw right through his body to Lee. I didn't recognize her as she shrunk and mutated before me. The smaller she became, the bigger I felt -- not big with stature or pride, big like a black shit-stain on a white dress, big like when you're caught in the *loo* with your pants down, like when you're Marv Albert and your photo is plastered on the front page of the evening edition. Big like Pee-Wee Herman.

"Thank you, but that's not necessary, " I said. *'I have a lot of friends I can stay with. They've been wanting me to move in for a long time."*

"But I'm your friend, too," Gene said.

"No, really. I can't disappoint them."

"Who, " Lee asked, as if still entitled to share my confidences.

"You don't know them. They're from my job......But don't worry. I'll be fine," I stuttered, as a back flow of acid rose from my stomach into my mouth, heaving up all the humiliation of these foolish words. Gene reached over again to comfort me.

"I think you should come to my place," he urged. "Someone's gonna have to look after you for a while."

"My friends can."

"Not if they're working," he said.

"You work!"

"I free-lance. I'm always home."

"That sounds like the best idea," Lee said maternally, the intellectual giant I'd idolized; the socialist with balls who wasn't afraid to tell her husband to go straight to Hell, who wasn't afraid to play by her own rules, the *She* giant of the great women who ruled the earth before recorded time, the seven foot tall earth goddess of mythology.

I looked at her through my half-sealed swollen eyes, cherry red from the blood vessels that exploded with the first wallop, my vision blurred and distorted. *Maybe it's the injury,* I thought. *Maybe that's why she looks so strange. Maybe that's why I hate her now, because I'm injured. Yes. It must be. Because I'm injured.*

KAL

GENE'S TINY APARTMENT was bare. It was obvious he was low on funds. One might have seen this as evidence, as Lee did, that he was a loser at heart, despite his talents and charm. But I didn't see it that way. To me he was responding to a higher call. He wasn't the guy writing trash 9 to 5 at some P.R. firm. He was a *real* writer, though I don't think he ever wrote much. He was "free-lancing," he said. That makes all the difference. I knew he'd write something great one day and I was honored to know him, especially when he made me laugh, which he did a lot no matter how bad things were. I think it would be fair to say I loved him and yet, to this very day, I'm not sure how he felt about me.

His kindness to me was everywhere, but why? I suspected it had something to do with Lee, some convoluted repayment for something, some message that only she could decode. I wondered about it, often. In good moments I thought maybe he was flaunting me in front of her, I the younger one, the one who was special, different from the rest. He was getting even and, in that script, I had some intrinsic worth. In lesser moments I was his project through which he'd atone, in her eyes, for his shortcomings. The sadder a case I was, the greater his redemption -- and I retreated in shame. At other times I thought that maybe he was just attracted to me -- *in spite of* her. And where once I'd been unresponsive to his flirtations **because** of Lee, now I gloated over them -- and shared his bed with pride. Also with relief. Alcohol had taken its toll on him-- and though his sexual limitations troubled him greatly, they were never sufficient to curtail his drinking. But I didn't care. In my condition, sex was the farthest thing from my mind.

And so the barter was struck. However he profited from the arrangement, it was I who came out ahead. His humor was a miracle, especially to someone who'd cried as much and as often as I. He was gorgeous though he had no idea. He was one if the smartest men I'd ever met. His wit and knowledge were gifts when a gift was utterly needed and appreciated. They rose from recesses in his off-script brain that startled me with their originality, their uniqueness, their ferocious take on the mundane and cowardly world. He was an intellectual warrior. His mind was courageous, off the beaten path, a take on life and situations that had absolutely alluded me. And yet with all this wealth, he was a hopeless alcoholic, invariably passing the evening in a stupor on the couch.

I would wash the evening dishes, put away his alcohol and tuck him under the blanket that kept him safe. And in that peculiar arrangement, through Gene's guidance and support, I took my first steps towards reconstruction.

One lunchtime a month or so after the assault, Gene met me, as planned, at the lake in Central Park to talk and enjoy the spring air before we each had to go back to work. My face was still swollen but I welcomed the chance to be outside, away from the wondering eyes of strangers. Gene called our lunch a picnic. It was sweet of him to describe it that way. It made me feel child-like -- that daddy was taking his daughter out for a treat, just the two of them. But as I waited at the deli counter to order my sandwich, a deep sadness over come me, as if I were seeing myself from the outside in. For a moment there was no shame and no reproach, just the abiding realization that *it wasn't right what happened to this little girl. It just wasn't right.* That's what I thought -- for just a moment.

But there was something else. When I stood at that counter with all the other working adults, it was with a great pride of accomplishment that I, a child yesterday, could afford to eat out -- even if it was only baloney on rye in Central Park. As we left the deli, I think Gene saw it all on my face, the sorrow, the confusion, and also the pride, because before we had a chance to sit down and eat, he took my arm and gently kissed me on the forehead.

"I want you to come with me to see my therapist," he said suddenly, out of the blue.
*"**What**?"*
"To see my therapist."
"You mean a Psychiatrist?"
"A Psychologist."
"What's the difference?"
"It doesn't matter. I just want you to come with me."
"I don't need to see one of those guys. I'm not crazy."
"I know you're not. I see a therapist and I'm not crazy."
*"**You** see a head doctor?"*
"A therapist."
"Why?"
"Because it's helpful."
*"**You** need help?"*
"Everybody needs help. If you're alive, you need help", he said, without judgment or condescension. *" Trust me on this. If you don't like it you won't go again."*

And that's how I wound up in the office of Dr. Kalman Rabinowitz -- staring aimlessly, twiddling my thumbs, squirming in my canvas wing chair. *Canvas wing chair? Is this guy nuts?* I thought. *Who has canvas wing chairs? He must be a real winner, this shrink! He can't* even afford leather! And look at this place. It looks like he just woke up. And his beard. Who does he think he is? **Sidney** Freud?

"Tell me about yourself," he began in a comforting voice.

"Vhat do you vant to know?"

"Your accent. Where are you from?"

"Vell.................." I hesitated, shifting in my chair.

"Did I make you uncomfortable with that question?"'

"Vell........................."

"Hmmm?"

"Vell................................"

"Are you feeling uncomfortable now?"

"Vye should I be uncomfortable?"

"You tell me."

"Vhat do you vant me to tell you?"

"Whatever you'd like."

And so on and so on and so on -- till finally he sat forward in his chair and I knew, instinctively, I was allowed to go. I made for the door as if he were a dentist, only to be met by Gene who made me promise I'd give it just one more chance.

"So you were going to tell me about your accent," Kal began our second session.

"I vas?"

"Weren't you?"

"Vye do you keep asking me the same question?"

"Why do you think?"

"How am I supposed to know?"

"You sound angry."

"Vell I'm not."

"I didn't mean to make you uncomfortable."

"I'm not. Maybe **you** uncomfortable!"

"Sometimes I am.......If you're alive you sometimes get uncomfortable."

I looked at him out of the corner of my eye, careful to shield myself, lest he see right through me -- lest he see what I thought my mother had seen before she turned away. *He's baiting me,* I thought. *He doesn't get uncomfortable. He's just stringing me along.*

"You look surprised."

"At vhat?"

"Maybe that I said I get uncomfortable too at times. "

"Vell I'm not!........................"

"Hmmm?"

" It's not important."

"Your thoughts aren't important?"

"Vell they've never been important before. Vhy are they important to you?"

"Nobody cared what you thought?"

"No."

"That must have been hard for you."

"It was.."

And so we were off to the races, sparring, baiting, provoking. Until the day I finally told him about running away. I faced him, directly. I was watching him with absolute vigilance. I could see his eyes blink. I could see potassium cross his cell membrane. That's how closely I watched him -- so I would have known if he was conning me, thinking ill of me beneath his poise.

"What a resourceful thing to do," he said, without a trace of blame, "getting out of there.

It must have taken a lot of guts.

Silence fell. I sat up, dizzy and mute. I tried to get my bearings in this unfamiliar place, light-flooded and up-side down. *A bad girl who might not be so bad? A crazy girl who might not be so nuts?* I tried to stay put in the world, as I knew it to be. But the floor kept moving. The colors kept rearranging their pigments, playing with my eyes, taunting me, mocking the foolishness of where I'd been -- till

STUMBLING HOME

finally, weary from clutching a life-line that was strangling me, I let go of my grip and embraced what was happening. It took a while for my guard to genuinely ease, but, in time, with his skill and patience, I finally spoke to him as I spoke to people in Brooklyn….. about Bea, Bea Starr from Sheepshead Bay.

MIRIAM

IT WAS ABOUT this time that a new *"temp"* came to work in my office who spoke this language I was beginning to understand. Her name was Miriam, yet, despite her education and sensitivity, no one ever called her "Miriam".

"Give it to **'the temp'**," they'd say. "Ask **'the temp'** to get it...Is **'the temp'** back from lunch?" Until the day she was fired, I don't think anyone ever used her name.

I was already a fixture by the time Miriam came to work in the office, or, as we used to say, *by the time she came to work for* **"us."** Not that I was a great secretary by anyone's stretch of the imagination, but I was entertaining and eager-to-please, the child who tries to keep her dysfunctional family afloat. At least that's how I think I was seen.

Miriam, on the other hand, wasn't seen at all -- except by me. She may have been "the temp" to the grown ups in the office but to me, only four years younger than she and virtually her peer, she was a giant. I watched everything she did and marveled at her poise, her college education, the money she seemed to have in abundance, her taste in expensive clothing, her reticence, above all. To me she was an upper-east-side widow, thin, elegant and frail, who dines alone each evening at the same time, the same table in the same fine restaurant, impeccably mannered and coifed, sipping her *Manhattan* and the ones after that, beautifully, yet simply dressed, except for the occasional white gloves that went out with *Victrolas* and snuff -- The matron whom the waiters know because she's a creature of habit and

STUMBLING HOME

everyone thinks she's loaded (with liquor, too) -- and they treat her gently because she's gentle -- and would **never** make a scene and they wonder when her husband died and know it's just a matter of time ....

Except Miriam was young and didn't drink. Had we not sat five feet away from each other, I at my proper desk outside Marty's office and she at a make-shift table for the transient "temp," it's hard to imagine how our paths would ever have crossed. I remember the first day we spoke. She was getting her coat just before lunch. It was a deep green cashmere coat with a full chinchilla collar. *That must have cost a fortune*, I thought. *I wish **I** had the money for a **real** coat. She didn't buy **that** in a thrift-shop!*

"That's a beautiful coat," I commented, as she was about to leave. "Where did you get it?"

"Bloomies."

"Where's that?"

"Bloomies, you know. Bloomingdales."

"I think I've heard of it."

"It's right across the street," she said as if to remind me of something familiar I'd inadvertently just forgotten in the chaos of the moment.

"I don't go to a lot of stores."

"Me neither. But Bloomies is different. I only go there when there's a big sale, like today. You could probably get a coat like this for $50.00. Would you like to come with me?" she asked innocently. "We could be back by the end of lunch."

"I'd love to but................ I go to my therapist at lunchtime."

She stopped in her tracks and looked me straight in the face as if seeing me from a totally different angle.

"You have a therapist, too?"

"Yeah. And you, too?"

"Yes..." she nodded. "That's so wild. You're the best secretary here. I can't believe **you're** in therapy."

"What does that have to do with therapy?"

"Well, I keep getting fired. I'll probably get fired from this job too. But you, you seem to be able to do everything. And you have so much confidence. I can't believe you have any problems."

"Everyone's got problems," I said, reassuringly. "It's the nature of living."

It wasn't long before Miriam and I were great friends. Sitting at my desk, wondering what I was doing there, I'd turn to her, pucker my mouth like *The Cookie Monster* and stare her down. She'd respond by crossing her eyes and sticking out her teeth as if they were bucked. Then we'd laugh, compose ourselves and start all over again. The moment when our eyes met, or rather, the moment when my eyes met her *eye*, we knew that life could be good and we fought to maintain the conversation.

It was the same outside of work, even when we weren't alone. Once, when Miriam and her boyfriend, Tony, met me for lunch in a diner, Tony really made me angry. When the check arrived, I suggested we split it in threes, knowing full well I'd ordered the least expensive sandwich on the menu, but he took out a pencil and starting separating out who had what for how much. Now, I never would have expected anyone to pay for me because, after all, I wasn't Sandra Dee. And I knew we were all financially strapped. But haggling, particularly with his girlfriend, about pennies was just too cheap. As he worked his numbers in deep concentration, I stared at the back of his head with my mouth puckered. Miriam crossed her eyes and pulled in her lower jaw and we commiserated in silence.

Another time we were shopping indecisively and the salesgirl rolled her eyes. We went into our routine and baffled her completely.

I loved Miriam's silliness, though it confused me. She was like me, yet she seemed to come from a different planet. It was only when she haggled back with Tony that I got an inkling that what she was haggling about had nothing to do with the check. She, richly dressed and put together with care and he, handsome, *normal*, though stingy and impoverished, were nothing like me yet utterly familiar. Of course, I never haggled about money and certainly, as the daughter of good communists, I never would have. But watching the two of them, I knew in my heart what it was like to be short-changed. It was only the fact that Miriam dug in her heels and haggled back with him while I gave away the kitchen sink that threw me off. Once I understood, though, my bond with her was unbreakable.

SKIPPING TOWN

I'D WORKED AT The American Jewish Committee (a.k.a. *The Institute for Human Relations*) for a year and was beginning to get cabin fever. The fact that I'd lasted as long as I did was no small achievement and I was the first to acknowledge it. *Bea Starr from Brooklyn* seemed more comfortable with herself, (though I recall continuing to feel offended when someone brought my origins to my attention). Or maybe it wasn't comfort. Maybe I just tired and gave up. Sometimes I like to think that, that I just succumbed *to Brooklyn*, not because I was really *from* there, but because I hadn't the stamina to fight for my rightful place in the world. I liked that one. My therapist, Kal, didn't.

At other times I was clear that *Beatrice from The Ukraine is damaged. She's a sick child. Her grandiosity,* Kal would say, *is her only defense against the disappearance of her self.* What a bunch of nonsense, I'd argue. I am different. I'm not like the rest of you. I'm not mediocre! The battle was still waging inside. Yet with each week, with each month, for some inextricable reason, the conflict was beginning to recede and other matters were taking the fore.

I've got to get out of here. I decided. *I can't do this job one more day. I'm dying in here. I won't die like this.* That's what began to stir. I knew that most people could tolerate routine, that they didn't **have to get out of here**. But I did. At the same time, I'd given up Russian; I'd given up Hindi. I'd moved into an apartment with two other nice Jewish girls from work; *What more do you want?* I'd challenge Kal? *My blood?* But this was a battle Kal couldn't win.

STUMBLING HOME

Without much drama, I took the money I'd saved from work and, along with my room-mate, Marcy, we *got out* the way *normal* people do when they're restless or bored. Well, almost. I didn't exactly change jobs or take a break for R & R or have an affair or get my nails done. I went to South America.

Now we're talking about 1960 or 1961 when nice young girls didn't go to Colombia (though we had no idea that Columbia, at the time, was in the midst of internal havoc, violence and armed revolt). Rather, they went to Paris or London or Rome or maybe even Brussels if they were a little far out. If you really wanted to be different and were *really* ahead of your time you'd go to Nepal or Marrakesh -- or join the Peace Corps. But nobody went to Colombia! The fact was all I knew about Colombia was that it was in South America and I didn't know of any young Americans who vacationed in South America. For me that was the best P.R.

And so we had to go to there -- precisely because no one else did. *I may have worked in an office for a year,* I told Marcy when we planned our itinerary, *but there's no way you'll get* **me** *to Paris. I'm the kind of girl who goes to Bogota and Medellin and Cartagena and Santa Marta. If* **they** *don't go there, I do!*

Colombia was like unhooking a corset that's three sizes too small. I remember everything we saw, every impression. Yet, despite it all, what I was most aware of was the overwhelming euphoria of having cut loose and, at the same time, the overwhelming need to reconnect. That was my summer vacation. That's what was memorable, not the sights nor the people nor the culture, as awesome as they were, but the magnificent feeling of freedom -- and yet the longing to go home. It startled me to feel that longing. I'd never felt it before, certainly not when I left Brooklyn.

What I felt in Colombia was **home** *sickness,* a sickness **for** home, a running **to,** like a kid at a carnival who wants to try all the new rides yet can't wait to go back to his old favorite. And maybe he'll even start crying and stomping his feet as though someone were preventing him, as though if he didn't get back there right now, the ride would disappear and he'd never be able to go on it again. But mommy will understand that he's just a little kid, that he's overwhelmed and that he's crying, not because he has too little, but because, at that moment, he has too much. And in her patience and wisdom, she'll help him sort it out.

At the time of my trip to South America, I hadn't yet understood this, that one could have so much that its absence hurts. In Colombia I got the first glimmer of that kind of abundance. There was a home I missed, a home I was home sick to return to and this insight alone gave me joy and quelled my panic so I could continue on. We climbed Montserrat in the middle of Bogota (where a handsome young Colombian boy fell in love with me, and I with him), yet even that couldn't change the equation.

And we travelled on a noisy, wobbling, primitive "bus" shared by the local poor and chickens (who had their run of the place) to Santa Marta, across from the sea, where we sat in an outdoor café and out of nowhere shots were fired. Two men, seated across from us were apparently hit while a young man, not much older than we, wearing a New York baseball cap was seated on a low brick wall, seemingly unperturbed.

When the havoc passed we approached him and asked him, in English, what was going on. He answered, robotically that "Hey, this is Columbia, man." Now this was long before we knew much about drugs or the sound of someone stoned. However, it was clear to at least these two neophytes that this guy was American and wasn't drunk but something very different. He seemed as out of place in this environment as we must have seemed to the local travelers with whom we shared the bus. Why he was there, at his young age, in the middle of an apparent war zone was as perplexing to us as, perhaps, we to him, though he didn't seem in the least bit curious about us.

Had Marcy not doubled over in pain several weeks later as we explored Columbia and been forced to have her appendices removed (which everyone was later convinced had really been an abortion), we might have stayed the full two months. Unbeknownst to us initially, she was taken to the Canal Zone hospital, the American hospital at which American citizens and service members were treated, while I was forced to find a hotel room, which, of course, I'd have to pay for.

For Marcy, the dilemma was easy. She'd had her appendix removed and treatment at the hospital was *apparently* free to American citizens. But for me, forced to pay for a room in the El Panama Hilton, the swankiest hotel in the Canal Zone (but the hotel closest to the hospital), the cost was outrageous. Fortunately, the first night at this swanky casino hotel had been a godsend.

When I walked into the casino on that amazing first night, two handsome young Columbians approached me and offered to buy me a drink, which I unhesitatingly accepted. It would be the first of their remarkable weeklong generosity, offered freely, without a price to be paid. For me, it was unfathomable, that they, without rhyme or reason, chose to subsidize my time in Panama. They never asked for a cent of repayment, explaining in their thick Spanish accents, that they, not I, were the lucky ones. Just having the company of an American girl whose English they could emulate was repayment enough. For a week we ate at the fanciest of this fancy hotel's restaurants and gambled at their casinos, laughing and exchanging trivia. I didn't spend a penny and they asked for nothing, nothing except for the pleasure of my company! It was the strangest curve-ball I'd ever been thrown. And that was how my unexpected vacation in Panama was spent.

When Marcy was ready to be discharged from the hospital, I said my reluctant good-byes to my amazing two friends who I promised to take around New York if they were ever able to visit. The week spent with them was the most unexpected, perplexing experience of my life, they in their hotel room and I in mine. Never once did they even knock on my hotel door, never once even a hint of impropriety. I had no way to explain their generosity except to accept the fact, as they repeatedly said, that my company was sufficient. Having only recently watched Miriam and her boyfriend, Tony, haggle about a few cents made their generosity even more remarkable, although I'd seen such generosity before, primarily from my father who had subsidized his two (*half*) brothers by setting them up in his rare book business.

I don't know if my two friends ever did come to Manhattan…for those were the days without internet or cell phones so even if they did visit, given how impermanent my moves were, I would not have known. What I did know, at least was beginning to learn, was that my parents were not typical people and that THEIR experiences as refugee Jews from the continent where Jewish lives were so cheap and so difficult, must have been formative. I never forgot that take on my childhood and I believe it, just as stridently, today.

Marcy's appendectomy took every last penny we had and we were forced to return to New York early. When we arrived home I got down on my knees and kissed the ground, a gesture from a child who'd been raised to mock such ethnocentrism.

Coming home was as mesmerizing as leaving it, but coming home early had a price. Our apartment on 113th Street, which we'd sublet for the summer, was still occupied when we got back. We were forced to take a room at The Hotel Albert on University Place in The Village until our tenants were gone. All we needed, after all, was a place to sleep and we planned to do just that when we got our room. Fortunately, as it happened, other events intervened.

Marcy, in her homesickness, decided that an old boyfriend was the true love of her life and she had to see him immediately while the handsome Inca boy I'd met in Bogota and made love to on Montserrat and swore to marry and live with on the mountain for a thousand years -- until *I got home* and forgot his name --- was unceremoniously forgotten. With Marcy now "occupied" with the "love of her life," I decided that Cedar Tavern, just across the street, was the logical place to visit.

The evening was warm, a perfect, sanguine New York night and Cedar, as always in the summer, was exploding with buzz and vitality. The bar, deep with scrappy men, was the finish line on a challenging course. My pulse quickened as I meandered my way through the brush like a skier down the slalom -- focused and euphoric. I waited patiently for a seat, staring attentively at nothing as if called to urgent mental activity, as if unmindful of the bodies pushing me from every side. Finally a seat was free. I pushed forward *accidentally* and claimed my place. I could have sworn I was caught in a time warp. In each direction men crowded the old mahogany bar, the same men, it seemed, who'd last been there, in the very same seats with the very same beers, as if they'd never left -- drinking men, serious drinking men. Even their talk was the same.

These weren't the men at a Grand Central Bar waiting for the 7:08 to take them back to Connecticut, men in $3,000 suits who'd kicked the stuffing out of themselves on their climb to prosperity, who knew despair when the vodka wore off but were helpless to know what to do about it. These weren't your average men, rich Joe's with three kids and a wife more distant than kin, men who'd done what was expected of them and never questioned it, who's thinning hair was their only clue that something was happening, and it wasn't good, who's kids did drugs, men who were never perplexed, who are morally certain and know the only way to live, who laugh at anything unlike themselves and tyrannize their households or abdicate it, who refuse to see their kid's psychologist -- *who has some damn nerve* bothering him with her pithy concerns, who misses his kid's soccer game because he has a meeting, who adores his daughter but never spoke to her and is a stranger to his son.

These men at Cedar weren't the sorry sights who ascend to "head of household" under the tutelage of their own fathers and the threat of their scorn, who are buckling under the weight of their roles and the rigidity of their heritage -- like three generations of cops who's last offspring got his genes from his gentle mother but who'd rather die than leave the fold. These weren't men in *Boxers,* going under at full speed, who'll have respectable funerals and be called "good men."

These were not "good men" and that was the appeal. This was a club for renegades, for artists. It was a club for men who left the beaten path or never saw it in the first place, for the painter or the sculptor or the poet who came to his work because he **had** to. Maybe he'd even wished he was one of those guys on the 7:08 but hadn't a clue how to get there and finally just let it slide. But whatever the case, he wasn't the guy on that train.

In short, this was a club for *men without brokers.* Maybe these men wished they'd had investments or the capitol to need one. Maybe they were even the one's who'd never be caught dead on the 7:08 yet their lust for money would prevail. But, at the time, colored as it was by my youth and naiveté, I was certain these men, my heroes, men in cords and work boots, **chose** to be financially poor in favor of culturally rich. So I sat at the bar like Marlene Dietrich, dangling a cigarette from my lips, indifferent to the *local color*. I was only there, after all, to grab a quick drink on my way to more important destinations. I watched myself attentively in the mirror behind the ornate bar and perfected my presentation.

I wasn't particularly struck by the two men to my right. They seemed unusually devoid of flash and were deeply involved in conversation. They weren't unattractive but I didn't sense any interest on their parts in me. I discounted them without further consideration. I waited. Soon an old lush approached me and described my body as he imagined it in the nude. I laughed so as not to offend him then turned away. *I don't want anyone seeing me with this guy,* I thought. *It creates a bad impression.* I waited some more. A handsome, young guy reached over my shoulder to get his beer.

"*I'm sorry,*" I said, as sweet as all get-out.

"*No. I'm sorry,*" he responded casually.

"*No, please. **I'm** sorry,*" I toyed. "*I'm s-o-o-o-o sorry.*"

He rolled his eyes, as if to say, *"whatever"* and made his way from the bar to a young, blond woman and handed her the beer. *Whatever,* I thought, and continued waiting........and waiting. I looked again to the men on my right, this time a bit more carefully. While they were still deep in conversation, the one farthest from me seemed distracted by my presence. I re-checked the woman in the mirror and tossed my hair back. I made it a point to look towards Mecca when I sensed he was watching me, and, for a moment, our eyes met.

He was ruggedly good-looking, a bit older than the men I was accustomed to but not too old. His long, thick hair was longer than fashionable, even for the artists of the day and it struck me immediately that this was a man who thought for himself. I liked that about him, and the haphazardness of his appearance as though he had better things to do with his time. Again I looked to Mecca and again our eyes met. This time I noticed his features. They were well-constructed features, strongly defined. The prominent chin and olive complexion suggested he might be Spanish or even Italian. I liked that. He was sexy in a way that only men who are unselfconscious can be sexy. It spoke of character and higher values. We searched each other's eyes when, for an instant. I got a glimpse of what existed inside. This was a serious man.

When I understood that, I raised another cigarette to my lips and leaned towards him invitingly. He reached into his pocket and took out a lighter.

JOHNNY MARINO

JOHNNY MARINO WAS his name. It was a fitting name. Short and to the point. No middle name, he said. That was fitting, too. This was a man unencumbered. What you see is what you get. I was aware of that immediately, his directness and seeming simplicity that you'd never confuse with simple-mindedness. To the contrary, what was evident from the first was that this was a man of depth.

When he looked at me, he looked nowhere else and when he spoke, his words were prudent and economical, as if his time was precious and shouldn't be squandered in shallow water. And when I spoke he listened to every word.

I was confused by him, by his seeming integrity and I lost my bearings. My head, tilted back aloofly. My eyes, first lazy in feigned disinterest, began to lower, then opened wide like a child in wonderland. I felt myself losing power. It wasn't a discomforting loss at all. It was a welcomed loss and long, long over-due. As we spoke, it was clear to me that I'd switched modalities. The girl from the D.P. camps receded, her accent long since silenced. But the transformation had been incomplete, tentative, like discarding an old dress before you're sure how the new one will look, before you've seen yourself in the mirror. That's how it felt at first with Johnny, that I was wearing an outfit I'd never seen – that I had no way to judge, as if I were blind and had to go it on faith. But as the hours passed, I managed to peek at the reflection in his eyes and was reassured. The girl from Brooklyn turned down the volume because she sensed she could still be heard.

But in doing so she knew she'd never be the cause of a Trojan war and it was a hard pill to swallow.

But Johnny made it easier. *"Delightful."* That's what he called me. That's what he called this undistinguished girl. And though I'd have preferred "sexy" or "gorgeous," I sensed that "delightful" was good enough and I was able to let it be. It was his graceful maturity that set the tone, like a sign in the road that you follow willingly because you know it's for your own good. That's how I saw it, letting it be. It was for my own good – like putting your foot on the break when the sign says "STOP." Maybe I couldn't start a Trojan war, but I was good enough.

We were at the bar until midnight. Thomas, his friend, had long since excused himself, first cupping his hand in a fist and affectionately jabbing Johnny's ribs, winking to him as he left. They were gestures that seemed to please Johnny for his face took on an air of pride despite its modesty and the blush of embarrassment. And they were gestures that pleased me too. I was the prize he had won. We talked about everything, or, rather, I talked about everything, but mostly about my trip to South America. The photographs, still in my bag from the morning, provided the visual aides. It wasn't your usual travel-log, polished and historically accurate, but Johnny seemed please. When we'd seen the last of the pictures, he asked me if I wanted to see his studio.

I was thrilled that he wanted to prolong our time together -- but then the words sunk in and, if the truth be told, the invitation to his "studio" was disappointing. While he'd told me from the beginning that he was a sculptor, I somehow didn't **really** think about it. I suppose if I had, I would have tried to envision the wealth and power of a prominent banker who just *happens* to be an artist, too. That way he'd have the wherewithal to triumph over life's struggles and rescue me from mine. That's how I needed to see him. And that's really how he struck me at first, prosperous, creative, yet substantial -- *normal*, in other words -- until he invited me to his "studio." As soon as he said that word, the picture of strength was replaced, instantaneously, by one of powerlessness and I was disappointed, not wholly disillusioned, but disappointed, somewhat.

When we left Cedar Tavern, though some of the fizz was gone there was also an authentic interest and respect. The only thing that suffered, in fact, was the part where they live happily ever after. The reality of an *artist* in his *studio* intervened. As we walked a few steps toward the curb I thought we were going to hail a cab. *Maybe he's an artist,* I thought, *but he can't be wholly down-and-out if he's got money for cabs.* My spirits rose. Then he reached for a bicycle leaning against a tree!

"Hop on," he said casually. "I'll ride you."

Ride me? I thought. *Is this guy kidding? Where's my taxi? And besides, this is*

"Beastress". "Pleasingly plump, cheerfully chubby and fantastically fat!" I wanted to disappear. *I'll get on this guy's handlebars and the tires will blow and I'll die of embarrassment.*

"Come on. Hop on."

He's got to be nuts. I'll just......**hop on?** Like a skinny ballerina, I'll just......**hop?** I declined.

"Come on. I can ride us."

I wanted to excuse myself inconspicuously but the conflict was too apparent. There was no place to run.

"Fine." I said, matter-of-factly, not letting on that I *knew what he knew that I knew.*

I stood on my tip-toes and raised my backside over the handlebars, then released my toes cautiously, as a child would who's about to sit on a balloon. *No explosion!* I raised my feet off the ground and tucked my red cotton dress under my thighs because, whatever else I may be, I'm *always* a lady! And off we went, smoothly, through the dark, warm, summer night, without a care in the world -- except for my unrelenting need to look graceful despite the fact that I was about to fall on my ass and my unrelenting fear that the tires would blow, any second, beneath us.

But he was strong, this sculptor, and a virtuoso on the bike. And I managed to maintain my poise and *"je ne sais quoi"* as he rode us downtown along Sixth Avenue then turned onto Chambers Street and stopped in front of an old industrial building off the corner. I was new to this area, at least after dark, and startled. I knew this area during the day but I had no idea it turned into the Fruit and Produce Market after dark. Though it was after midnight, the street, from Church to the Hudson River was filled with light and activity as if it were midday. Men were scurrying in every direction, buying and selling in the open-air markets and hoisting huge crates from loading-docks onto the trucks that would take them to markets throughout the state. The street was littered with occasional melons and peaches that had fallen to the ground and, everywhere, the lights and sounds of commerce masked the night. For a girl for whom darkness had always signaled the beginning of a waking death, this street was magical.

"Have you ever been to the Washington Markets?" Johnny asked, as he dismounted the bike.
"I've only been here during the day. It's been empty. I had no idea this went on at night."
"It's the fruit and produce markets. They're only opened at night."
"That's wild."
"Yeah. I love this area."
"I can see why."
"Here," he said, picking up a peach from the ground and handing it to me.
"You mean we can just take it?"
"Sure. Here's another one."
"I can't believe it," I said, astounded by the abundance, by the fact that here one needn't worry, that food was free for the asking, like the sight of a rich harvest in a drought. I held the magic fruit in

my hands as Johnny unlocked the gate to the ground-floor storefront and wheeled his bike into the ante-foyer toward the front door. It was dark and still, as if it were the entrance of an abandoned building. All I could make out was how old the building seemed and how dilapidated. As I waited for Johnny to unlock the front door, I noticed a display window on either side of me and imagined it filled with expensive gifts or millinery. *Why are these windows painted over?* I wondered. *It makes the whole place look like wartime. With just a little effort, this wouldn't be nearly so bad.*

The front door opened before me. I followed Johnny inside -- then stopped abruptly, as if frozen. This was a Great Room, a cathedral with its vastness and majesty. A ceiling soared to the heavens. But instead of columns, towering trees made of steel -- bearing "fruit" the size of dinosaur ova rose from the floor. And, instead of pews, one small wooden stool sat in this forest of welded metal from which Johnny Marino grew his crop.

There was no gold in this church, no ornaments, no stained-glass windows, nothing "pretty" or unnecessary. Not even a bed, except for a mattress hidden in a loft that you'd never find unless you knew where to look.

"It can't look like anyone lives here," Johnny explained, unsolicited. *"The Fire Department comes by once a month to check -- because I weld. If they think I'm living here, they threaten to give me a summons and I have to pay them off to leave me alone."*

That made sense, what he said, but, somehow, I suspected there was more to it. I couldn't stop staring. Even the ashtray, actually the lid of a jar, was merely functional, like the pure white walls, bare and unadorned, that served only to enclose the space. And that too was barren except for scraps of metal and welding torches that lay neatly at the feet of the trees.

Most people wouldn't call these objects "trees," certainly not Johnny nor his artist friends nor the galleries that showed them nor even the occasional patron who bought one. But to me, there was no doubt. I wanted to ask him then and there for confirmation, and be done with it. But I couldn't speak. All the whiteness, the space, all the purity and the splendor of the trees. Above all, the splendor of the trees. I was dazzled by their brilliance. There were no lies here. I knew that the moment I walked in. Nothing to make you look like what you're not. No lefties who play the market, no saints who speak in forked tongues, no feisty virgins from Sheepshead Bay, *or was it Kiev?* This was a place to work, plain and simple, a sanctuary where anything, even trees made of steel, can thrive.

So when I said earlier that I was disappointed when Johnny invited me to his "studio," it's also true that the disappointment was brief and ill placed. It took only an instant in this cathedral for my fantasies to be re-arranged. I'd no longer be rescued by his money and status in the *acceptable* world, I thought, but, rather, by his talent and status on the fringe, like the child-lover of a young Picasso, still poor but world- renowned.

COUPLING

A HALF-REFRIGERATOR AND small industrial sink stood hidden by a pin-board on which drawings and templates for future works were posted. The drawings, whether brief and spontaneous or elaborately rendered, were placed as a surgeon would his scalpels, ordered and systematic.

The term "obsessive-compulsive" hadn't yet entered the vernacular but if it had, an unenlightened observer might have used it to describe this space. The studio was impeccably organized and efficient, but to see it as "compulsive" would have missed the point. Even then, as unschooled as I was, I somehow knew that the order in this place was no shield for errant impulses. This wasn't a man who organized his world lest he spin into chaos or shoot his neighbor. This was a man who took great care because that's what great art required and it made me admire him all the more.

"Purity," that was Johnny's word. He liked his environment pure.

"It's like a museum," I commented. "The walls are so white."

"I don't like nonessential things," he explained, "like a living-room in Queens with a couch and two matching end tables, a "painting" that was only bought because it matched the sofa. Where every surface holds an object, just to fill up the space. I can't live like that. It's too distracting. I need the space. Someone might call it 'empty'. To me it's opportunity."

This was a man to be taken seriously.

The *"bedroom,"* accessible by an unobtrusive ladder in the corner of the studio, was like the rest of the space, functional and unadorned, a small mattress on a 4x8 foot plywood loft floor, the lid of a jar that served as another ash-tray and a copy of Art Forum. We didn't even bother to remove our clothes. No need to get all carried away.

I suppose I would have liked it, though, if there had been a bit more drama to this first encounter -- but things were happening so fast, I didn't give it much thought. The only thing I really wondered about, in fact, was the kissing. Johnny kissed me with his mouth closed. It was peculiar, not "bad, " as if it hurt, just odd. I'd never been kissed like that before, certainly not while making love. I didn't know what to make of it. I think I just shrugged my shoulders and chalked it up to his *purity*.

In those days, though, it wasn't altogether unusual for a man to kiss a woman with his mouth closed on the first date. To the contrary, it would have been *taking liberties* to do otherwise. But this wasn't a *date* in the first place and, secondly, we were making love, for Pete's sake, so why stand on ceremonies. I was perplexed but **everything** here was sparse. I was young, without the psychological equipment to probe further. (But when I finally understood, late in the game, it was cataclysmic, like Adam in the Garden of Good and Evil, and it signaled, without recourse, the beginnings of my adulthood. But that, of course, comes later, much later than this story allows right now).

When we finally descended the ladder from the loft, a streak of daylight was sneaking through the bottom of the studio's only window, blackened, I thought, to obscure a view from the outside in. It was a strange sight, the black window above a strip of bright light, as if to sit on the light, to snuff it out. Or maybe it was the other way around. Maybe it was the daylight forcing itself in, like a suitor who won't take *"No"* for an answer -- as if to thumb it's nose at the blackened pane. As if to let Johnny know there's only so much a man can do before nature takes its course.

STUMBLING HOME

It was an unusual sight, a window painted over, like painting over a Botticelli. *Windows determine the rent.* I thought. *The more there are, the higher the price. Doesn't he know that? Doesn't he care? Doesn't he want people to know he's got one! Show it off like the teeth of a prized mare. For Christ sake, don't paint it black! Would you paint the mare's teeth black? If you don't want people looking in, put up drapes. Maybe something in floral -- with a matching chair.*

As we walked through the cavernous space toward the door, I noticed again the strips of metal beneath the "trees," lined up in perfect order on the floor, waiting their turn obediently, to become. *In vitro fertilization! That's what's going on here.* I turned to Johnny to see more in him. My eyes screened out the periphery, holding steady, intense and undiverted, respectful and awed by my subject -- and his work. And then it occurred to me that maybe the painted window wasn't so much to block the view *in* as much as it was to block the view *out*.

The thought delighted me. A man with so much inside he needs to ration it. And I, empty as a lake in a drought, who can't get enough, whose only goal is satiety! What symmetry. What a perfect mix! We walked out onto the still and lifeless street. My heart wasn't fluttering with passion. It was swelling with admiration. Now Chambers Street was as I'd known it before, empty and inert. It was almost dawn and the flurry of activity the night before was gone, as if it had never been. The transformation saddened me. The world was bleak again - like leaving a party at 5:00 AM to walk the streets devoid of movement or light. The taxis, otherwise in abundance, were nowhere to be found, no children, no people like yourself whom you might call upon for assistance if the need be. I thought of all that with the Market's closed, till Johnny, once again, saved the day.

"Want to go for breakfast?"
"Now? What's opened now? It's 5:00 o'clock in the morning."
"The Market Diner. Come on. Hop on.

And, of course, I did -- and the diner **was** opened and his stock continued to soar. Since the day I left home, I'd never had a *proper* breakfast. In childhood, breakfasts were important -- not only for the nutrition they provided but, more importantly, because they reflected the quality of mothering. The child who left home with a meager breakfast was a pitiable sight. *"The poor kid!"* An observer might comment. *"What kind of mother does she have?"* No one ever questioned the "fathering" or whether the kid just didn't like to eat a lot. No. The better the breakfast, the better the wife and mother. So while my mother may have been deaf to **my** needs, she always made a *proper* breakfast: bacon and eggs, juice, pancakes, toast, jam, the works. I missed that when I left home – and, of course, I didn't have the money to buy it for myself. But Johnny and I ordered such a breakfast at the Market Diner that morning.

At first, I was reluctant, figuring in my head what each item might cost: *"Let me see, if I get eggs without the bacon........What if I get the bacon but not the toast?..........How much are the pancakes alone?"* I finally thought, *"The hell with it. How many times do you do this?"* And I ordered the works. It crossed my mind whether he might pay, but I dismissed it, he being the struggling artist and all. *"It won't kill me to splurge this once!"*

When the check came, there was a bit of tension, at least on my part. At that time, it was the custom for men to pay and, with Sinai or Alfredo or others, they did. But I never took it for granted. So the situation was ambiguous and I took out my purse. As I did, Johnny reached over and picked up the check without a word or inkling of hesitation.

"Please," I said. *"I've got some money,"*

He just smiled.

This was very significant. I was watching everything. And everything was being weighed, like an accountant. Had he accepted my offer of money, things would have been different. It wasn't the money, per se, because I knew he didn't have much. It was the **feeling** of being cared for. Without it, nothing was possible, at least not a love affair. So once again, his credit rating rose.

It was after seven when we finally left the diner and, though neither of us had slept, we were ready to keep going.

"You want to walk around?" he asked, as we headed for the bike.

"Sure. Where should we go?"

"How about the village?"

"Great!"

"O.K. Hop on. We'll be there in two minutes."

Eighth Street was my favorite street in the whole world. It was the center of the universe, the cafes, the kookie shops, the counter-culture and bohemia. It was where I belonged. So to be there that morning with Johnny was like bringing a guy home to meet your parents. It was that kind of test. The shops were hours from opening but we parked the bike and began to browse, past the funky clothes stores, the subterranean clubs and the occasional little "head shops" that were just beginning to crop up with their pipes and "roach holders" and paraphernalia for drugs. As we looked in one of these windows, at what was completely unfamiliar to me, I noticed a sign on the adjacent store:

"Sam Kramer Pierces Ears Perfectly and Painlessly."

Hmmm, I thought. *And it's opened.*

"Do you want to go in?" Johnny asked, noticing my temptation.

"I do.......But I don't..... I'm too scared."

"Come on. I'll go with you."

"No............Well........maybe...........No. I can't! I can't. I've wanted to get my ears pierced for years, but I'm too scared."

"There's nothing to be scared of."

I looked at him, half believing and confident, half terrified like a child about to go on a roller coaster for the first time.

"Come on," he prodded, taking my hand. *"I'll be with you."*

At first I walked behind him, six paces, as if to slaughter, but when we got inside, the sight of the earrings gave me courage -- until Sam

Kramer appeared from behind a screen.

Where have those hands been? I recoiled. *What's that stuff under his nails? This mechanic is going to pierce **my** ears?* I tightened my grip on Johnny's arm and was about to turn to leave.

"Can I help you?" Sam Kramer asked, coming toward us in his mechanic-stained clothes.

"Yes....." Johnny answered.

"No!" I interrupted.

"It seems there's a difference of opinion."

"She wants her ears pierced."

"That's what I'm famous for!" the mechanic answered.

For giving them lock jaw? I thought. *This guy amputated limbs in Normandy! On the beach! With no anesthetic!! That's where he learned his trade. And he wasn't even the medic! And what's behind the screen, anyway? Is that the toilet? I didn't hear a flush! Damn! I hope he didn't poop!*

It was too late to turn back. I couldn't look like a fool. Sam Kramer reached for something from behind the counter with his right hand.... then approached me.... with a hole puncher. His left hand moved spastically towards my ear, then clutched the lobe while I clamped my eyes and shuddered. I could hear the flesh rip. I must have whimpered. Yet all I remember is Johnny Marino's hand on my shoulder. A simple gesture, not self-serving, an anonymous gift that saves the day with nothing asked in return. It was for me, in that brief, consoling act, all I'd ever wished for and more than I'd ever known.

THE ALBERT

IT WAS OBVIOUS to me that a marker had appeared in the road, one I hadn't expected yet one I was eager to follow because I knew it would take me home. He'd sensed my homesickness and had come to help. I knew that with such clarity and assurance that my path was certain and I knew it would be O.K.

So when we left Sam Kramer's, it never occurred to me that it was time to go our separate ways, if only till the next time we'd meet. From the moment we left that store, I never doubted, never questioned that there was any place for me except with him. So, with Marcy at her boyfriend's and with the two of us exhausted, it was as natural, as if we'd been married forever, to head to The Albert to sleep.

We walked past the concierge and took the elevator to the fourth floor. I groped for my key and motioned for Johnny to wait. The thought of his entering an untidy room was out of the question. I didn't create trees from scrap metal but I was a good woman and I kept a clean home. It was important he know at least this. I unlocked the door, opened it cautiously so he couldn't see the disarray, then switched on the light.

Two bodies, one small and white as talc the other big and black as coal, moved rhythmically, in unison, up and down, up and down on the bed. I switched off the light, closed the door and shrugged my shoulders.

"I'm sorry, Johnny, but my room-mate's still asleep," I said, hoping he hadn't seen them, lest he think, by association, I'm too "easy" too.

"That's O.K. Do you want to come back to my studio?"

"Sure," I answered. "Sounds great."

It was four PM when we finally awoke. Outside, the markets were just beginning to come again to life. Johnny disappeared for a moment and returned with a panoply of fruits to accompany a late lunch of peanut butter sandwiches.

"I have to work tonight," he said, without apology. "Would you like to stay?"

"Oh. I didn't realize," I answered, a bit confused. "I don't want to be a nuisance."

"You're not. I like having you here."

"I like being here."

"So why don't you stay?"

"But you have to work."

"Yes, here."

"Oh! You mean your sculpture."

"That's my work. Three nights a week I bartend but **this** is my work."

"Oh! I didn't understand."

"So what do you say? You could read.........or draw. You said you love to draw."

I hesitated. All the signals. All the inner voices. There was no question I liked this man, that I liked him a lot. There was no question I was comfortable in his presence the way I'd longed to be comfortable all my life. But a "bartender?" How it diminished him. The hastily constructed fantasy seemed to wane with each new revelation. Where were the artists who made money from their art? Was Johnny a bartender because his work wasn't good enough? Was I awed by his work because of my ignorance? But then again, I argued, what about the great artists who were dirt poor? Echoes in my head, like a warring jury deciding a man's innocence or guilt. And what about Miriam and her boyfriend? Tony was a painter -- and penniless. If it was O.K. for Miriam, why wasn't, it O.K. for me? But Tony was young, I argued. That was to his credit. It shifted the scales. Johnny was 39, after all, twenty years older than me. It effected the balance of power. But at least I didn't have to haggle with Johnny about money the way Miriam did with Tony. And besides, the deliberations continued, Johnny was sexy, much sexier than Tony. And even though he was 39, he didn't seem old, just mature and caring and solid as a rock. He calmed me down and made the winds subside. Still, I'll never have a nice apartment like Ellie will if she marries her lawyer. And what about Becky? She already **married** hers! Even **his** father was a lawyer, a judge, in fact. Now that's marrying well! They'll never have to worry where they'll sleep the night. They'll never have to fight the world with their mitts drawn, kick and scream and lie and finagle to stay above water. They'll be protected from the cataclysm the way women are supposed to be and their hearts will stop racing with dread.

So maybe there's no problem after all, I finally decided. *Maybe I'll just wait it out, enjoying Johnny's company, hoarding his kindness and wisdom, repairing my wounds, recuperating from war, buying time and reparations, till a "perfect" man comes along.*

"I'd love to stay while you work," I finally responded.
"Good. When I'm done we can go out. I always go out at ten."
"Great. I'll just sit here and relax if you don't mind."
"That's fine. I've got The Sunday Times. It'll keep you busy." His stock rose immediately.
"That'll be great. I'll do the puzzle. It's my favorite thing."
"I love it too. If you don't finish it, we'll finish it together later."
"That sounds so nice."
He nodded.

I curled up on the small, industrial-looking sofa, posed myself carefully to minimize exposure of my heavy calves and turned my attentions to the crossword. I loved the crossword. It was one of the few ways I'd learned to relax. Not twenty feet away, directly in my line of sight, Johnny stood high on a ladder welding the top of one of his "trees." The image was stunning, he with his torch aglow, his eyes covered by goggles, the blue-white flames and sparks flying like the Fourth of July. Had I not known otherwise, I would have assumed he was a steelworker in a mill or an underground mine.

As the evening passed, from time to time I lifted my eyes to follow his work. His stamina impressed me, the way he stood awkwardly at just the necessary angle without regard to time or what must have been fatigue. I only noticed him change positions once. I looked up, for a moment, from my puzzle and there he was, seated on his wooden stool, staring at me without a word. *What is he thinking?* I asked myself. *What does he see?* It disarmed me. I instinctively hid my fingers, my nails bitten to the quick. They'd always embarrassed me, these nails that told the whole story I was unable to hide.

"What are you looking at?" I asked flirtatiously though embarrassed.

"At you."

"Stop," I said coyly.

"Why?"

"Because I'm embarrassed."

"Of what?"

"I don't want you to see my nails."

"Why not?"

"Because I bite them."

"I know."

"You do?"

"Of course. They're lovely."

"***Lovely?*** *You've got to be kidding.*"

"They're lovely. They're just like you."

STUMBLING HOME

I didn't know what he was talking about, but it didn't matter. He'd seen them -- the scared child, lost and chasing her tail. He'd seen the evidence of my damage and disease that I'd hidden all my life, the evidence that separated me from **real** girls whom lawyers marry and who take care of them because they're worth being taken care of. And he thought I was lovely? How could it be? I didn't understand. It didn't matter. He saw them and they were lovely. I died and went to heaven.

As was Johnny's ritual, the work stopped at 10PM sharp when he disappeared behind a free standing partition that enclosed an industrial sink. When he reappeared, a few minutes later, clean and shaven, I was struck by "the look." He had it, the ruggedly handsome face, the long dark hair, the brown corduroys and denim shirt. The only thing missing were the work boots. In their place were rich brown leather shoes, simply styled and well broken in. You could tell they were comfortable and expensive, not *showy*, expensive or flashy, but well made to do what they were meant to do. It seemed so appropriate, this departure from *the* working-class style. It made perfect sense. This was a man who took his cues from no one. Once again, my respect for him grew.

We didn't need the bike now. We were only going down the street to the corner of Chambers and West. The city was in evening mode, except for the Markets where daylight stood still. The late summer air was mild and clean and a warm breeze from the river embraced us as we passed the trucks and loading docks and open-air produce stalls. Every few feet we stopped for a moment to say *"hello"* to this guy or that -- and they to him, like old, dear friends,

"Hey, Johnny, have a coupla peaches."............... *"Hey, Giovanni, take a bite of this."*.................. *"Ay, is that the misses, Johnny boy?"* ....*"Where'd you go last night? We didn't see you round."*

"I was busy," Johnny answered, smiling and taking my hand.

"Well, don't do nothing I wouldn't do," one of them said with a wink.

The West Street Bar, Johnny told me, was one of the oldest bars in New York, a worker's bar for the Washington Markets. Not a *"pub"* or a *"tavern"* or a *"cafe,"* just a beaten-up old bar as old as the markets themselves -- that had seen it all and knew better days (and was once even visited by a prince, he said.). Charlie had tended bar there for forty years. Johnny said he knew him before his hair turned white, though his Irish smile and whimsy hadn't changed a bit. You could tell he probably tended bar better than anyone in New York (even better than Johnny -- though, of course, Johnny wasn't a "bartender." He was a sculptor who *just happened to tend bar.)*

Charlie had a glow about him, a kind, old soul yet playful as a kid. And the minute I met him, I loved him and I think he loved me. At least his face lit up whenever I walked in.

"Now sit yourself down, me pretty lass," he'd say. *"You must be hungry as a bear."*

"I'm fine, Charlie. Really,"

"Don't give me your guff. You'll eat this sandwich, you will. You're skinny as a rail."

That's the part I loved best. I was *"skinny as a rail."* Me! And he treated Johnny like that, too. To Charlie, Johnny was a young upstart, wet behind the ears. I loved when he spoke to Johnny as if he were a kid. And I think Johnny loved it, too. There we were, two kids under Charlie's wing. It made me feel we had more in common -- and that felt good. That's why I had a martini that first night at Charlie's -- because that's what Johnny drank. I'd never tried one before. I'd heard they were lethal. I hardly drank except for an occasional glass of wine but tonight was a first.

"Johnny, boy," Charlie said, handing him his drink. *"It's been waitin' for you. Just the way you like it, dry as a bone. And you, you pretty lass. What can a get for you?"*

"I'll have the same, please."
"Are you sure," Johnny asked, parentally.
"Yup," I said, sticking out my chest.

"It's good we didn't take the bikes," I think I said an hour later as we were leaving.
"You've got a buzz, huh."
"A buzzzzzzzzzzz."
"Yup!"

When I opened my eyes the next morning, I was alone and, for a moment, lost -- until I followed a humming sound to the studio below. There, at dawn, just as he'd been the night before, was Johnny on top of his ladder, welding. My confusion disappeared and in its place, joy and gratitude filled me, as if awakening in the midst of a wonderful dream to find, in fact, it's become real.

It was Sunday, not that I'd have known it unless Johnny reminded me. So much had happened in forty-eight hours -- euphoria engulfed me – until reality broke through:

"I've got to work tonight," Johnny said matter-of-factly.

O.K. I thought. *That's fine with me. I'll just sit here like I did last night.*

"What are your plans?" He continued, piercing my dream.

"My plans?" I asked myself. *Oh! God. He wants me to leave. I **knew** I should have played hard-to-get.*

"I have so many people to see today," I blurted out, *" and so much to do. You know I was gone a whole month! My friends must be worried sick. I probably should have been home last night. The phone must have been ringing off the hook."*

"I'm glad you didn't go home."
"You are?"
"Of course."
"Oh! " I muttered foolishly.

"Why don't you stay?"

"Stay?"

"Sure. I don't have to be at the restaurant until five."

"Oh! You're working in the restaurant tonight!"

"Yes, but why don't you stay anyway. You can call your friends while I'm gone."

"Gee, I don't know," I hesitated, not wanting to seem too eager.

"I've got a better idea. Why don't you see your friends tonight while I'm working and pick up some clothes. I'll give you the keys and you can come back here when you're done."

"Oh!............"

"Didn't you say you had to stay at the hotel until your apartment's vacant?"

"Yes, but............"

"So, why don't you just stay here instead."

"Johnny........" I sighed, as if pulled to safety from a sinking ship.

"I'd like it if you did," he added simply, his voice gentle and direct.

"You would?"

"Very much."

I raised my eyes to meet his, searching for a clue. *Who is this man*, I asked myself, *so calm and soft-spoken? Can all this sweetness be real? Where is the drama, the raised voice, the fist? Where is the jealousy, the dread? How can it be so easy? Just get your clothes and stay here. Till when? Till what?....................Till it's time to go.*

I went back to The Albert that afternoon. Marcy and her boyfriend were still in bed like they'd been the day before. I tiptoed in, pretending not to notice and grabbed my suitcase still unopened.

"When will you be back?" I heard Marcy ask, half-asleep. "Are we inconveniencing you?"

"No," I answered, raising my index finger to my lips and tip-toeing out of the room. "I'm fine. I'm sorry I woke you. I'll see you later."

"If you need the bed, we can go to Mark's house," she offered.

"It's fine. Don't worry. I have a place to stay."

WITH JOHNNY

I NEVER RETURNED to The Albert nor to the apartment on 113th Street, except once, a week later, when Johnny and I packed my belongings and moved them to his studio. To others, it must have seemed reckless and impulsive in the extreme, but to me it made perfect sense.

(In retrospect, it reminds me of a story a friend told me of a man who had witnessed the slaughter of his wife and children before being dragged off to a concentration camp in occupied Poland. The man was almost 40 then but strong and steel-willed -- as only one could be who's beyond hope or pain. Somehow he managed to escape the camp and the Nazis and was found, near death, by a gentile family who hid him in a drainpipe under ground until the end of the war. For two years he lived like a sewer rat in the earth and only ate, (at the family's peril) when they signaled it was safe to come out of hiding.

When the war was finally over he made his way to Paris, wandering aimlessly, as if drugged, through a village square. There he saw a young girl, maybe sixteen, standing limp, hopelessly lost, a stick figure in a stupor, her arm grotesquely tattooed, a symbol of horror no less alarming than Edvard Munch's "The Scream." He didn't know if she was pretty or not. Maybe she had once been and might be again – but it didn't matter. She was part of his ever-diminishing family of Jews and he had to reclaim her. He did so, as if kin -- and they talked, the way the dead might talk on the other side. She was so young, this pathetic girl, so dazed, so weary, so bereft. Not that they had much to say, at least in words. Mostly they talked in code, in gestures, in the shorthand of the dead. Her languid eyes hid from his glance, not shyly like an adolescent, but vigilantly, with great reserve, like an orphan who'd stolen candy and was about to be exposed – except, of course, she'd stolen nothing. He understood at once – for he too had been falsely accused.

In that moment, he, in his 40's, knew their paths were joined and that, together, they'd rebuild a life -- and she, a mere child – who'd lived a thousand years, knew it, too. This man and this woman, my friend said, went on to marry and come to America where they had two children and eked out a living on Delancey Street on the lower East Side selling neon, flashing crucifixes. He knew their story well. He was their son.)

Now certainly neither Johnny nor I had known such horror but when I heard their story years later, it struck a chord. I'm sure if Johnny had heard it, it would have done so for him as well.

There wasn't much that had to be packed, only what I'd taken with me from Brooklyn several years before and the few additions I'd collected along the way: The now worn and fetid black, crepe dress that had served as my uniform for so long, the shapeless and threadbare silk opera-length gloves and the black shawl I'd draped over my shoulders on the day I ran away. These would remain the cornerstones of my wardrobe. In time, I promised myself, I'd be able to afford dry cleaning on a regular basis. Until then, cologne would have to suffice. The Cappezio ballet slippers would be packed, the make-up, *The Dialogues of Plato, A New Anthology of Modern Poetry, The Living Thoughts of Spinoza,* (all still unread though highly valued) and, of course, my guitar.

New was the red cotton dress I'd worn throughout Columbia, three saris, one Nepalese jacket, two kimonos, one long black, velvet hooded cape, *Blood Wedding and other Plays, The Poems of Garcia*

Lorca, and a tattered and barely readable copy of *The Kama Sutra.* (The two "office" outfits I'd worn to The American Jewish Committee had been tossed into the garbage the day I left).

A few shopping bags, that was my dowry. But it didn't matter. There wasn't room, after all, for all the "stuff" of a prosperous and settled life. And even if there had been, Johnny would have reminded me we weren't living in the suburbs. And that would have been just fine with me. His words, sparse though they may have been, were Gospel. I adapted to austerity with ease because it didn't feel like austerity. It felt like abundance. There were no pretty lamps, no sconces, no chandeliers -- like the home I grew up in. But there was another kind of light, a kind I'd never seen in Brooklyn.

Before long we settled into a routine that was better than either of us had expected. With Johnny's encouragement, I enrolled in pottery school and got myself a part-time job as a counselor in the Greenwich House After-School Program. My mornings were spent at a pottery wheel until 2:00 PM when I'd walk to P.S. 41 to pick up my "charges" and take them back to the program.

At first these modest activities embarrassed me. But the brief walk through The Village each day to the public school dispelled all that. These were the same streets I'd walked several years before in the dead of winter waiting for Bernie Eisner to get home. These were the streets I walked till my feet froze not knowing where or how or if I'd get through the night. These were the streets before Judson, the last stop on a space-launch that had no itinerary except the trajectory of my own cries.

And now I walked them carefree and safe, proud of my little clay pots, eager to pick up my hoard of children who'd race toward me with arms outstretched when they saw me come – who'd jump me all at once and giggle and fight to grab my hand so I'd walk with *them* and not the other, who'd talk at once to get my ear and tug and tug then hide behind me until I searched and found them. I knew these games well, not because I'd played them before – but because I didn't.

These streets, these modest little activities, this was my Freedom Road -- and every day I walked it, I filled with gratitude at the remembrance of what had been.

Johnny and I took the subway from Manhattan to the Bronx, to his mother's apartment on Hunt's Point Avenue, if my memory is correct. I remember a flutter of apprehension running through me as we descended the old, decaying stairs from the elevated train station to the dark, menacing street below. Outside, a sullied underpass reminded me of an Edward G. Robinson murder set and did nothing to quell my anxieties. *What crimes have been committed here,* I wondered, *hidden by this isolation? What am I doing here? Who is this man I'm with who once called this place home?*

Beyond the station, daylight was muted by the grayness of the landscape, by the run-down buildings and stores that had taken to selling *anything* that could pay the rent. It was a kind of bleakness I was unfamiliar with -- that spoke less of the neighborhood's poverty than it did of its lifelessness, a neighborhood in transition, without yet having decided what or if it was to become. It was a kind of bleakness that comes from erosion, not only of place but of spirit -- like a woman who's buried her only child. It was a neighborhood waiting to take its last breath. I didn't know anything about real estate, in those days, but you didn't have to be Donald Trump to know this was not a high-rent district.

By the time we approached the building where Johnny's mother lived, I was prepared for whatever I might find. We opened the rusted exterior gate and entered a small foyer, which even in its prime must have drawn the blinds inside one's head. On a sidewall the panel of apartment bells had been vandalized, it's wires severed and left dangling. Johnny rolled his eyes, as if a mere candy-wrapper had been tossed on the floor, and asked me to wait. He turned, walked back outside and knocked on a ground-floor window. A second later, a door opened and an old woman appeared in the hall.

The moment I saw Grace Marino, I sensed I'd known her my whole life and had always loved her. I'm not sure what it was about her that made me feel that way because she looked quite unremarkable, short, heavy-set with gray hair pulled back in a net the way women did years ago who never left the house -- and an old apron covering her robust frame that was as much a part of her as her name.

She walked awkwardly to her door, laboring beneath her excess weight. I followed behind her, observing the shabbiness of her housedress, so unlike the propriety of my Brooklyn home. Johnny supported her arm then stopped for a moment to kiss her on the cheek. She beamed and kissed him back. *Are they really family,* I thought. *How odd.*

Inside the tiny ground-floor apartment the walls, pocked like acne –betrayed their true age. The furniture, though clean, might have come from a coupon catalogue fifty years before, accented with plaster figurines and dime store candy dishes that made me blush. Not a book in sight. I knew I was out of my element – but it was O.K. because, however much I liked these people, I was only passing through.

Mrs. Marino had prepared a fine meal. No green vegetables and nothing that looked back at you from the plate. *Spaghetti* and meatballs in a rich sauce, in layers, bursting with fresh tomatoes, sausages and herbs – all of which were delicious though unfamiliar to me. My mother, after all, wasn't a cook. She was a communist! Mrs. Marino, on the other hand, must be an artist, I thought, like her son. *"It's all in the sauce,"* she said, raising a wooden spoon from the pot to my lips. I melted -- not just from the taste.

And the bread! *"Lard bread,"* she called it, filled with chunks of something so good you forgot the neighborhood.

"What are these? " I asked her, pointing to the chunks.

"Lard," she said. "That's the lard."

"Oh!" I muttered, still in the dark. *"And this spaghetti is s-o-o-o-o-o-o good!"*

"Lasagne." Johnny corrected, winking at his mother.

"What?" I asked.

"Lasagne," his mother repeated, smiling at me.

I fought back the urge to climb in her lap – when we heard a knock at the front door.

" I come to fix the faucet," the old man announced as he opened the door.

"Thank you Mr. Russo," his mother said, her Italian accent more pronounced. *"It's been leaking all day."*

"It's O.K. Mrs. It'll just take me a minute," he boasted, wrapping his pliers around the metal washer. "There," he said a second later. " No more leak. If it starts to drip again, just holler like a Jew!"

Mrs. Marino heard it even before I, or so it seemed, as she jumped to her feet.

"Don't ever say that, again, Mr. Russo," she struck back, angrily, waving her finger in his face! "This is my son's girlfriend and she's Jewish."

"Didn't mean nothin' by it, Mrs." he apologized, lowering his head as he walked ruefully from the apartment.

Mrs. Marino leaned over and placed her hand on my shoulder as if she'd known me all my life and was responsible for me. *"I'm sorry,"* she said simply with unfamiliar kindness. *"Some people are stupid!"*

I sensed then that she was my *REAL* mother, my birth mother whom the foolish nurse had inadvertently taken me from by mistake and placed in the hands of a stranger.

The oddest sensation came over me as Johnny and I returned to Manhattan. I felt bigger – not taller or fatter, but bigger the way a pregnant woman might feel bigger who's glowing with pride, bigger like an identical twin might feel who'd never known loneliness. The boundaries of my being had enlarged, and what filled me up looked like Mrs. Marino. Not that I was old or gray or heavy-set, but somehow a part of her was added to a part of me -- and it made me bigger. Maybe it's what people mean when they say they feel *connected*.

that the priest made a deal with the lawyer who made a deal with the D.A. to throw the book at Johnny if they'd let the other boy off. And that's apparently what happened: Johnny was sentenced to 7-15 years in prison on a **first arrest** and the other boy was released on probation.

"Remember," he said, *"this was a time when the whole system was corrupt." This was before labor laws, before civil rights. The mob ruled the streets and the courts."* Johnny despised priests after that, almost as much as he despised crooked lawyers, especially the one who made him the sacrificial lamb.

As it turned out, his arrest was not unlike so many others we've come to know exist despite all official protestations to the contrary. He was *interrogated,* he said, while withdrawing from heroin, intimidated, beaten and promised drugs if he'd admit to whatever the police demanded of him. Now Johnny WAS a burglar, a child burglar. Of that there was no doubt, nor any claim to the contrary. He was a father-less boy, a heroin addicted boy forced to earn a living for his family after completing only the 3rd grade in the midst of the worst Depression America had ever known. Even his gentle, decent mother, illiterate and uneducated as she was, learned to make alcohol in the bathtub of her small apartment until Prohibition was finally repealed, a mixed blessing for a family that managed to get by in part from the sale of her outlawed liquor.

Regardless, Johnny was a junky who supported his habit by stealing from whomever he could steal from. He'd sneak into apartments and steal whatever he could carry. But he never held a gun and never committed armed robbery. He was a petty thief, a "second-story guy" as the black and white movies of the day romanticized; a Jimmy Cagney who'd lost his way. Despite the reality of his offenses, he was young, frightened, and sick to his stomach. *With the help of his "**attorney**", the police readily elicited from him confessions to crimes he'd never committed, crimes, which, when solved, would be*

STUMBLING HOME

a feather in the precinct's cap. Without his druthers or the benefit of counsel, he was easily convicted of whatever he'd been charged with. 7-15 YEARS ON A FIRST OFFENSE! After several years in prison he was finally paroled only to return to drugs and ultimately to prison again. It was during this second incarceration, he said, during the most desperate period of his life that his real awakening occurred.

Perhaps it was age, perhaps fatigue, perhaps insight that had no traceable origin. But whatever the source, Johnny began to find purpose. He studied the trombone and joined the prison band. Jazz ultimately helped him to survive those years. He read everything he could get his hands on and found himself intrigued with art, psychology and the workings of the mind. When he was finally released, this time for good, he got himself a job as a bartender, found a psychoanalyst, and enrolled in art school. He was on a fast train, desperate to learn, to grow and to make up for the years he'd lost. (I had the good fortune to meet him many years later, after his psychoanalysis was complete and he had already built a rich and productive life as a sculptor. I even met his psychoanalyst when Johnny asked me to join him for a session after he'd asked me to marry him on several occasions.

The Doctor, a wise and caring elderly Jewish analyst obviously cared for Johnny a great deal as Johnny did him. I think they both wanted to make sure that I was not frivolous and understood the depths of his feelings for me and the realities I'd face as his wife).

The truth was I had no intention of marrying him and shuddered at the story the wise and caring elderly doctor told me, not only at the injustice Johnny had endured, but, at the *unwholesomeness* of his plight. Of course I understood Johnny was a victim of these injustices but it didn't alter the fact that he was *tarnished* by them, as well. It was all so *alien* to me, his addiction, his imprisonment, the church's complicity in this outrageous miscarriage of justice. It was all so *unclean,* such a peculiar reaction from a child/woman who had been as abused as I was. But true to form, this was part of my family's mythology. I could feel myself recoil as he was rendered more and more unsuitable, more removed from the bourgeois social circle I wanted to claim as my own. This wasn't the world I knew. As bad as my world had been, it never struck me as **unwholesome**. To the contrary, despite all the abuse, my world was elevated in comparison to Johnny's world. Maybe I got frightened. Maybe that's what underlay the unwholesomeness, frightened at how vulnerable you are when you're poor, how you have to grovel and suffer indignities. I withdrew as though he'd told me he had boils.

While my own psychotherapy several years before had exposed the distortions I'd grown up with so that I knew full well that my father was not a *proper* English poet and my mother was not a saint, these insights were intellectual and not experiential. I still saw myself as *"Beastress"* and believed on some very primitive level, that the problems lay with me. It was in that context that Johnny and his history were seen as "unwholesome."

But there was another feeling, too, as the story unfolded, maybe not as pronounced at first, but perhaps more enduring -- that this man who said so little, who **never** spoke about himself, had shared this story with me the way he did, unsolicited, unadorned, without apology or interpretation. *"There's something you should know about me,"* he'd said not a day after we'd met, and that was that. He never lied. He never hid it. He never tried to make it something else. And this profound honesty managed to redeem him in my mind so that I didn't reject him out of hand. He was not my father, after all, a successful *British* poet nor my mother, a saint, who just happened to ignore every word out of my mouth.

In retrospect, it's clear to me, as I recall these events, that the masquerading that existed in my family was obviously *also* learned by me, so well that it became part of my own unconscious mind, as if I too saw the world as they did, as if their illusions were *real*, and of course, at the time they were. That's why my father's view of Johnny

STUMBLING HOME

was also, on the deepest level, my own view, like a child born with some grotesque birth defect who feels utterly defective, even though those defects were totally corrected at age five. She would remain "defective" regardless of her new reality, until, miraculously her unconscious world found a way to correct these distortions.... But on a *conscious* level I knew my father's perceptions were inaccurate and I had to repeatedly correct my own flawed, inaccurate world view...... my father wasn't an English poet, my mother wasn't a saint and I was no longer an exchange student from the Ukraine.

(As I'm recounting this period, I came across a photo from my childhood. I was ten years old at the time and my parents had taken my brother and me on one of the many cruises we'd been taken on in those early years. On this particular cruise a masquerade party was held and each passenger came in costume, if he or she chose. Now again, I was a ten-year old child. What costume might a 10-yeear old find fitting? A princess? A queen? A rabbit? Not for me. I was dressed as ½ man, ½ woman!!!!!!!)

If I ever doubted the truthfulness of the unconscious mind, those doubts were utterly, forevermore vanquished when I saw that photo and remembered that event. Of course, years of schooling had intervened between then and now so that when I saw that photo, I saw the unconscious mind doing what it was meant to do...to reveal its own truth, unadorned and unconcerned. That ten-year-old **girl** in that photo, obese, and only half woman *was* my unconscious truth!

Johnny was persistent about marriage. I couldn't understand the urgency. Life was so good to us. *Why couldn't we just stay the way we are*, I asked myself, *until I fall in love with someone? Then I can leave him. But not now.* I hemmed and hawed to no avail. But when he upped the ante and insisted on a commitment or we'd have to part company, I finally got wise. I agreed to marry him, "*but not now, Johnny. Later.*"

"When?"

"I don't know. Later. It's so soon. I need a little time."

That bought me a few months. And when "later" came, I pressed for more time.

"For someone as unconventional as you," I said haughtily, "your attitude about marriage is **so-o-o-o** bourgeois. It's just a piece of paper. What does it have to do with love? And frankly, the idea that The Government has to approve it, well……………"

He didn't bite. He was a "*simple*" man. We got down to the wire again, then again, then one last time – till I finally agreed to go with him to City Hall to apply for a marriage license.

That's all I'll do, I promised myself. *I'll just* **apply** *for the license. You don't ever have to* **use** *it……………and even if you do, you don't have to use it for months. Who knows what'll happen by then?*

I needed the time. Not to meet Mr. Right necessarily, just to maintain the status quo. That's all I wanted. And for a while, it worked, especially when Johnny had a major piece accepted at The Whitney Biennial, the "frontal" piece, to be exact, the piece in the center of the entire show. That focused his attentions back on his work and away from the question of marriage.

It was a magical time for us, the month before The Whitney. We got the license at City Hall and, at the same time, he was offered a one-man show at New York University's Loeb Gallery that promised to put him on the map. I was able to breathe again, free to like him even more. And because I was convinced we'd never actually marry, I stopped comparing him with other *boys* — where invariably he came up short.

He gained stature in my eyes, especially compared to that first night when he'd told me he was a **bartender.** But now with The Whitney and N.Y.U., things were starting to shift. He seemed taller to me -- and even better looking, not that he wasn't good looking all along. He was. He just began to look a little younger, a little more **wholesome**. Even in his *cords* and work boots, he began to look like he was wearing a suit. I was told I had a sparkle in my eyes.

And I was becoming a major fan. It's true I loved his work before The Whitney, but that was just **me** loving it. It didn't mean he was *really* good or that the world would value him – like they would if you said he was a lawyer. It didn't make him the kind of man you'd want to marry. It was just **me** loving his work. But now with The Whitney, that too was beginning to change.

I even remember coming to his defense when John Canaday wrote a review of the Biennial in *The New York Times* and failed to give Johnny's centerpiece special mention. I wrote Canaday a scathing letter:

"Dear **J.C.,**" I began, cleverly. "….No wonder you're so arrogant! Your initials have gone to your head."

"Dear B.S.," he wrote back, "Anyone with **your** initial shouldn't be criticizing someone with mine!!"

The point was, of course, I was proud, proud enough to bring my friends around, especially to the opening at N.Y.U. *That would be the perfect occasion for introductions.* I spent days preparing for the "black tie" *Opening*: the press, my gown, my hair. But mostly what I labored over was the guest list. I sent fliers to everyone, every man who'd never given me the time of day. Every friend of my brother's who'd heard him call me *"Beastress."* Every Gwyneth Paltrow who'd felt I was *"so nice, if only she'd lose some weight."* Every neighbor who thought my parents were just *"amazing.......... But what about that strange daughter of theirs?"* Every girl I'd ever wished to be (which was **every** girl, except maybe the one who was fatter than me), every relative who sympathized with my perfect parents for having to endure the humiliation of a daughter who leaves home for no good reason, every boy who looked like Jimmy Dean, every girl who's mother wasn't deaf and smiled a lot, who's father was an accountant or a little-league coach, who's mother never heard of Emily Dickinson. Every girl who was blonde and had a **pixie** nose, every girl who could wear short skirts and all the boys who ever liked them!

I sent out dozens of fliers! I was exhausted by late afternoon when Johnny told me of a job at the restaurant where he was bartending

"Hat-check girls at 'Momma Laura's' make a lot of money," he said. *"If the girl wasn't fired today, you'd never get this chance. They need someone. If you want the job, it's yours."*

It wasn't quite the job I had in mind, I thought, especially in light of The Opening, but I did need the money. It was a simple job, Johnny assured me, in a little booth at the entrance to the restaurant. I'd take the patron's hats and coats and, for the minor service, be rewarded with an astounding tip. I can even do my crossword puzzle when I'm not needed.

"They're very rich people who eat there," Johnny persisted. *"And I'll be right across from you at the bar in case you have any problems!"*

And so it was that I was wrenched back to the real world. As it turned out, I made more money that night in less time than I'd ever made in my life, especially for doing virtually nothing. It was almost too good to be true – like what a girl must feel who's parents give her ten dollars when she only asks for five, *"Just in case, honey. Just in case."* But there was a down side, too. I'd never minded working in The Catskills. *Everyone* did, all the *kids*, all the kids who'd later become the important people of the next generation, even some kids whose parents had money. Like Princess Di baby-sitting. It didn't lower her rank. But at "Momma Laura's," the *hired help weren't* kids. It wasn't just a pit stop on the way to the Senate. For these people, middle aged and settled, "Momma Laura's" was The Senate. And they prided themselves on being there.

Johnny didn't feel the same way, of course. He rarely let on where he worked, except to his closest friends. They understood that artists are poor and have to work odd jobs to do their art. It doesn't diminish them, because they're **Artists.** But it did diminish me, because I wasn't. I tried not to think about it. I tried to keep counting my money – and there was plenty of that, because *"Momma Laura's"* was a gold mine.

It was the fanciest restaurant I'd ever seen. Not fancy like an Italian restaurant in Brooklyn pretending it's in Rome, but understated, seriously understated, small, quiet, reserved. *"Reserved"* isn't a word that comes to mind much when you're from Brooklyn. Nor a word I would have thought of to describe an Italian restaurant, at least not the Italian restaurants I grew up with. *"Momma Laura's" was* more like a restaurant you went to if you were fasting, if you wanted to meditate, a restaurant you went to if you were very, very tiny and only required a sprig or two to keep you going, a restaurant you went to if you were Presbyterian or from a small town that people called "sleepy," a restaurant you went to if you wore little tailored suits and "pumps." That's another word that doesn't come easy, *"Pumps."* Jewish girls don't wear "pumps."

"Momma Laura's" didn't seem to be a place you'd eat at if you were Jewish or even Italian, for that matter, or anyone who worked for a living. I could tell it from the tips, their sheer enormity – given without fuss or fan-fare, without the vaguest notion on the part of the donor of their value to the recipient -- enormity without generosity, because to the donor it was nothing but pocket change and he hadn't a clue of its worth. A donation without conversation, with but a slight nod, a slight, obligatory smile that's not meant to engage, not meant to equal the playing field, a donation so big it feels to you like a windfall, yet so incidental to him that it underscores the disparity in your stations and you're left astoundingly aware of all you don't have.

Like the time after the *attack* -- when I was staying at Gene's apartment and he asked me to sing at some rich guy's party. I was only eighteen or so and the chance to make twenty dollars was irresistible. I had sung the year before with a Catskills band and loved it but the money was barely pocket change. Twenty extra dollars was sorely needed.. It was an elaborate party, a real band, women in fancy gowns and men with manicures. I stood with the musicians, flaunting sex appeal as only a teen-ager can do, separated from the *guests* as if there'd been a mote between us. But I could tell my voice made an impact. All eyes were on me, like when I sang in the Catskills to supplement my income. Still, no matter how young or sexy or talented, I wasn't a guest and probably never would be. But at the end of the party, the handsome *thirty-something* host asked me if I'd like to go back to his apartment.

Entering his penthouse apartment was like walking into a Hollywood set. A world reserved for the rich and famous that I could only have imagined. The glass-enclosed sculpture garden was the size of a tennis court. I threw my head back indifferently and tried not to gawk. It was an *Oscar* performance, black dress, bedroom eyes, a sassy wit. But I knew it was insufficient. He was surrounded by sexy

231

ladies, women who were rich! It wasn't until I saw his chess set that I felt my value rise.

The set was ornate, ivory, the kind of set no serious player would ever use. It didn't matter. I could play without a set. I assume my host saw the game as part of the seduction. *I'll give him a good run for his money*, I thought, *but not so good that he'll **really** lose.*

But I won, despite myself. I just couldn't resist. I tried not to make it look too easy, since what I really wanted was to marry him, tomorrow. I feigned surprise. *"You must just be tired,"* I said. *"Maybe a bit under the weather."*

He seemed disarmed – and a little annoyed. *Damn!* I said to myself. *You've really done it now! Do you **always** have to act like a man!* I felt myself mutate. The sultry damsel-in-distress chipped away at the *bitch* until she was nowhere to be found – and I could see my host begin to relax. He took my hand and led me into the bedroom. I sensed the wedding bells might chime after all.

He fell asleep quickly, after our brief excursion. I'd done my best, I reassured myself. *Rita Hayworth* and all. I lay seductively in my palace bed thankful for my good fortune yet somehow believing it was destined to be. I couldn't sleep a wink, though, not because of the kingdom that lay ahead, but because I couldn't risk disturbing my pose. Being caught asleep with your mouth open or your thighs any which-way can change the direction of any man's voyage, even when God is at the helm. So I lay motionless, constructing my wedding list in my head, till the early hours of dawn when my body reluctantly surrendered to the hazard of sleep.

When I finally awoke, I was alone in bed. A brief note lay conspicuously on the night table beside me:

"Please let yourself out and take the twenty dollar bill for cab fare home." Now this must have been about 1960 or 1961 and what I saw was not a twenty dollar bill but a thousand dollar bill, far more than the taxi fare and more than a call girl's fee for service and it allowed me to appreciate his gentlemanly gesture.

That's how it felt to be a hatcheck girl at "Momma Laura's." Money was abundant but so too was its meaning. And watching Johnny shake martinis only made matters worse. It made me miss my father. **He'd** *never shake martinis. He'd never be caught dead in some silly red vest with his name on the lapel! He was an English poet, after all.* And it made me wonder, as I studied Johnny, if my father was right. But the full magnitude of my dilemma was yet to come.

An elderly gentleman, tall and reserved, approached my hatcheck booth and handed me his hat. I sensed he was important – like a statesman or wealthy landowner who'd been immune to the struggles of the lower class. He reached over to his elegant, though aging, wife and removed her fur, a graceful act, seamless and matter-of-fact. A younger man, strikingly nondescript though not unattractive, perhaps the son, followed suit. Nothing could be assumed of him except, without doubt, that he'd been privileged. That was inescapable. And perhaps a certain gentility that comes from wealth and entitlement. Their presence awed me, or maybe it was dislike. I kept my distance, barely managing a respectful smile – till a screeching, tenement voice hollered out my name. The restaurant turned to witness the source of this bizarre greeting, though I knew its source, immediately.

"Bea!!!!!!!!"

Becky's voice was unmistakable. And though I hadn't seen her in months, she was exactly as I'd last remembered, overwhelming the moment, grabbing me, hugging me, screaming out my name.

What in the world is **SHE** *doing here with these people, in this wealth?* I thought. *Making a scene, calling attention to herself AND ME? And what am* **I** *doing here, checking* **their** *hats?*

"Bea, Bea," she screamed, landing a big, kiss on my flushed cheek as I tried to pull away, as I tried to evaporate, while the young aristocrat watched obediently from the sidelines. *"This is Walker,"* she gushed, reaching for his arm, *"my new husband, and this is my father-in-law, Judge……………"*

That's when I missed my parents the most – not a yearning for what is, but a yearning for what never was and never could be -- like missing your ex-husband whom you used to want to kill but who now seems perfect, except that he's just remarried.

And that's when I understood for the very first time why my father forgot Poland. Had it not been for Ellie's visit the next night, I don't know how I would have recouped.

REGROUPING (PART 2)

I HADN'T SEEN Ellie since her pregnancy. We'd spoken several times but an implacable schism had kept us apart. When she called to tell me she'd gotten married, it was with great ambivalence that I invited her to the studio. *If I **must** see her*, I thought, *at least let me do so with The Whitney at hand.*

Ellie was as pretty as always, maybe even prettier because she was no longer a girl. Not that she wasn't still young. She was, but she had a new sophistication that made you take her more seriously, more as a woman. Where once she'd tried hard to look the part, now it came with ease – with fine clothes that spoke of her style and creativity, clothes she could once only wish for. Her make-up was art-full and her carriage regal, like a cover of Vogue. That's how she struck me when I opened the gate to the studio to let them in. She'd become a woman. Maybe there was also a new hardness I saw. I wasn't certain. She was restrained, poised, superior, like a visiting ambassador on a fact-finding mission to Biafra. I was put off. She seemed a thousand miles away.

And Raymond, her new husband, was the beleaguered minor officer assigned to serve her. He surprised me initially, though her description of him two years before was still fresh in my mind and remarkably accurate. But he wasn't quite as short as I'd imagined him to be or quite as bald or quite as devoid of charm. He had none of her flair or sophistication, yet he had a sobriety that seemed to compliment her well.

I was jealous of this elegant and talented woman. But it was a new kind of jealousy and strangely liberating. A jealousy that had nothing to do with a man, nothing to do with a fear of losing him. Like the dread I felt with Alfredo's betrayal, that any woman could wrap your man around her little finger. That dread was as incomprehensible to me with Johnny as a Russian accent. I never worried that he'd *stray*, not even with Ellie. I don't know why that was. It certainly wasn't because I felt as good as Ellie or as pretty or appealing. None of that existed. Maybe I still saw her as I did when we were young, as so far out of my league, that comparisons between the two of us were absurd. That may be. Maybe it was even that I trusted her **that** much, that I trusted she'd never make a move on my man. I doubt that. Not because she wasn't worthy of my trust, but because, at the time, I wasn't capable of it. Maybe I just trusted Johnny. Maybe it's as simple as that. Maybe I just trusted that in his eyes I measured up. I doubt that, too. Not because he **didn't** feel that way, because I sensed he did, but because my reasons were probably more obscene. Maybe it was **Johnny** who didn't measure up. Maybe that's how I felt. Maybe I sensed that **he** was so far out of **my** league that he could only be grateful to be with me. I hate to think that that might have been how I saw it. But whatever the reason, the absence of that dread was a blessing, though it didn't assuage, in the least, the envy stirring inside me. Yet I must admit, despite these wrenching admissions, it's also true that the longer I'd known Johnny, the more I adored him. I say "adored" rather than "loved" because I was still trapped in the destructive sexual politics that were part of gender roles in America at that time. It would be several years before I understood how much I'd been steeped in those absurd roles and how much I did really love him. This was the '60's, after all, the most turbulent time in our history and everything, everything was up for grabs!

If, in the moment of Ellie's visit, I could have re-costumed my life as I did at sixteen, I would have jumped at the chance. But that magic was no longer available to me. I was what I was. And it was clear that's all I had to work with. Yet, it's also true that, if left alone with Johnny, if removed from the markers against which I judged myself, my life was happier than it had ever been and I was absolutely at peace. It was only in the context of *others* that I wanted to shrink into oblivion, and it was in that mode that I greeted Ellie at the door.......... until she entered the studio and, with Raymond at her heels, froze before the majesty of Johnny's work.

I could see the saga in her eyes, the wonderment, as if standing at the foot of the Grand Canyon for the first time, her eyes dilated to take it all in, to absorb the work, our lives, the austerity of the walls, the tools, the gear, the incidental sketches, each precious, yet a mere prototype for what was to come, the oak table top, eight feet round, sitting imaginatively on a tree stump. I think it was that table that wiped the superiority off her face.

Ellie loved oak. She was ahead of her time. Mahogany was the prize of middle class Americans in those days, with its rich texture and shine. Oak, matte and unpolished, was the choice of the artists and the counter culture. It was **different** and Ellie knew it. I, by contrast, despite my peculiar odyssey, was really quite conventional in my taste and remarkably devoid of an artistic eye. Where I'd have winced at dining chairs that didn't match, she'd have preferred it. There was no Macy's in her either. Ellie was the one who taught me that oak was **artsy**. "*Mahogany was* **so** *bourgeois,*" she said. I took my cues from her. That's how I new Johnny's table was **really** *hep*. Like the way she dressed that day -- shiny black boots laced up to her calves. Victorian boots, expensive, **good boots**, unlike anything I'd ever owned. Even when we were kids, she always wore beautiful clothes.

I remember going to her apartment one afternoon. We must have been thirteen at the time. It was her birthday. She came to the door in a brand new leopard-skin jacket, like Natalie Wood at a film premiere. Her mother had just bought it for her, she said, her mother who had barely a dime to spare. So it wasn't just the jacket that made my jaw drop, (though leopard-skin was the rage at the time and every movie star wore one). It was that I knew it must have been a hardship

STUMBLING HOME

for her mother to buy – but she adored Ellie and knew just what she'd love. My family could have afforded it, several times over, but never would have bought it, even if they'd known that I'd love it, too. Ellie was just worth more than me, and she knew good stuff when she saw it. That's why I began to relax when I sensed her wonder (and maybe even envy) as I met her at the door.

"Oh," she exclaimed, "*This is so **interesting**.*" That was **the** word! "*Interesting.*" She glanced at Johnny seductively! That look I'd seen a hundred times at Bernie Eisner's place when she rated the *boys* and set her mark. Yet it didn't scare me in the least. I know Raymond saw it, too, and I felt badly for him.

"*And the bikes*" she continued. "*How great. I wish **we** had bikes. It's **so** bohemian. Oh! And the guitar. God! I haven't played a guitar in years. Are you still playing?*"

"Yes," I answered, matter-of-factly, as if to conceal my pride. "And I'm singing, too. I've even got an accompanist."

"Wow. That's really hep, Bea," she gushed, her imperious tone giving way to an effort-full smile.

"They've got an audition tomorrow night at The Bitter End........." Johnny said brimming with pride.

"He should know," I interrupted like a fluttering peacock. "**He's** my manager."

"Really?" Raymond asked.

"Not that she needs a manager," Johnny added.

BEATRICE MANNO
companied by George Fernandes

Personal Manager
John Manno Wo2 017

"You should hear her voice."

"I'd love to," Raymond said.

"Why don't the two of you come with us to the audition. You'll give Bea some moral support."

"Oh, could we, Ray? That would be so hep."

"I have a late meeting tomorrow night………"

"Oh, Ray! You're so **bourgeois**," Ellie shot back. "Why can't you be a little more of a **non-conformist** like Johnny? Maybe you can re-schedule it for the following night." And he did.

THE SHOW

I DON'T RECALL ever waking up in those days when it wasn't sunny, regardless of the weather. The plans for the N.Y.U. show consumed me. Johnny never failed to tell me how I impressed him, how I could take an idea, however distant or slight, and give it form and make it real, at least in the service of someone else. And, of course, each moment of praise further energized me, renewed my purpose and hope and sense of being loved. I flew like a bird that had never been wounded and gave Johnny's talent an impressive forum.

The show was a stunning event. Miriam, long-gone from The American Jewish Committee, was still with Tony and, together, they came to celebrate Johnny's work. She looked lovely, my staid, elegant friend, belying the quandary I came to know later was steaming beneath the surface.

"Are they trees?" Miriam asked admiringly of Johnny's massive works.

"Don't be simplistic," Tony chimed. "They're metaphors."

"Well, they look like trees."

"That's because you're not an artist."

Then there was Lee who showed up with Freddie Versace, Johnny's childhood friend from the Bronx. I'd seen Lee intermittently after the attack yet we'd never spoken of it. My deep sense of hurt formed an insurmountable wedge between us though she continued to remain exalted in my eyes. I introduced her to Johnny and several of his friends the week before. I was filled with pride. I wasn't surprised she came to the show with Freddie. She was captivated by him. And that had pleased me greatly -- that there was something I brought to the table that impressed her. I knew Johnny's friends weren't the men she'd been used to, the guys who sat in the back seat. These were artists, musicians, and occasional *second-story* guys from his childhood in the Bronx. Freddie was one of the latter. Not that he was a criminal. He was just one of those poor, *hep* ghetto kids who was hit over the head by the Depression and never quite got on his feet; a smart kid, a bit shady, but hungry to break free of *the neighborhood*; a guy who hung out with the jazz dudes on 125th Street, who smoked reefer and would rather have died than manage a shoe store in Queens; a guy whose parents barely lived to middle-age, whose education stopped before his growth spurt, who hustled and conned and fit in nowhere – and everywhere.

Freddie was proud of Johnny, like a kid brother might be. He tagged along enviously as Johnny found his way out of the Bronx to a purpose that came from his character and talent. Freddie wished he'd had either. Instead, tall and ruggedly handsome like Anthony Quinn, he mastered an irresistible smile and spent his few bucks on fine clothes and new teeth.

"*Look at this,*" he said to me when I first met him, hoisting his head backward and opening his mouth wide as a salt pit. "

I got 'em last week. You think they're fake, Huh. They're not. I got 'em at the dental school. They're screwed into my jaw. I didn't pay a dime. They look good, huh."

"*They really do, Freddie,*" I assured him, concealing my embarrassment.

"*Look closer. It's not a regular bridge. See? They look good, huh.*"
"*They really do.*"

Lee had a different take on Freddie. I think she saw him as boyish, as vulnerable, as raw as they come. Maybe she thought he was Stanley Kowalski in *Streetcar*. I don't know. He was as far from her left-wing cortex as they come, she, who'd never surrendered to the philosophy between her legs. Boy, did Freddie give her a lesson in Descartes! She was almost as smitten with him as I think she was with Johnny.

But it was obvious she'd fallen for Freddie and obvious he'd fallen too. That's how you knew *he could have been a contender* – for Lee's appeal was nothing she wore on the outside. It was her smarts and her politics and her sophistication, and it said reams about him that she was the one he chose. He could have had a blonde – and he could have worn a *Zoot* suit. But he didn't. He was gray cashmere, herringbone and tweed – despite his grammar and his teeth. I think what he wanted most in the world was not to be Freddie Versaci, a throwaway kid with no scratch, no schooling and a whole lot of cavities. And the fact that Lee was a Jew only sweetened the pot. For some poor Italian kids from the South Bronx, a Jewish girl was the ticket out, though I had no idea why.

And then there was Becky and her new husband. Walker was good-looking and rich. A *WASP* (whose father was a judge), as henpecked as a chicken, being led around the gallery while Becky, shlepping her A & P bag, slapped her wet kisses on anyone she pleased. He had been whipped into shape, like a crash course they give diplomats who have to learn a language in six days before they ship them overseas. I don't think Becky looked at a single sculpture that night, or any night, for that matter, because for her "art" was like a thousand dollar Gucci bag when you're starving, superfluous. Walter was the only sculpture worth showing.

And, of course, Ellie showed up with Raymond at her heels, adoring and rapt. It reminded me of our childhood when she'd talk with my father about Goethe or Rembrandt or Kant, as if she knew them personally, and my father would beam with delight. Usually that bothered me, when she came on so uppity. But when she talked with Johnny that night, about Art, **that** night, Johnny was a giant and I was so proud that he was mine. I don't know how Raymond saw it but I think he must have felt like me, just brimming with pride.

My parents were there too, despite my father's continued

THE SHOW

disapproval. I think they came because my relatives did, because the announcement of the show had been so impressive, because it was mentioned in The New York Times -- or maybe they were just pressured to *give the guy a chance.*

"*After all, Sam, it's N.Y.U.,*" I imagined my Aunt Betty had said to him. "*And he's in The Whitney and The Museum of Modern Art......... So he's twenty years older. He seems to be good for her. She seems happy. Don't give her a reason to choose between the two of you.*"

Good, old Aunt Betty. She was my father's younger half-sister and she adored him. He was the oldest of the siblings and he was her pride, and theirs -- he, the poet, the playwright, the one who made the big money – and gave to them generously when the need arose. But Betty, in particular, idolized him. First thing in the morning when she was a child, like my aunts on my mother's side of the family, she would race out, behind her mother, to buy *The Jewish Daily Forward* to find his poems. He was her mentor and he taught her about the higher road. So when he encouraged her to pursue art (instead of the usual secretarial job of the day), she followed his advice. She wasn't a **real** artist, like Johnny, some naysayers might contend. But in those days a woman's art was subordinate to her familial roles. She was first and foremost a wife and mother, but she knew a **real** artist when she saw one. And he was that, above all.

The first time they'd met, we'd been invited to her home in Queens – no doubt so someone in the family could get a first-hand look at the ex-con, ex-junky, penniless, Italian sculptor. For someone with less character than Johnny, that visit might have been intimidating, full of ego. But Johnny was too steady to care. His sense of himself was implacable. He had no axe to grind. And so the evening was more wonderful than anyone could have imagined with Johnny talking with Aunt Betty about art, about her work and his, encouraging her, counseling her, taking her under his wing as I'd imagined my father had done with her forty years before. Mostly they talked about sculpture, about welding, about how you get this patina or that, how it is to work in bronze. I saw her blossom, my Aunt Betty, from somewhere in boredom and middle age to youth and vitality. I saw her eyes widen with possibility.

By the time we left her home that night, it was obvious she adored him – and so it didn't surprise me that she might have urged my parents to give him a try.

My father walked through the gallery with his nose in the air and a sneer across his face like a *DANGER* sign at a sanitation ditch. But my mother, the Gypsy I'd longed to know, resurfaced, for a moment and filled me with love, **just for a moment**. She studied every sculpture, their magnitude, their material, her face lit with curiosity and respect. I noticed her follow Johnny and tap his shoulder timidly. Her soft, engaging smile was, at first, unfamiliar then vaguely reminiscent of something I'd known years before but had long forgotten. I inched closer.

"This is so interesting," she said to him, pursing her unpainted lips as a virgin would – or an anarchist.

"You know, Johnny, some of the greatest artists in the world were Italian……Michelangelo, Di Vinci, Botticelli………..And some of the greatest poets, too."

"That's nice of you to say."

"Have you ever heard of Christina Rossetti?" she asked.

"I don't think so," he responded.

"Well, let me recite something for you."

"Ma," I interrupted, "That would be great but maybe you could recite it a little later."

"But Sissy, I'm sure Johnny would like to know more about his people."

"Ma, I'm sure Johnny knows about…………."

"I'd love to hear you recite something," Johnny cut in.

"Ma," I interrupted again, grabbing Johnny's arm. " We've got to say hello to some people."

"You, know, Johnny," she continued undeterred, "Your sculpture reminds me of poetry."

"Ma!………….."

"That's very kind of you to say, Mrs. Starr."

"Sissy," my mother said to me feigning an aside, "your young man is so nice. But let me ask you, Johnny. Are these meant to be trees?"

"I'm not really sure," he answered modestly.

"How interesting of you to say. Tell me, you must know Robert Browning."

"Yes, I've heard of him."

"Well, he was once asked about the meaning of his poem, 'My Last Duchess.' You know it's a very obscure poem. In any case, he thought for a moment about the poem's meaning and then responded. 'When I wrote it,' he said, 'I knew what it meant and God knew what it meant...... Now only God knows what it means'................. You see, Johnny, I told you you remind me of poetry."

Her soft laughter was infectious. Her scholarship filled me with pride. Johnny leaned forward and gently kissed her on her cheek as she beamed with delight.

"I'd love to hear you recite poetry," he said. "I'm always ready to learn something new."

"What an exceptional young man, Sissy," she whispered to me for his ears to hear.

I nodded.

"Sam," she said, reaching for my father as he passed by, "Sissy's young man is so interesting. He's quite an artist, isn't he?"

"A craftsman!" my father muttered, with unveiled contempt.

When we finally got into bed that night, a distant scene kept surfacing: the day when mommy had taken her little girl to school for the very first time. The little girl was only five and yet mommy walked quickly, too quickly for the child's short and reluctant legs, too unaware of the little girl's growing terror as they approached the dark and unfamiliar building she was expected to embrace. Mommy's grasp was firm around the little girl's hand, tugging her along, decisively, purposefully, as she charged straight ahead. They would not dilly-dally. They would not be late. It wouldn't look right.

"Kindergarten is such fun," mommy would say in the days before. *"You'll have such a good time."* And the little girl agreed and went on with her business, maybe because she never really expected to go – until that final day. Until that first day. The very first day of school. And even when mommy woke her that morning, the little girl agreed it would be fun. Even when mommy dressed her she agreed. And even as they left the house to walk the few blocks to school, her little feet skipped, as if they were taking her on an outing, a rare and welcomed outing away from mommy's demons, away from mommy's tomb-house, away from mommy's husband and the deadly roles that were thrust upon them by their histories. Yes, it would be fun, this special day with mommy. Two girls out for a stroll, just mommy and her little girl.

"No, no. I don't want to go, mommy," the little girl cried as they neared the school.

"Of course you do, Sissy."

"No, mommy. I don't. I want to go home."

"Don't be silly. You want to go to school."

"No mommy, please. Please let's go home. I want to go home."

"That's ridiculous. Everybody loves school."

Dread filled the child as it did each night when she tried to sleep, while mommy read indifferently in her bed close by -- as the little girl pleaded with her to close the light so she might sleep, as mommy's deafness shut her out, as the little girl waited and waited and waited for mommy to hear, to turn out the damn light so the damn kid could sleep -- till the little girl's mind found its way to a coffin underground from which there was no escape and the terror of a waking death consumed her, ate out her innards and her wish to live – till she vowed, this little child, to end her life in the morning so she'd never know such terror again.

The little girl yanked her hand out of mommy's hand and bolted toward home.

THE SHOW

"Sissy, come back here," mommy screamed. *"You've got to go to school.*

The little girl ran as fast as her little feet would take her as mommy dashed after her. Faster, faster the child ran, to the right, to the left, passed the single-family homes where all was well and nondescript, passed the deafness of Brooklyn and The Great Plains, passed the house where the boy lived who'd hung himself just a few years before (and everyone said he died in a car crash)………….and just when mommy almost caught her, the little girl darted back on her heels like OJ. evading tackle. She would not be caught, this child. She could not be caught. She'd run and run and run till the shuddering inside her stopped, till running took her out of her, till she found some place to rest.

We slept so well that night, after all, Johnny and I – in the glint of the show that dazzled us all. It was a deep sleep, as deep as the center of one's self, as far back as a kindergarten child who'd run so far that all the danger had past, who'd come upon a place where the view was different, where she could see that the goblins weren't goblins at all. And when morning came, it was clear something amazing had shifted.

CLOSURE (FOR NOW)

A KNOCK AT the front door awakened us. We'd come to expect Mark's visits on Sunday mornings. Despite the hour, Johnny and I were never put upon to see him out front at 6:00 AM. To the contrary, it pleased us. He was my *kid* cousin, after all, only 15 years old, going out of his way after a long night's work at The Herald Tribune to bring us bagels and coffee and the Sunday paper right off the presses. And always with a big smile on his face, as if proud to have something to give, beaming from ear to ear. Why did he do that? I wondered, put himself out? What did he see in us, he and his younger brother, David? So smart my kid cousins, so talented, so ambitious. What did they see in **Johnny**? It made me feel important, like I did when Lee met Freddie Versaci, that I brought something to the table that other people valued.

It wasn't until that particular morning, waking in the glow of the night before, that I began to understand, for the first time, Mark's visits. And when the phone rang *off-the-hook* till noon, my take on our lives had clearly changed.

"Bea," Mrs. Marino said on the phone, *"You're such a good girl."*
"I am?" I asked bewildered, hoping she'd say more.
"You made Johnny's show so nice."
"It was so nice because his work is so good."
"And because you're such a good girl, " she added. I melted.

My mother called, too, and threw me for a loop. *"What a nice young man you have, Sissy………."*

I couldn't figure it out. Where was the scorn and disapproval? He was nothing like the man I'd envisioned she'd approve of. What had become of the woman I knew? But try as I might, I couldn't make sense of it. It wasn't time yet for that. It wouldn't be for years to come. So I just took it in, her pleasure with him – and his stature continued to rise.

"He's wonderful," Lee said. *"And he's really handsome………….."*

"He's so in love with you, isn't he?" Miriam asked. *"Are you going to marry him?"*

"Oh! God, Myr. He keeps asking. I don't know what to do."

I'd put the question of marriage on a back burner – and appreciated the many events that demanded more immediate attention like Johnny's shows….. until that Friday morning when his insistence was unavoidable. I'd known the question was front and center for him but N.Y.U had given us some breathing room. I knew it would eventually resurface. In anticipation I'd spoken with several friends about my dilemma and it was Lee, in particular, whose counsel was determinative. Without a tinge of moralizing, her pragmatism came out of left field, nothing I ever could have imagined. Now this was the early 60's when I'd met Johnny. Certainly there were rumblings that "the times they were a' changing," but that hadn't happened yet, at least in my world, and I wouldn't have known even if they had, not in my field of vision.

"Look, I know he's not your Mister Right' she counseled, "but I know you love him and I know he loves you so marry him and if ever your Mister Right comes along you can always get a divorce!!!!"

The statement stopped me in my tracks. It wasn't the concept of divorce that threw me for a loop, for certainly I knew that divorce existed, (although, at the time, no one in my family had ever been divorced, EVER, and I couldn't imagine such a scenario existing.) The concept of a divorced woman was, for me, in the late '50's, as anathema as the concept of a transgender woman. It just didn't occur and was not part of the vocabulary, at least my vocabulary. I'd never even thought to ask Lee if she and Gene were divorced. I just assumed they'd simply decided to not live together at that particular time. Even that, was revolutionary. A woman never left a man and made sure that a man NEVER left her. If she was, in fact, a "good enough" woman, he'd never leave. NEVER. Even if they hated each other as much as I hated spinach they'd still stay together, maybe throwing up all over each other but still married. Couples stayed together till death. That's the world I knew so Lee's mention of divorce was akin to Kalman Rabinowitz saying my mother was a bitch. It shocked the stuffing out of me. But Lee's reference to divorce had none of the repellent responses that I'd felt with Kal. It was shocking, yes, outrageous, in fact, but extremely liberating. Lee, a woman I looked up to, was giving me an out, if I needed one. And the fact that she was a "lefty" made the suggestion all the more acceptable. Lefties were smart, utterly moral and courageous, at least the Lefties of the 30's and 40's. And while Lee slept with a lot of men, you never would have described her as "loose." She was *liberated*. When Johnny readdressed the subject of marriage that Friday morning, it precipitated none of the claustrophobia it had before.

"I want to marry you, " he began, *"but if we're not going to, we have to split up. I'm much older than you and I don't want to wait any more."*

I knew from his tone that he meant business, that the time had come to make a choice. It froze me in the moment – as I was preparing to take a teen group from the YWCA on a ski trip for the weekend, my second job, just a few hours a week as a youth worker. Johnny was a man of few words. He didn't say anything superfluous. What he said he meant but why he chose that particular morning for a showdown confused me since the night before had been so loving. I'd hosted a teen dance at the "Y" and he showed up unexpectedly with his mother and brother to hear me sing.

"Can you believe her voice," I heard him say to his mother as I belted out *Hava Negila* at The Young Women's *Christian* Association.

"Isn't she amazing? " Of course I never thought to NOT sing a Hebrew song. Those were the songs I knew and this was at a time before my "awakening," before I really understood anti-Semitism, before I really knew its depth and how many minds were twisted by it. I have no idea how the staff felt about my choice of music but if they had any misgivings, they never shared them with me.

Mrs. Marino was beaming. I could see her pride. Her smile lit up the room. She took me to her heart. I knew it without a doubt. I saw it in her face. And I saw Johnny's pride. I couldn't believe they'd come just to see me, just to hear me sing. I couldn't explain it, why people would go out of their way to delight me, to surprise me. No one had ever done that before. I was levitating.

So why this morning as I'm preparing to leave for the week-end? Why now does he drop the other shoe?

"But honey," I argued later in the evening, as Johnny pressed the ultimatum. *"I have to take the kids skiing. How can I think about marriage now?"*

"We can stop at City Hall before you leave."

"Today????"

"Now. "

"But honey, I have to pick up some things on Canal Street now."

"Like what?"

"Like…………………a…………like a broom……………..like a broom and a mop."

"We'll pick them up on the way to City Hall. We have the license. It won't take long."

"But I'll be in my ski clothes!"

"So?"

The morning was frigid and still. The markets were closed on Chambers Street as they always were in daytime. We were scouts in this no-man's land, pioneers in an outpost not yet included in city life. Only at night, when the markets awoke for business, like the Las Vegas Strip at 4:00AM, was there a soul on the street, in *the neighborhood*. But now it was desolate. Not a person. Not a car. Not a sound. It wasn't new to me, this morning stillness, but on that particular day I shuddered.

We crossed the silent grid to Canal Street without a word. The mop and broom hung absurdly from my hand till we neared the City Hall steps when they fell to the ground and my body exploded in laughter.

"What's so funny," Johnny asked, weighted down by a sack of new tools.

"I don't know," I howled in a fit of uncontrollable giggles.

"Well, something's funny."

"I don't know," I roared, my knees wobbling beneath me. *"I don't know."*

"Let me carry the mop," he offered.

"The mop? The mop? " My laughter overcame me. *"Never mind. It's................"*

"It's what?"

"It's............it's......................Oh! God! I have to sit down."

"You can't sit here on the steps. You'll freeze to death."

"I'll what? I'll freeze to death with my mop?" I dropped to the steps of the great building, ski suit and all and surrendered to the seizure of laughter I could no longer contain.

"Oh God I can't drop my broom!!!!!!!!!!!!! Do you have any idea why we................................"

"What?"

"Why we......................" It was useless.

Johnny, in his overalls, wool sweater and cap, picked up the mop and broom and led me up the great stairs -- as tears of laughter flooded my cheeks and my body shook from a hysteria I couldn't explain.

I can always get divorced, I reassured myself. *I can always get divorced.* That's how I steadied my feet to take me to the Marriage Bureau. That's how I barely contained the giggles as we approached a love-struck couple just ahead of us in line.

"Excuse me, " I said to them, reasonably enough, *"would you mind if………………….."* The laughter interfered. The couple joined in.

"Would you mind," I continued, *"if……………………….."*

"If you'd be our witnesses?" Johnny interrupted.

"Not at all," they cood adoringly, *"if you'll be ours."*

It was almost midnight when I finally reached the ski lodge. It had been an otherwise ordinary day.

"I've got to run, Johnny," I remembered yelling as I raced from City Hall after the brief "ceremony," *"or I'll miss the bus. I'll call you when I get there."*

"Don't forget."

"I won't………….Oops! Take the mop. I'll call you later."

When I got up to the ski resort, I was fully aware that whatever had made my knees shake and my body tremble, whatever had caused the peculiar outbursts of laughter had passed without a trace. And there, in a drab and darkly forbidding room, a hundred miles from home, I felt a wellness and a lightness, as if purged. I had married that day, yet its meaning eluded me, except for the lightness, for a slight smile that filled my consciousness. A knock on the door reminded me of my circumstance.

"When do we leave for the slopes tomorrow," the girl asked.

"At eight," I replied, *"but we'll have breakfast first. Tell all the kids to be up by seven."*

"Can you wake us?"

"I've got my clock set."

"Thanks," she said, turning to leave. "See you in the morning."

"By the way, " I began haltingly, *"before you go………………. I………..I got married today."*

"What?"
"I got married today."
"Really?" she asked, staring at me in disbelief.
"Really."
"Oh………..," she replied, "that's………………..uh…………..….nice."

I remember the quiet of the room when she left. I remember being surprised by her bewilderment. *Why is this odd to her?* It crossed my mind that maybe most people don't go skiing on their wedding night, alone. But that was just a thought. It had no real meaning. Like pretending you're Russian in an Indian sari. But I didn't see it that way. I didn't see it **any** way. I just did it. That's how the "wedding" was. I just did it. It made its own particular sense. So why was she bewildered? Especially when the lightness seemed so evident and so deep. The stillness of the room intoxicated me. There was such order then, such painlessness, such light. I reached for the phone, but hesitated. It was late, too late to call. *No,* I thought. *It's fitting, just one call.*

"Ma?" I said, almost questioningly, when she answered the phone.

I'd thought for a moment how to tell her, how to put it right – how to explain what to others might seem odd, how to make her know it was right. She was miles away yet I could feel her by my side. She was part of the quiet in the room, part of the order and the peace. Four-feet-ten, rotund, her white hair and aged skin, her wisdom and the sparkle in her eyes, without a dime or a book, she knew it all and never needed reminding to be nice. She loved me -- and I knew it, she and her son, Johnny Marino. So simple, this remedy – like a tiny, tiny pill that can stop a stroke or put a giant to sleep. So simple. Yet, so hard to get.

"Ma," I fluttered.

"Who is this?" asked the gentle, sleepy voice.

"It's, me, Ma, Bea."

"Bea?"

"Yes. It's me, Ma, your new daughter-in-law."

"Oh my God!" Mrs. Marino cried.

"Johnny and I got married today."

"Oh, my God. I'm so happy. Where are you? Where's Johnny."

"I had to take some kids skiing for the week-end………. and…………….. Johnny's home."

"Home?"

"Yes."

"Oh my God!"

"It's O.K., Ma. I'll be back Sunday."

"Oh, Bea, " she laughed lovingly. *"It's just like the two of you."*

"It's O.K., Ma. …………………….Now you have **THREE** daughters-in-law."

"No, honey, I have two daughters-in-law ……….but now I have a daughter."

AFTERMATH

FOR MANY PEOPLE, settling in to married life requires an adjustment, a process of adaptation, but that wasn't the case for me. There was no adjustment, no chiseling of the edges to fit together harmoniously, no accommodation to make, however reluctantly, for the greater good. In fact, nothing had changed. I was as comfortable with Johnny as I'd been before, as happy to be with him, as pleased with his company. Maybe it's because I'd allowed myself an exit route, allowed for the possibility of divorce that I didn't see the wedding as an imprisoning life event.

Whatever the reason, the fact of our marriage was, in and of itself, inconsequential, except, perhaps, for my father and his biting expressions of disappointment during our very infrequent contacts. My mother, on the other hand, with all her propriety and conventional rigidity, was far more accepting of the union, pleased by it, as if she'd idealized Johnny as she'd once done my father, ennobled him – so that his painful history became proof of his artistry. Drugs, poverty and prison, it seemed, were his price paid for greatness, a requisite, perhaps, for greatness itself – as she'd construed my father's temperament and violence as proof of his creativity. It was in keeping with her times and her romanticized, if naïve, world-view and it endeared her to me in a way I hadn't known before. Her pleasure in Johnny, her affection for him, her delight was an acceptance of me. When she saw him she smiled, a deep, adoring smile and kissed him ever so tenderly like a warm blanket cradling *me* in love and safety, filling *me* for a minute or an hour or an evening with the incidental spell of her mothering. It was so like her, her gentility in the presence of a worthy man, even his Catholicism was extraneous to her as it was to him. She could have cared less about it as he did, particularly in light of her reaction to my brother's betrothal a year before.

Manny was completing his internship at Yale Medical School when he met a lovely young Connecticut girl, Florence Ruchelli. They fell in love and hoped to marry. My father hadn't a thought about her. She was a woman, after all, and not held to the same standards of philosophical development as a man. His contempt for religion showed no favoritism; his anti-religious sentiments was for the adherents of any and all religions, people who should be made of stronger mettle, the men who cowered before their gods; who demeaned themselves in an attempt to ward off their fear of the unknown, the punishment that might await them, the death they feared and bargained to forestall.

But when my brother said he was marrying in a church, my mother, my ecumenical, leftist, poet mother was apoplectic. While she remained a woman with an almost childlike acceptance of all people individually, she was terrified of the *institution of the church*, terrified of its teachings and its power to incite the flock. She could embrace Florence but would not enter a church. It wasn't that Florence was Catholic; it was the structure of the *church*, a structure which had a unique and abhorrent symbolism after the war.

The *Reichskonkordat* between Germany and the Holy See, protecting German Catholics and constraining the German clergy, the pictures taken in front of the Vatican of Jews being deported and sent to their death, of Jews begging to be allowed to find shelter in that enormous institution, Pope Pius X11 complicity in the war (despite post-war Herculean efforts to sanitize the issue, to spin it, to negate it) all served to frighten Jews and remind them that anti-Semitism was born from centuries and centuries of church doctrine and liturgy.

STUMBLING HOME

Now, mind you, this was almost fifteen years after the end of the war and survivors had only recently begun to tell the world what had occurred (at least that part of the world that gave a damn, which wasn't a whole lot of people, maybe a few blocks in Brooklyn). But my mother gave a damn. The deaths of her mother's family, the death of virtually all of her grandmother's family, in Russia, were still part of family lore, although it wasn't until World War II that my mother began to grasp the larger picture, the picture of anti-Semitism. The photos and stories out of Europe had really just begun to be absorbed into American consciousness. The war had been, for more than a decade, a war of military battles, strategy, generals, acts of heroism on the battlefield. The destruction of European Jewry was only a footnote, if at all. It was only incidental.

At first the tales of horror and tragedy were dismissed as exaggerated, overly dramatized, Jewish propaganda to win world sympathy for the creation of the state of Israel, *they* said. Even after 1948 when Israel, through UN fiat, was granted its statehood, it faced brutal, deadly attacks from every direction.

Actually the United Nations Partition Plan of November, 1947 recommended the creation of two independent states, independent Arab and Jewish States and the Special *International* City of Jerusalem. The Jews accepted the plan but the Arabs rejected it, refusing to accept an autonomous Jewish state on what they argued was their land. In fact, the land was owned almost entirely by absentee landowners, Arabs, Jews and international landlords, under British administration. It was sparsely occupied land as one would imagine a desert in the 1800 and 1900's, a desert with no natural resources, no water, with little habitable ground, and few people who actually *lived* there. But some Jews, particularly at the turn of the century and through the close of World War I, began to see the handwriting on the wall and began to buy up land from wealthy absentee landowners, some of whom were Arab, who were only too happy to sell to anyone, any sucker who'd buy it.

No sooner had the United Nations offer been signed in 1947,

Islamic nations, indigenous Arabs refused to accept its existence and vowed to see Israel plunged into the sea, a vow that exists just as passionately today.

Even stories from returning American G.I's, who had liberated camps and seen with their own eyes the horror that was the Holocaust were doubted. At the war's end, the few Jews still alive in Europe were in DP camps or wandering aimlessly in search of family they hoped, however fruitlessly, had been spared.

And the role of the church in Hitler's grand plan had not been lost on these survivors but was unknown and perhaps irrelevant to the rest of the world. Even when it became known, it was denied vehemently by the church or spun in ways to absolve its role. Even when it became known that Hitler, himself, Himmler, Heydrich, Streicher, Hoss, Goebbels, and so many of the other henchman were born and raised Catholic, were even alter boys, it didn't seem to bear any weight. Of course, witnesses and survivors knew differently.

Now this was more than fifteen years after the end of the war. And the more my mother learned, the more she wanted to learn. Her life became utterly and irrevocably intertwined with the Holocaust and the distance between herself as a Jew and those who were not increased. Her fear of non-Jews, especially those who wore a crucifix, became apparent especially as she learned more of the betrayal of Jews by their "friends" and "trusted" neighbors, a reality that only became fully apparent after he war. For example, it was not unusual for a Jewish family, in anticipation of being sent to *"a work camp in the east,"* to entrust Christian friends and neighbors with their most prized possession, their child, till the war's end, for an ample sum of money or property, often entrusting them with the family's business, their home until, they believed, the Allies would win the war and they could return from the camp. Of course, as it turned out few Jews managed to survive the war. Those who did would try to find their way back to their town, the home they'd left in terror, in their frenetic, dazed belief that somehow, unimaginably, they would return and resume their lives. As it happened, if their home had not been destroyed, it was invariably re-occupied by these very same Christian neighbors who now claimed it and all the its possessions as their own and denied any agreement had ever been made to the contrary. And it was not unusual for a Christian family to refuse to return the child they'd been given for "safe-keeping". Often the child had been baptized, was being raised a Catholic and would remain a Catholic in their surrogate family. And indeed, what could this survivor do? If she protested too audibly she'd simply be shot. Who could prove otherwise? Jews were utterly expendable.

Under the best of circumstances, she'd find shelter in a DP camp and survive the dismal, agonizing years lamenting the death of her family and the theft of her children until some country agreed to accept her. On the minds of so many survivors, in 1945 and afterwards, when they were not reliving the hell that had been, was Palestine and its fight for statehood. It was only there that they believed they'd be safe. Of course the post-war nightmare could have been ameliorated had some country, at the Evian Conference in 1938, agreed to accept even some of these desperate Jews beyond their meager immigration quotas, but rather, they were turned away, often with a gun. None were accepted. **Not a one!**

Of all imaginable *or imagined* crimes, the crime of deicide, as it's leveled at all Jews, was and is the most heinous and the most unforgivable. No torment on this earth is sufficient punishment for this sin; a sin that can never be atoned for, for the killers can never be released from the hell they must endure both in this life and beyond. This is the anti-Semitism of all history and specifically of the Holocaust.

Incidentally, at the Second Vatican Council in the late 60's, the Vatican, which had opened its archives after generations, announced *in a whisper, in a closely* guarded whisper, that indeed **Jews had NOT killed Christ,** a rumor spread by *misguided* parishioners who **had misinterpreted** church teachings, but the damage had already been done. And the charge of deicide is still alive and well today around the world and sited, where needed, to explain continued acts of horrific anti-Semitism.

(As it turned out, some of the survivors of Hell had to wait a decade to leave the vast Jewish cemetery that was Europe. In the case of "Palestine", that debacle was the direct result of Britain's policies during the Mandate period following the end of World War I. The Treaty of Versailles had divided up the Ottoman Empire between the victorious powers with "Palestine" to be administered by England whose policies of deception, subterfuge and double dealing ultimately led to the ongoing Israeli-Arab wars that continues till this day.)

So while my mother remained a woman with an almost childlike acceptance of all people individually, she was terrified of the institution of the church, terrified of its teachings and its power to incite the flock. The crucifix, above all other symbols, elicited terror in her and any Jew who experienced anti-Semitism, even today. Thus, my mother could embrace my brother's fiancé but would not enter a church. The sight of a crucifix, even a small crucifix dangling from a child's neck sent a wave of fear through her. Of course, despite her apprehension, she was ultimately able to separate the woman from her church and attend their wedding with her usual poise and grace.

My marriage to Johnny was a very different event. While he was born a Catholic, he, like my father, rejected all religion. His mother, Grace Marino, a practicing, devout Catholic, was too inherently decent to harbor any of the hate that had marked history and the war years. Maybe it was her priest's betrayal of Johnny so many years before, maybe she, like Johnny, were simply not "sheep." They made up their own minds about people and who they could trust.

Ultimately she and my mother developed a lovely, respectful, even endearing relationship, two kind and innocent women bonding over the new couple they both endorsed. In retrospect I suspect they each saw in the other the very quality that had been denied them by their circumstance. Mrs. Marino was a mother, a mother and a woman first: a safe mother and a safe woman. She was poor, without formal education though smart as a whip. She could read people the way a scholar reads text. She could cook and feed her family; she could say lovely things to and about her children; she could embrace her children and hold them close when they needed comforting. My mother, on the other hand, could do none of these things, not because she was unkind but because she was the product of her unique family, a unique offspring of European Jews before the 20th century. She was poor, like Mrs. Marino, but came from a family who by dint of their history as Jews had to be cautious, at times mistrusting and insular. She, like so many Jews throughout history, who had been denied entry into professions, learned to value study, scholarship, artistry, pursuits that could not be taken away from them. Like so many Jews who throughout history were not allowed to attend a school with non-Jews, the state could not prevent her parents from teaching her privately. The limited, seemingly constricted world in which she was forced to live as a Jew, had the paradoxical effect of allowing her to focus on those things she was allowed to do, Darwin's concession to Jews. Clearly many such Jewish women were women like Mrs. Marino.

And of course, I had not married just anyone. My mother adored Johnny (and his mother as well) and saw my marriage as a stabilizing, welcomed event, endearing her to me and certainly to Johnny. Mrs. Marino was as unconcerned about my Jewishness as my mother about his Catholicism; At times I even thought that Mrs. Marino was pleased that Johnny had married a Jew though I could not tell you why. To both women ones religion was extraneous. The fact remained, however, I kept my distance from my parents.

Whatever had occurred in my family occurred long before my marriage and, despite my wish to the contrary, it seemed resistant to change. Though I no longer ran from my parents as I'd done that awful day in Brooklyn several years before, I remained guarded in their presence and avoided them as much as possible. When we did see one another, I continued to fight back tears. What had changed, though, was the extent to which I tried to win their favor, or rather, the extent to which I *behaved* as if I were tryingo win their favor. I no longer entertained my father as I'd done before. I was more somber in his presence, more constrained, *as if* my efforts to please him had begun to humiliate me. I say "as if" because I don't recall *feeling* humiliation or anything I would have defined in those terms. Certainly I was ill equipped at the time to accurately identify most of my inner life but I do know things began to *look* different. Everything was becoming muted, the make-up, the clothes, the decibel level, the involuntary movements of the hands and eyes that define anxiety, the staccato chatter that accompanies the need to be heard when one knows full-well hearing is impossible.

From all appearances one might have assumed I'd matured, that I was taking myself more seriously, that I was more comfortable with myself, more self-accepting, that I'd stopped chasing my tail because I was more at peace. And certainly that was true but most importantly, I suspect, is that I'd come to know love, not the tumultuous, pained love that accompanied Alfredo's betrayal, but a love for Johnny that invariably put a smile on my face.

Yet in my parent's presence, all bets were off. With them I was still a child in Macy's who can't find her mother. First she calls out to her "mommy" without great alarm, assuming she'd just wandered to the very next aisle. Then, with increasing pitch, she calls her again, sensing she'd gone a bit further, perhaps out of hearing distance, then she begins to run, to shake, to wail, to race frenetically throughout the store screaming from a place inside her self she'd never known existed, pushing other shoppers out of her way, imploring them to find her mommy, find her mommy.

Most of these mommies are found just down the aisle, just beyond the rack, maybe in the next department, maybe even on the next floor, having assumed her little girl was right next to her, just behind her, right there in her shadow. Maybe the mommies are as frenetic as their child, in a state of unimaginable dread, maybe they're found just chatting nonchalantly with another mother they knew from their neighborhood who also just happened to be shopping at Macy's.

But what of the child whose mother is never found? Does the child ever stop screaming? Is there ever a moment when she accepts that her mommy will never return? Is there ever a moment when she resolves to go on? The little girl is deposited at her little kindergarten class but mommy fails to pick her up. Mommy died in the interim, never to return again! What does that child feel? Is her pain allayed by the fact that mommy had lived 28 years -- so her loss can't be nearly as painful as if she'd only lived six? What if mommy had been 38? Would the little girl cry longer? What of the baby who never knew her mommy? Does she still cry for her? Does Mother's Day make her want to swallow nails? Or does she somehow, through some great unfathomable mercy, find a way to cope, to ultimately tally up, to weigh the indescribable gifts against the unspeakable agonies and have something left over to hold on to? Maybe when that happens, when we "come to terms, " a light goes out and we're muted a bit, dulled, enervated, and our voice, once screeching with terror or euphoria drops by a single tone. Maybe that's what "closure" means. Maybe that's why I became less frenetic in my parent's company.

As a married woman, I suspect what I felt with them was something akin to the kind of acceptance that follows loss, *however one experiences it, whatever or whomever happens to be lost*. I came to know that what I'd fought so hard to find was, forever, out of reach. I needn't run anymore, nor scream nor make deals for what could never be. Closure without completion. And it allowed me to go on.

SPACE

SOMETHING WAS IN the works. Though I kept my distance from my parents, in their presence I observed them as one would Bin Laden. I studied their every expression, their moods, even their choice of words in their language of kings. I was no longer simply reactive. I was no longer the kid who just happened to have been in the line of fire when the stock market took a tumble. I had somehow become less involved, less of a participant and that meager distance allowed for a slightly different perspective.

My mother's fondness for Johnny was what continued to claim my attention. I'd seen her sweetness before, her charm, her graceful gentility, but at a distance, at a far distance that had nothing to do with me.... and in those moments I saw what others saw in her and were so enchanted by. Yet her kindness repelled me, too, perhaps because I mistrusted it, perhaps because I was never its object. But it wasn't unfamiliar to me. Around Johnny, she was adoring. She listened when he spoke, she nodded, she smiled, she applauded. If you didn't know of her asexuality, you might even have thought she was flirting with him. And perhaps she was. It made me wonder if she'd ever flirted with my father, if her *vaginismus* was a natural consequence of years of gender inequities, a natural consequence of living with a man like him. I wondered if his heavy-handedness would have been so pronounced had *he* lived with a different woman. That was easier to entertain since

I'd experienced his moments of accessibility. I could readily recall the thousands of times he'd kissed me, threw me in the air with delight, looked me square in the eyes and smiled. Despite everything else, I never doubted that he loved me. NEVER. I never felt that about my mother.

If I concentrated really hard I could recall a way she occasionally looked at my brother, early on, very early on, a look of unmistakable love, a mother's love for her son. I could even recall, at least I think I could, a vague, elusive, fleeting image of a mother at the foot of her daughter's bed, reading to her at bedtime. She seems to love her little girl. Her face is gentle and warm. Her daughter is transfixed by her mother's aura, by her mother's long braids, by her colorful "gypsy" clothing, by her magic. She doesn't care that it's Emily Dickenson she hears. It's her mother's voice. She's enraptured.........But...wait. Is that love in mommy's eyes? It was! It was. I saw it. It was there a minute ago.

She looked at Johnny that way. I tried to understand. In those early months of married life I tried to make sense of these discrepancies, to reconcile this emotional generosity with her steely detachment towards me, the mother I was most familiar with. Somewhere in my efforts I remembered a story I'd been told, that **she** told me when I was very young. I doubted the recollection, as a child learns to doubt herself when she's not acknowledged. She couldn't have told me. Perhaps I made it up. But I hadn't. She told me! She did! She told me that when she was in college she fell in love with an older man. She'd fallen in love with her *Spanish Professor* but was forced by her parents to end the relationship because he'd been divorced, a definite deal breaker in her time. He wanted to marry her but it was out of the question. She was devastated, she said, inconsolable. She thought she'd never recover. Several years later she met my father. Her family, fearful that Gypsy, a bit of a rebel and now older than proper, might never marry, encouraged the alliance – like the cops *encourage* a suspect to admit the crime.

The memory of this story haunted me as I tried to make sense of the woman I momentarily got a glimpse of. Where was the woman who had fallen in love with a divorced man? Where was the GYPSY I'd heard about? Where were the braids? Where was the loving sound in the voice of the woman who sat at the foot of her bed so many years before? It was only through her affection for Johnny that she showed herself, her spirit, her rebellion, her willingness to transcend. And I came to love her for it -- and sensed that somehow for her, of all the relationships in her life, mothering a daughter was fraught with trouble. I didn't understand it at the time, why she couldn't embrace me as she'd embraced Johnny, but I came to believe that, as painful as her distance was, it had less to do with me than it did with her. And that realization allowed me to let go.

My father, on the other hand, had little use for Johnny. This orphan from Poland, penniless, self-taught, who'd been kicked in the *kishkas* only to pick himself up and reinvent himself as a proper English poet couldn't abide any of these very same struggles in Johnny. Had we seen more of my parents, perhaps the situation would have become more problematic. As it was, it was tolerable, at least for us. A man of lesser character than Johnny might have reacted to my father's slights by seizing the gauntlet. To the contrary, Johnny extended an olive branch. Though the effort was fruitless, it served to highlight his ever-increasing stature in my eyes.

It was with Johnny's family that we were most connected, with his two younger brothers, Basil and Vincent, with their wives, Nina and Gloria, with his cousins Jimmy, Josie, Anna, Mary and Frank and with his mother whose company I cherished. It was a stunning family, the three brothers, their striking good looks matched by their charm and side splitting wit. Basil, the middle brother, was a showstopper and Vincent, the youngest and equally handsome, gave him a real run for his money, and their welcoming, charming wives.

Without serious formal education, at least of the Proustian sort, the two brothers were both successful commercial artists who gravitated instinctively to the edgy New York of the 50's and 60's yet still maintaining their traditional Italian roots. Their beautiful wives, Nina and Gloria, were their perfect counterparts. Though both were from first-generation Italian homes (Nina, in fact, was raised in Italy), I always felt welcomed in their midst. My mother-in-law, Grace Marino, with her infinite wisdom and kindness, would have had it no other way. There's no question that had she been born in another age, in another circumstance, her accomplishments would have had no limit. She was Golda Meir, though considerably shorter, a bit heavier, as innately smart and capable but far more accessible, at least to me.

The Marino's reminded me of Ellie's family in Brooklyn though on first glance one might not have noticed the similarities. Ellie's parents were old and life-worn. The Marino's, with the exception of the elder Mrs. Marino, were young, attractive and stylish. Yet, both families were down-to-earth and welcoming. Both looked at you when you spoke; both acknowledged even your most trivial comment -- for language had no hierarchy of intrinsic importance. If you had something to say, they wanted to hear it. If it happened to be foolish, they'd just laugh good-naturedly and slap you on the back, as if to say, "It's O.K. I said the same stupid thing last week." They could laugh at themselves without losing face and laugh at each other without inflicting mortal wounds. They were a safe harbor, without judgments, without reprisals and without "culture," at least the "culture" that sets people apart from on another.

In stark contradiction to my own home in which 50's modernity was devalued in favor of antiquity, Nina and Gloria epitomized the period. Their homes, like themselves, were right out of Ladies Home Journal with every new appliance (irrelevant in my home for my mother devalued cooking and the time it consumed) and every element of 50's décor. I found myself looking up to the two of them as a child would her two beautiful, older sisters, admiringly, in awe of their new gismos and fluff. I didn't care that they didn't read Kierkegaard. They read Vogue and that was a breath of fresh air. I was proud to be one of them -- and with that pride, unspoken reservations I'd harbored about Johnny had changed.

Sundays Johnny and I usually took the train to the Bronx to visit with his mother. His brothers and their families and, occasionally, his cousins came as well. All these people crowded into a tiny tenement apartment, barely three miniature rooms, would have stretched the patience of most people, but not here. Warmth, laughter and the aromas of southern Italian cooking filled the hours. I quickly learned that "sauce" was "gravy," a Magnus opus, that "spaghetti" was just one of many "pastas," and in no time at all I became "Mom's" most eager and appreciative culinary student. Escarole soup, Lasagna, lard bread, ravioli. And, above all, THE. "gravy".

I watched. I listened. I took notes. "You're such a good girl," she'd say, periodically and I'd inflate as though I'd eaten a house. Mostly, just standing by her side, in that tiny, dilapidated old kitchen was all the food I needed. Occasionally Johnny would see us side by side fussing over the stove and me imitating his mother. "You're such a good girl," he'd mimic lovingly. I thought I'd eaten two houses. Life was perfect.

I wanted for nothing and never thought beyond the moment. The only "future" we ever discussed was brought up by Johnny. New York was clearly the heart of the art world in those days but California was making a name for itself, particularly with potters and sculptors who worked on a massive scale. The climate and abundance of cheap studio space allowed for artists to live and work more easily, and most appealingly, to work out of doors. For a welder like Johnny whose works were often eight or ten feet tall, the prospect was utterly fascinating.

Working out of doors and working in bronze were the two opportunities he yearned for. The latter was out of our reach financially but not the former. The thought of spending a year in L.A. intrigued me as well. Though, unlike Johnny, I had no particular goal in mind, it struck me as a great adventure, cutting loose, flight, but this time safe in the company of a mentor and trusted friend.

(Basil, Johnny, Flo, me, Manny and my parents
at the airport to see us off).

Johnny had moved his massive sculptures to the sub basement in the old commercial building, a basement if not unknown to recent building owners, was certainly unused. Only the day before we were to leave for LA, to my utter amazement, I found out I was pregnant. Johnny was thrilled. I was, as well, but also in a state of total disbelief; It must an error, I assumed, a false positive; the one error in the doctors otherwise perfect diagnostic record. Of course I had never used protections (except on one occasion at Sinai's insistence), since it struck me as utterly superfluous. I couldn't get pregnant as other girls did. I was not like other girls. I wasn't even fully convinced I was a "girl." That's not to say I questioned the *appearance* of my physiology. I just felt so unlike other girls, so much an imposter, a fraud. If I could get pregnant it would connect me to that strange, foreign sub-set of people who thus far had utterly eluded me. I had neither been invited to join their ranks nor was I ready to force my way in.

I assume it must have been similar to what a boy (or a girl, for that matter) in the '50's experienced when he saw that all the other boys were flirting with girls and he knew he didn't have the same feelings towards her. It's the terror of some confirmation that he was *a mutation, a freak, an outcast*. He has no peer group, no community, no like-minded others and it would be that way till the end of his days. In 1965 (four years *before* Stonewall) and the year in which I got pregnant, my position seemed as perilous as his and my flirtation with suicide just as predictable as his. It wasn't my sexual identity I doubted. It was far more primitive than that. It was my identity as even human. (But for this boy, and others, there was a growing chorus to affirm him and oppose the marginality that had been inflicted upon him and it was getting louder day by day.)

In 1965, there's no question that the depression that had engulfed me had lifted but my underlying sense of inauthenticity diminished yet still existed. There was no chorus doubting my affliction. And because of that, this "pregnancy" remained, to me, dubious.

LOS ANGELES

OUR DEPARTURE FROM New York was seamless, as if we had unlimited funds, a home awaiting us in LA, and not a concern in the world. I suppose in part it was the times. This was the sixties, 1965 to be exact. All rules were suspended, at least those having to do with the old proprieties.

We arrived in LA greeted at the airport by Guy and Marlene Williams, two artists and old friends of Johnny who insisted we stay at their house until we found our own. That night they hosted a welcome party for us to introduce Johnny to their friends and some of the most prominent LA artists of the day, John Altoon (and his beautiful wife, Babs), John Baldassarri, Paul Sarkissian, Mel and Fran Liau, Jim and Ruth Bradley and a host of others.

The party was overwhelming. I was a kid in a grown-up world of laughter, art, gallery openings and a weekly game of poker that I would join. Guy suggested we call a fellow artist and architect who had a house in Pasadena that was scheduled for demolition to make room for the Pasadena Freeway. Since there was no way to predict if the house would be razed in a week, a month or a year, the owner had bought another home and had already moved in. He was, however, concerned that if the Pasadena house was left vacant, vandals might occupy it and he would be liable for any problems that might arise. Hence he welcomed us occupying the house temporarily until its demolition. While it was clearly a temporary fix, we were grateful to have at least a home for the moment.

The house, it turned out, was an architectural dream, a two-story *hacienda* with a huge landscaped garden and fountain surrounded by a six-foot high Spanish-tiled wall. The main floor was one huge white, windowed open space, as if the owner had recreated a gorgeous New York artist's loft. And indeed, he had. On the second floor were 4 large bedrooms, enough for anyone to visit and stay a while. Outside was a 3 car-garage that was ideal for Johnny's studio.

We couldn't believe that even though our occupancy would be brief, this would be ours. To make the arrangement even more unbelievable, the owner was not interested in being a landlord. He wanted only to be assured that the house would be occupied by reliable people whose occupancy prevented vandalism on his property. All he asked for was $28.00 per month to cover the utilities! We stood dumb-founded! Good New Yorkers that we were we assumed we were being scammed. We kept trying unsuccessfully to find out what the scam was. Finally Johnny called Guy to ask him what this guy was up to. It was all above board, he was assured. The owner was a fellow artist as well as an architect who could be taken at his word. In fact he had built the house for himself, conscious of all the parameters an artist might have if he had the freedom to plan his own living environment. He wanted nothing more than to protect the property and anyone who happened to venture on it. To make the deal even more unbelievable, the owner had left some furniture in the house that he no longer needed, enough that we virtually bought nothing. Of course, in time, I assumed, I might need to buy a crib if indeed I was fortunate enough to really be pregnant. Now all we needed to do was find jobs.

Johnny got a job bartending and I managed to find a waitressing job in downtown LA for an Israeli couple, whose daughter, Yael Bialybroda, ultimately became one of my closest friends. I worked the lunch shift in their busy, run-down diner whose clients were primarily the construction workers hired to build the high-rise office buildings slated to modernize the downtown area. I say I worked the "lunch shift" as if there were a dinner shift or late-night cocktail hour.

STUMBLING HOME

Clearly there were none of these since, in those years, all of downtown LA closed up when the workday ended. That was perfect for me since it gave me time to nest in our fabulous Spanish villa.

When indeed it became obvious, even to me, that I was pregnant, my joy and anticipation were boundless. Not only would I have someone whom I could unconditionally love and who would unconditionally love me, I was human, after all; an authentic female, a fact no amount of accents or pretense could negate. I was utterly, inextricably human and utterly, inextricably female and that fact alone served to release me from the hell I'd lived in most of my life. The only discomfort came later in the pregnancy when I was waiting tables one day during lunch.

The crowd in the diner was not a crowd my father would have esteemed. They were construction workers, after all, not philosophers or academicians. That fact, for me, was utterly conflict-free except on this particular day. It was towards the end of my ninth month of pregnancy and my stomach protruded directly in front of me like a slingshot pulled to its greatest tension. But I was young and strong so this reality didn't interfere with my work. I could carry on my tray all the meals and platters I needed to without a tinge of discomfort.

As I was walking to a table in the front of the diner, passing men, most of whom still wore their hard hats, someone pinched my backside and whistled. (I would have said "pinched my ass," but in those days, while I was relieved that I was human, I couldn't be vulgar, not a word, not a reference that wasn't clean and polished and certainly not a reference to a body part that one never talked about.) But that's beside the point. At that moment when I felt the pinch, a flush of embarrassment overwhelmed me. It was an utter indignity, beyond the pale. I was pregnant, for God's sake, not a slut! Didn't the fool know it was a virgin birth? I was still my mother's daughter, after all. There was no sex involved. The humiliation stopped me in my tracts. I had intended to work until the very last moment, even if I could have afforded to do otherwise, which, of course, I couldn't. I was due to deliver the second week of April and it was then the very end of

March. Regardless, I decided that would be my last day. The insult to my self-esteem was too great. I had to leave. The extra few days, I rationalized, would allow me time to fix up the house in anticipation of my mother's visit.

My mother had offered to come when I gave birth and help me with the baby, an offer that, while pleasing, made no sense, whatsoever. It's what mother's did at the time and while my mother had done some of the things expected of mothers, like taking me religiously to art classes at the Brooklyn Museum, this was completely unexpected. It had nothing to do with a baby, of that I was sure. It was about doing the "motherly" thing, about being appropriate. She was the last of all her friends ("the girls") to have a grandchild (and certainly the last to have a child) and I'm certain she learned from them what is expected of a mother.

Throughout my childhood, "the girls" were the only connection to "Gypsy" that remained in tact. There were five of "the girls" (all my "Aunts') as they were referred to, whom she'd had since her girlhood in Brooklyn. They were all very similar in that they were all intellectual, all prized creativity and all (with the exception of my mother) were brighter than their husbands. I'm actually not sure that my mother was not smarter than my father. I didn't really know her well, at least not well enough to know what she actually thought. My mother only said to me what she thought a mother "should" say to her daughter, and that, god knows, was utterly skewed (except for the few impromptu complaints about other women being horny that she just couldn't abide.) My mother never, ever told me that my father left her; she never ever mentioned a word about anything other than fine, polished, wholesome, "right" feelings towards everyone.

I remember once asking her what sex is like. "It's wonderful……………" she said, after a long, long hesitation…….. " If you're really, really in love…………then it's the most beautiful thing in the world!!!!." WHAT? What I'm sure she meant to say is that it's bearable. It's part of your wifely duty. So do it and don't complain and…… Don't ever fuck just anyone!!!! Those messages I got loud and clear.

STUMBLING HOME

She was terrified I'd be a whore! Why? Was she afraid she'd become a whore? Was that the worst she could imagine if I went wrong? That I'd be a whore? Not that I might get cancer and die young, or get hit by a car or fall from a cliff. No! The worst thing she could imagine is that I'd be a whore *and then no man would marry me*. But I have to see this for what it was. She knew the world to be unbearably harsh toward women, unforgiving. You had to be sexy so your husband would want to fuck you but you couldn't enjoy it and you couldn't actually *look* sexy because the world would think you're a slut. You had to be smart so you can keep up with your husband but not too smart that he doesn't think he's the man. You have to be tall and short, fat and thin, competent yet "in distress." "Make him think that………………….." the most oft used start of any sentence between my mother and me, at ANY AGE. Don't be better at sports than a boy. Don't be better at school…..Don't be better at art, at guitar, at ballet,……………. Don't be funnier. Remember to always laugh at his jokes. Ask him questions as if you can't, for the life of you, know how this silly thing works, like starting up a car, like turning on a TV! Make him feel that he's stronger than you, smarter, sexier, more accomplished, more creative. The ONLY things you're allowed to excel in are patience, poise, modesty, morality, pain tolerance, cooking, cleaning and stupidity.

Only one of "the girls" had two children. All the others had only one child whom they delivered 10 to 15 years before my mother, so clearly none of these women were "mommas" like Mrs. Marino. They were all Eastern European, all spoke Yiddish and all came to America at the beginnings of the 20th century. None of them were into clothes or make-up or appearance. They were ideational women who prided themselves on not being "superficial" or prissy or trendy or conventional; I suspect they all had similar conflicts related to men, given the generation though they all seemed far more powerful in their marriages than my mother did. I'd say they were men's women in that they had more in common with men, at least superficially. I doubt, though, that men would have appreciated them as much as men might appreciate them today. I can't imagine my mother ever confiding in "the girls" though I know she had. I just can't imagine her ever being "real" after Gypsy died.

Eating in any of "the girl's" homes was like eating in my own. No aromas of anything cooking, certainly not anything anyone enjoyed cooking or would want to eat. Cooking was not a prized pursuit. Nor were their homes decorated in any particular way. They were utilitarian. It was clear that no one in the home took pleasure in the way things looked. In that regard my own home was very special, filled with sculptures, statues, art work from my parents many world travels before my brother and I were born. I think my father was the inspiration for most of this because they were all bronze, mostly fine reproductions of Homer, Dante, Michelangelo, drawings of Heine, Aristotle.

Attending lectures was what "the girls" did, reading, bearing witness, joining the picket line. They were all of left leaning persuasions, all marched for civil rights, "Negro rights", for worker's rights for Julius and Ethel Rosenberg and later, for the creation of the state of Israel. Several were staunch Communists and the others certainly leaned in that direction. Now certainly sex roles were far more rigid at that time. Women rarely worked (except for most of "the girls" who had all, with the exception of my mother, graduated from college and become teachers, one of the few fields acceptable for women at the time). In fact, most men at the time were utterly against their wives working "out of the house". It was a sign that the husband didn't earn enough money for the family. It was a sign he didn't measure up, like wealthy people in the 1800's who would never allow themselves to be thin for fear it be construed as evidence of poverty.

A woman only worked if she needed the money. Divorce was strictly frowned upon so even if the spouses despised each other, they still lived in the same home and adhered to the same characteristic roles. Women didn't drive cars; Most played Mah Jong or occasionally Bridge (though certainly not "the girls"). They never played poker or even chess. I'm certain in the years when my mother was childless she saw, as the "girls" began to have grandchildren, they all rose to the occasion. It's simply what mother's did, hence my mother's offer to come to California. I doubt it had anything to do with children or enjoying the presence of a new born, even if it was her first grandchild.

And so I left the restaurant that very day in anticipation of my mother's visit and the delivery of my first child. My mother had bought a round-trip ticket that theoretically allowed her about two-three weeks with me and the baby before she had to return to Florida (where she and my father had moved after I got married). Her flight was scheduled to return on April 24. As each day passed my "due date," (if I recall correctly was in the first week in April) my mother was clearly more and more uncomfortable. She worried relentlessly about my father, she said, what would he do in her absence. How would he eat? How would he wear clean clothes? He'd be so bereft. I finally spoke to a doctor at UCLA where I was to deliver who offered me no clarity. It'll happen when it happens I was told. Since we had no health insurance nor had ever even thought about it, I would deliver in their maternity clinic and it was already eminently clear that this was not a first tier facility (or even a second tier).

As each day passed, my mother's anxiety increased. She finally mentioned that she'd have to pay a huge fee if she had to extend her return flight. It was one of the few times that I was able to see her anxiety. My mother was a master of invisibility. The only affect I had ever seen was related to the slaughter of Jews and on one occasion, a long, long time before when she saw a woman in a pharmacy whom she recognized. Her face tensed, a look of anger that was totally unfamiliar to me. She leaned over as if to tell me a secret: "That woman wants your daddy!" she said. I could have keeled over right then and there. For her to confide THAT sentiment was, to me, completely anathema, especially since I was then still a child. I thought she might even cry which would have been a first. "It's terrible not being able to hear....," she said ruefully. "Women know I can't hear what they're saying to daddy."

It never occurred to me that my mother might feel jealousy, or envy, or anger or any other authentic feeling. How interesting that the only time I'd seen affect on her face was related to feeling threatened as a female. She didn't regret her deafness because she could barely hear what her daughter was saying. She regretted it because it disarmed her in her competition with other women. In retrospect it makes complete sense, knowing what I'd come to know about my father and his affair with my mother's cousin. I suspect this was not the last of his dalliances though I'd never know that for sure.

(Years later when Marcy and I came back from Colombia and we moved into the Hotel Albert for a few days until our sub-tenants moved out of our apartment, my father came to visit. I met him in the lobby of the hotel and we began to walk towards the elevator. As we passed the front desk, he said to the desk clerk almost incidentally, "This is my daughter." Why in the world would he offer that information? No one had asked him. What was he thinking? It later occurred to me that he wanted the desk clerk to know I was not a prostitute, he a much older well-dressed man and me a dolled-up, flashy eighteen year old. He was my father and not a "customer." How odd. That possible confusion had never crossed my mind. Why had it crossed his? When it occurred to me that this was what he might have been thinking, I felt defiled. Did HE see me in sexual way? I can't imagine that he did but he was probably used to others seeing HIM in a sexual way. He was handsome, after all, extremely charismatic and always the center of attention....particularly the attention of woman, it seems.)

In any case, I knew my mother was getting anxious and I had passed my due date several days before so I suggested to her, in all earnestness, that she return on her scheduled flight. After a prolonged conversation she agreed to go home as planned. As it happened, the birth was three weeks later than expected. One interesting event that I wasn't able to integrate for a long period of time was that I went into labor sometimes passed midnight at our home in Pasadena, over an hours drive to the UCLA Medical Center. When we arrived Johnny came to the delivery room with me. Mind you, we were clinic patients so there was very little attention paid to my condition. I was now a good eight hours into labor when Johnny announced that he had to leave to get some sleep. The statement bothered me but I also understood that he had had no sleep the night before. I have no idea where he went though I can't imagine he'd drive all the way back to Pasadena. Most husbands in that position would simply doze off in a chair in the room or force themselves to stay awake. (Until very recently, it bothered me that he left, until a cataclysmic event years later in New York.)

After several more hours it was clear that the baby was not any closer to delivery. A doctor examined me and said the baby was upside down and would have to be inverted. Of course I had no idea how that would be done until the doctor simply took his hand, placed it inside of me and literally turned the baby to his proper position. The pain was unlike anything I had ever experienced, as if a spiked bowling ball was lodged in my stomach and had to be inverted, every spike tearing through my insides. Finally when the torture was over the baby's birth followed easily.

By the time Johnny returned he was greeted by the most beautiful 9 lb.8 oz. male baby ever born, cooing, angelic, a miracle sight. We named him "Roni" in keeping with the 60's counterculture and because we couldn't agree on another name. (Later Roni would complain about his name, wanting a more common name like Steven or Tony or Ed. I told him he was born in the '60's and was lucky we didn't name him "Moon Unit." He ultimately decided to change it himself to Ronald since most people assumed that was his name all along.)

I'm not sure how to describe my mood when we finally returned to Pasadena except to say it was probably what most people feel when they say they are utterly and completely at peace. Certainly there were times in my life when I felt happiness but that was always, I suspect, relative to the times I felt unhappiness, like the times my father was in a good mood and I knew my brother and I were safe. It was always conditional. This was different. It was a sense of absolute peace, not contingent on anyone or anything, a sense that all was right in the universe, just because …. and would remain so for years to come.

STUDENT LIFE

NO SOONER HAD our son been born, I knew I could not go back to waitressing. I asked one of my husband's friends how I would go to college in California, given my college experience in New York. I don't know why I even thought of returning to school but it seemed completely natural and anxiety-free, what any adolescent would think about except I was no longer an adolescent. He told me that California has Community Colleges that are opened to ANYONE, at least for one semester, till you prove your seriousness.

Pasadena City College (PCC) was a short, bus ride away so when my baby was just a few weeks old, I put him in a baby sling and went to the admission office at PCC. Roni was born on April 30 and it was on one of the first weeks in May that I registered for summer school at Pasadena City College. I was allowed to take two classes during each of the two summer sessions. The admissions counselor, however, strongly suggested that I take only one class, given the new baby and my poor history at college. She also suggested I take an "easy" class so as not to be overwhelmed, so as not to stack the deck against myself. Her suggestions were immediately dismissed.

I don't know what the key had been but no sooner had I heard that I could go back to college, some puzzle was unlocked. I was absolutely determined to go back and to do well. Instead of taking one class, one "easy" class I took 2 classes, the maximum I could and they were solid academic classes, required courses, in fact. I was on a roll. It was the summer of 1966. I knew the moment I entered my first class that I would do well.

I carried Roni on my back though I occasionally moved him to my chest so he could see the world as I did, the classrooms, the faculty, the chalked writings on the boards He remained in that sling for about a year. Fortunately he was the sweetest, calmest baby I could imagine, and absolutely beautiful as well. If he wasn't asleep, he was cooing, observing everything in his field of vision and utterly delightful. Since I hadn't grown up around babies, I didn't know it could have been different; that some babies were "fussy," "colicky" irritable, that I was very, very lucky. I knew that I was lucky from the moment he was born, not really because he was an "easy" baby (which he certainly was) but because I was the happiest I had ever been, the happiest I imagined any woman had ever been. That void in the center of my being was absolutely gone. In its place was wellbeing, joy, utter pleasure. I think I was always smiling.

When the first summer session ended and I'd earned two A's, the advisor gave me the green light to enroll for the second summer session and when I got two more A's I was offered two teaching assistantships, grading papers in several fall classes. Of course I registered for the maximum allowable credits for the fall semester in which I likewise got all A's. (If I recall correctly I had to petition to take an extra class beyond the usual allowable maximum, which I think was 16 or 17.). I transferred to California State College in LA for the following spring semester and graduated in June of 1968 with a major in Psychology and again with grades of all A's, having competed a four-year degree in just over two years, including six summer sessions, two back-to-back each year with all "A's.

I knew Johnny was extremely proud of me. He didn't say it in those words but he made it known. He had gotten a job teaching sculpture at the Pasadena Art Museum, a job that made a world of difference in his self-esteem. Having been a *New York* artist with a show in the Whitney, a sculpture in the permanent collection of MOMA, and a host of other credits, he was a hot commodity. He was offered a full time teaching position at Cal State LA, the same school I was attending and from which I would eventually graduate. For a man who never went to high school, he was doing superbly. Between his income and mine from my teaching assistantships we were able to afford a baby sitter and eventually a lovely preschool (The French School) at Cal State, as well.

We had settled into a beautiful routine. Johnny taught at Cal State several days a week and worked in his studio in the back of the house the rest of the time. I took as many classes as I was allowed and spent the rest of the time with Roni, a few friends that I'd made from school and preparing meals for my family. Together Johnny and I played poker with his artist friends at least one night a week. It was a rotating game, always in a different home. When it was our turn to host the game (which I adored) I made a huge bowl of pasta, garlic bread, donuts for dessert and several gallons of cheap Mountain wine. Clearly I had not as yet become a chef but we were poor and it was easy.

One of the bright spots of these evenings, apart, of course, from the poker was our refrigerator. It was the one appliance we had to buy and we were able to get one at the Salvation Army. It was a really old refrigerator but it served its purpose. When, after some time, the door handle ultimately broke off I tried to figure out how we could afford another refrigerator. Before I had resolved the dilemma, Roni had a screwdriver in the hole from which the handle had broken, raised the tip of the screwdriver upward and opened the door! He couldn't have been more than two. It happened on a night of our poker game and everyone went crazy, laughing, kissing him, making a big fuss. As it turned out, whenever we had a game at our house, everyone asked Roni if he would be kind enough to open the refrigerator. It was a highlight of those wonderful evening.

Another special event was a year when the Rose Bowl was played in Pasadena. I don't recall the date and neither I nor Johnny kept up with sports. Neither of us would have ever even known about the Rose Bowl except that from early in the morning on that particular day the traffic in our neighborhood was getting dreadful. We apparently lived within a few blocks of the Rose Bowl stadium and people began to ring our bell asking if they could park their car on our property. Initially when we were asked, having no idea about the game or even where the Rose Bowl was, we just told the first few people who asked that they needn't pay us. They could simply park. When we finally realized what was happening we put a large sign in front of our driveway and directed the cars to every available inch of our large property. We made more money on that one day than we'd probably made in 6 months.

By the time I graduated in June of 1968, I was exploring the possibility of going to medical school. At the same time I applied for a Master's degree in Psychology at Cal State while I explored my various options. My mother-in-law had visited shortly after Roni's birth and I picked her up at the airport with the large van John used to transport his sculptures. When she saw me pull up in that huge truck she smiled approvingly ear to ear. "Look at you," she said, proudly, " driving that big truck! You're really something!" I suspect her approval was coupled with great relief. Here, her first son had been in such trouble earlier in his life, such despair, and I'm certain part of her love for me was that she knew I would not condemn him, I would not expect of him things he could not deliver. To the contrary, I celebrated the fact that he was an artist and joined him in his dream. I even drove that old, monstrous moving van. Our visit was wonderful.

The following year, when I was getting my MA, my parents decided to visit. In preparation, I spent my free time making the house welcoming. Now, granted, the house itself was an architect's dream, although it was modestly decorated. The furniture was the furniture left by our architect landlord. I splurged on new sheets, blankets and pillows for the full-size bed in the second bedroom upstairs next to Roni's room and new towels and toiletries for the upstairs bathroom. I assumed my parents would be comfortable upstairs with far more privacy. I made the house more welcoming and attractive and cooked a lovely meal for their arrival. It was a very proud moment in our lives since I was graduating and Johnny was a professor of art at Cal State. I picked them up at the airport as I had done with my Mother-in-law and we drove back to Pasadena. I was proud as I opened the gate into our Spanish garden enclosed by its six-foot high Spanish-tiled wall with fountains and sculptures.

When my parents walked thru the main door to our home, I had never thought twice about the fact that Johnny and I slept on a large mattress on the living room floor. However, my father had apparently seen the mattress on the floor, and exclaimed contemptuously: "What a gypsy existence THIS is!" I was devastated. I never forgot that insult and never forgave him for it.

To make matters far worse, when they brought their bags upstairs to the bedroom, I told them cautiously: "If you have any pills or medications let me store them out of Roni's reach. When they finished unpacking they came back downstairs with Roni, happy as a lark, right behind them, his mouth and tongue deep blue. I screamed and ran back upstairs to see what he had found. On the floor of my parents bedroom were blue pills scattered all over the floor. I found the pill bottle which said they were for blood pressure. I didn't bother with niceties. I grabbed Roni and literally raced the three blocks to the hospital emergency room, running all the way. By the time he was examined, he was groggy and slightly limp. There was no antidote, I was told. He'd simply have to be watched overnight to see how bad it got!! I was beside myself, in a state of absolute terror. Johnny finally showed up and the two us kept a vigil as our son's life was in danger.

Finally, in the morning, they discharged him with apparently no lasting ill-effects of the medication. When we got home, my parents were frozen with dread. They saw that Roni was well and we scarcely said a word about what had ensued. My father did say that he had forgotten about his medication and was sorry. For a man who never apologized about ANYTHING, this was quite remarkable. Nothing more was said.

They only stayed for 2 more days, which was all I could, in fact, tolerate. Johnny was gracious and welcoming although I don't know I could have been so restrained had the situation been reversed.

In June of 1969 I got my MA in Psychology (also with straight A's) and, as I did with my BA, graduated Magna Cum Laude. I was offered several full scholarships for Ph.D studies, with The University of Southern California (USC) making the most attractive offer: a full tuition scholarship in addition to an extravagant living allowance that amounted to more, in fact, than we'd ever earned. While I would have preferred going to medical school, the decision was relatively easy. I could not turn down USC's offer. (I seem to recall having been told that medical schools would not award female students full tuition loans although I'm not, in fact, sure that was the case. Maybe it was something I conjured up in my own head to justify not, at least, applying. I was, after all, a wife and the mother of a toddler whom I adored spending time with and medical school would have put us in debt for years to come.)

In the midst of these life-changing events, my brother called to tell me that he and Florence were splitting up. He was leaving his internship at Yale and eager to transfer to a medical school in California to complete the rest of it. I told him I had planned on attending USC for my Ph.D and he decided to transfer there as well. He arrived in Calif. just prior to my graduating from Cal State and rented a small apartment in LA.

USC

THROUGHOUT MY YEARS at CSLA, Johnny, Roni and I were at the same location and all doing wonderfully. About the same time construction of the long-overdue Pasadena Freeway was about to begin. The timing could not have been more perfect. Just before I began my Ph.D studies in June of 1969 we moved closer to USC and John got a fabulous storefront in South Central LA that would be his studio. I continued getting all A's although the novelty had begun to wear off. In addition, the anti-war movement was in full swing in Los Angeles and I was beginning to feel badly about not participating. I ultimately joined my peers and made a trip to the Haight-Ashbury district in San Francisco for an anti-war rally. I took Roni with me, as I usually did, never questioning the decision. As it turned out the crowd was infinitely larger than any had been in Los Angeles.

With Roni in my arms, we were in the midst of a huge crowd packed against each other with little room to move. I assumed he'd be upset by the tumult but, rather, he was fascinated by the Hippies and the Flower Children who were everywhere. Their clothing was not altogether new to him but in their sheer number it was a visual feast: ever color in the rainbow, tiaras, half-nude girls, a guy with a parrot on his head.

Then, out of nowhere, an explosion, and the air thickened. Tear gas had been shot into the crowd by the police making it hard to see and even harder to breathe. I hid Roni's face in my chest and pushed my way through the crowd as if I were a line backer. We finally managed to get out of the center of the crowd and into a hotel lobby where I washed out his eyes and mine, as well.

For a three-year old who was frightened and in pain, he was a trooper and apparently more able to cope than many kids his age seemed able to do, partly, I think because he was brilliant. He was speaking earlier than any of his peers and was able, at this particular juncture, to express himself so well, evidence of his amazing intelligence. He talked all the way home.

Going to San Francisco on that particular day was memorable for another reason, one that surprisingly was not as upsetting to me as the tear gas had been. In class, before we left, the instructor, apparently annoyed that so many of his students were taking off class to demonstrate, had warned us that we MUST be present for an exam the following day, the day I was to leave for San Francisco. I had not skipped a class since I'd returned to school. Whereas getting to class was such a source of pride, having once been unable to do so, attending class now, when others were protesting what needed to be protested, was beginning to make me feel ASHAMED!! I decided, knowing full well the price I'd pay, to go to a protest demonstration in Haight-Ashbury, regardless. It was really a pivotal moment I have come to realize. I did not have to turn myself inside out to feel good about myself. I no longer felt foreign. I no longer felt like a genetic mutation. I always suspected I was competent (at least in certain spheres) but now I knew I was competent in the real world; Bea Starr was competent, a mother, a wife, a student, Bea from Brooklyn, New York. That stunning awareness allowed me to forego the perfect grade. And, in fact, as a result of that rally, I got the one and only B of my college experience .... a source of pride for years to come, not because I hadn't gotten more B's but because I had gotten THAT one B!

Getting that grade was significant in another way. Shortly after we'd moved closer to USC, I was walking through a mall in LA when someone tapped me on the shoulder. I turned around and there in front of me was Carole Klein, a neighbor from Brooklyn and classmate at James Madison High School.

"Carole," I said, astonished by the familiar face, "What are you doing in LA?"

"Writing music," she responded casually. Poor girl, I thought.... What a shame and she's so smart too.

"And what are you doing here?" she asked.

"I'm in the doctoral program at USC," I answered lowering my tone so as not to call attention to my achievement.

We chatted for a few minutes about Brooklyn, hippies and how the world had changed when I said I had to get back to my house and make dinner for my family. She wrote her number on a slip of paper and made me promise to call her. I didn't think much of it except that I knew I'd have no time to socialize before I'd have to start my dissertation. When I got home Johnny was reading the paper. I mentioned running into Carole Klein when I noticed a huge ad on the very page he happened to be looking at. There, right before my eyes, was a full-page photo of Carole **King**, apparently one of the most famous singers and songwriters of the time. It was Carole Klein!

I don't know if I would have called had I not seen her staggering celebrity.. for my free time was always very stretched, but I do know that having seen that ad, my embarrassment was overwhelming. It wasn't simply that I was so removed from the world that I'd never heard of Carole **King**. It was my initial reaction, that this very smart young woman was ***only a songwriter,*** a songwriter, a dime a dozen! I wanted to crawl under a rug!

(Interestingly enough, years later I got a call from my son who, at that time, was an attorney in the White House. A woman had been referred to him since she was very involved in conservation and was told that he was the person to speak with. The woman was Carole King. She and my son talked in his office and he apparently mentioned that she had the same "accent" as his mother. She asked where I was from and he responded "Brooklyn."

"I'm from Brooklyn," she said. "Where in Brooklyn?"

"Sheepshead Bay."

"I'm from Sheepshead Bay....What High School did she go to?
"James Madison," he answered.
"You've got to be kidding! I went to Madison. What's her name?"
"Bea Starr."
"OMG. We've got to call her."
And they did. Actually Carole called and spoke first. I almost fell off the chair. "You must be so proud of your son," she said in an instant. And of course I was but I was more struck by her character, that she, as famous as the Beatles would have the poise to compliment *me* and that *I*, those years before in LA responded to her telling me that she was writing music with a hidden haughtiness that continued to shame me.)

The final hurdle in my Ph.D studies was my Orals, the Oral Examination that one typically takes after completing ones dissertation. A dissertation was expected to be a unique contribution to your field of study, which must add to the knowledge of that field and thus, required you to know everything there is to know in that particular area, at least that's how it was at that time. Given that, the examiners would have to be scholars in that field. I didn't know any of my examiners personally except for Dr. Al Marston, the Chairman of the Dept. of Psychology at USC and the sponsor of my dissertation. I'd never met any of the other members but knew their names, their work and their reputations. Clearly one's Orals are very intimidating at least they were for me. (I must add that this was 1971. Computers were just beginning to be known to the general population. I was, in fact, one of the first USC graduates to have written her dissertation on a computer, a huge "appliance" the size of a refrigerator.)

As I prepared to get Roni ready for his pre-school and get myself ready for my orals, Johnny was also getting ready. I was confused because that particular day was not a teaching day for him. It would be, I assumed, a day he worked in his studio. His studio time was very prized. I asked him where he was going.

"With you." He responded matter-of-factly.

I was completely perplexed, until I saw the expression in his eyes. Johnny rarely said more than needed to be said, but I knew when I looked at him that he was coming to be my cheering squad, my moral support, perhaps my protector. I don't think he knew, as I didn't, that no one was allowed in the examining room with me but I doubt it would have made a difference. I had no idea what I was in for and I suspect he assumed that whatever it was, his support would be of help. We had never discussed my dissertation. I had never expressed my anxiety. I had never in my wildest imagination thought of asking him to accompany me, but that was Johnny, a man of few words and as devoted as the day was long when he understood his actions to be expressions of devotion.

When we got to USC, Dr. Marston met us in the Psych Department. He had met Johnny before and greeted him cordially, motioning me into an anteroom and Johnny to remain in the waiting room. I didn't know how long the examination would be but I noticed that Johnny had brought along several copies of Art Forum, his preferred reading as he kissed me good-buy.

There were six examiners in the room apart from Dr. Marston, a very intimidating yet awe-inspiring group. There was virtually no small talk and the substance of the examination began immediately, questions about my research, "The Timing of Reinforcement in A Covert Aversive Conditioning Paradigm," why I used a particular statistical model; how did I resolve my results with so-and-so's in 1961, with so-and-so in 1968? What do I think of this theory or those results, this behavioral model or that?

After what seemed like hours of questions and follow-up questions without any feedback whatsoever, not a nod of affirmation, not a raised eye-brow of confusion, not a hint of reaction one way or another, out of the blue, without any preparation, one of the examiners asked me to leave the room. I was devastated, beside myself. I had no idea what I'd said wrong, if I'd said anything wrong, but, even if I had, I certainly didn't think I'd done so poorly as to be literally thrown out of the room. When I saw Johnny in the waiting room, I burst into tears. He put his arms around me and asked me what had happened. I told him I must have screwed up royally. Just then, Dr. Marston came out. He extended his hand to me, smiling proudly as a parent would, "Congratulations, Dr. Marino."

It was the first time for a long time to come, that I would hear that salutation. To this day, I find it hard to communicate the enormity of that event, for this girl, this foreigner, this school phobic, this imposter, this girl who speaks in tongues.

RETURNING HOME

I GRADUATED IN June of 1971, having finished long before expected. In anticipation of graduating, Johnny and I had decided to return to New York and so I applied for my internship at the Veteran's Hospital in New York City. I was accepted immediately. I flew back to New York with Roni and Johnny drove his truck back with all our belongings. We stayed at my mother-in-law's apartment in the Bronx while I began looking for an apartment for us in Manhattan. It took Johnny almost a week to drive cross-country and in the interim, Roni began running a high fever. We called a doctor Mrs. Marino knew who came over immediately. When he was done examining Roni, he turned to me with a serious tone and told me that he has a hole in his heart! I would need to take him to a pediatric cardiologist. It did not have to be done immediately but it had to be done. I couldn't absorb what he was saying. What does that mean? What are you saying? He has a hole in his heart that he was born with, the doctor said. He didn't know if the hole was in the lower or upper chamber of his heart but it was congenital, not terribly unusual but something that would need to be corrected.

Children are born with a tiny hole in their heart, he explained, which usually closes by itself as the child grows. If it doesn't close properly, it needs to be closed surgically! I was beside myself! This was the first I'd ever heard of this but it was also the first time in his young life that he had ever run a high fever. The fever, I recall the doctor saying, is probably what had re-opened the hole before it had fully closed itself.

When Johnny got back to New York, we took Roni to Bellevue Hospital Pediatric Cardiology Unit which was right next door to the Manhattan VA Hospital where I had already begun my internship. My health insurance that had covered us at USC had not yet begun through the V.A., thus, we were again relegated to being "clinic patients." By the time Christmas came, we still had no insurance coverage and Roni was being followed by doctors at Bellevue. Despite my attempts to fully understand Roni's health situation, my questions were continually rebuffed and dismissed as if to say, "You're clinic patients and we've already given you enough time"… Had we not been "clinic" patients, there's no doubt in my mind that his doctors would have been more responsive and communicative.

My internship was hectic. We were overloaded with Viet Nam vets wounded in battle and while I was in staunch opposition to the war from its beginning, now, having seen the cost up close, my heart was heavy. There were also World War II veterans, some of whom never recovered. One veteran who survived the attack on the Arizona, struggled with flashbacks of such magnitude that he was never free of the sights, the screams, the smell of flesh burning, his buddies drowning in the water, being eaten by sharks just out of his reach. I'll never forget some of the experiences revealed to me in therapy that to this day continue to haunt me as they did my patients.

As "Clinic Patients" at Belleview, it was the first time since childhood that I understood what my mother had tried to make me aware of, not just the enormity of racial hatred toward Jews that resulted in the Holocaust but the enormity of racial disparity between white and non-white Americans here in America and the suffering that ensued. It was why she marched when she did and attended rallies and stood on picket lines, why she was a member of "subversive" organizations that Jewish and non-Jewish immigrants who had no experience with the Holocaust avoided. It's why she was a staunch supporter of civil rights and why, in these arenas, her voice was clear and powerful.

In retrospect, I don't ever recall her having difficulty hearing anything said on TV, on the news or in conversation, about either Anti-Semitism or Racism. Perhaps I'm wrong but that is my recollection.

Waiting in Belleview's Pediatric Cardiology Waiting Room was a staggering awakening. The waiting room was lined, on each side, with dozens of mothers and their young children, mostly Black and Brown parents and children ....facing one another awkwardly as you'd expect given the circumstances....and then there was Roni and then there was me. While I have no doubt these other parents and children were as worried as I about the health of their children, they "appeared" far more able to contemplate whatever the outcome, I assume as Jews "appeared" able to contemplate what lay ahead of them when they climbed up the railway cars to their final destination.

Much has been written about Jews walking to their deaths "like sheep to slaughter," ignorant conjecture by people who were not there, by Jews and non-Jews alike, wholly unfamiliar with the lives of Jews in Nazi-occupied Europe. I sensed that these parents and their children were as traumatized as I by a system that seemed to operate independent of them, in spite of them. The only difference, I suspect, was that my child and I were White and new to this trauma and had not, as yet, been beaten down by its realties.

My anxiety over Roni's atrial defect continued to haunt me. The fact that the "clinic" experience at Bellevue was what it was made my worries all the more pressing. On the most recent occasion I was so disheartened by the workings of the clinic that I decided to reach out to the chief cardiologist at the VA. Hospital for advice. I introduced myself to him and told him about our experiences at Bellevue, about our most recent visit where I was told by the doctor (who was never the same as the doctor we'd seen on previous visits), that I was to bring Roni back that particular Friday for surgery. I shook. Not an explanation, not a word of clarification, not a word of comfort as he left the examining room abruptly with me running after him beseeching him to "Wait! Wait! What is wrong with him? What is wrong with my son?" His pace quickened as he hurried down the long hall, refusing to stop, seemingly deaf to my fears! Instead, a social worker approached me, grabbed my arm to stop me from this outrageous display of ingratitude and patronizingly asked why I was yelling. Behind her were two men ready to do whatever needed to be done to stop this over-reacting mother who was obviously out of control and probably high on who-knows-what! (It was then I knew I had to see the Cardiologist at the VA and get his help. And I did so that very same day.)

"Did you tell them you're Dr. Marino?" the Chief Cardiologist at the VA asked me immediately. It had never occurred to me to do so. It never occurred to me that it would make a difference. My title was so new and, as yet, I was wholly unaware of the advantages that accompanied it. He wrote a name on a piece of paper as he got on the phone to speak to someone. "I'm sending Dr. Marino over to see you now. I'm sure you'll answer all her questions." When he hung up the phone he told me to go back to Belleview and speak to the head of Pediatric Cardiology, a woman whose name I cannot recall. He told me to head over there as soon as I left his office and that he would speak to the Chairman of the Psych. Internship to let him know I had an appointment and would probably be out the rest of the afternoon. I raced the few blocks to Bellevue and went directly to the office he had called.

So you're Dr. Marino, the female doctor said, greeting me cordially. On her desk was Roni's full medical record, graphs, x-ray reports, notes from each of Roni's prior visits to the clinic. She invited me to review the record though I assume she knew I was a Psychology Ph.D and would have limited knowledge of its meaning. Just her willingness to allow me access to the records was heartening. No procedure, no outcome was secret or malevolent.

"If I were you, Dr. Marino, she whispered conspiratorially, leaning closer to me, after I'd read the record as best I could, I'd take him to Mr. Sinai. I've already taken the liberty of contacting Dr.

STUMBLING HOME

Leonard Steinfeld, their Chief of Pediatric Cardiology, and he's willing to see you both this afternoon." I was stunned but also dreadfully disappointed.

"I gather you don't know we have no insurance," I said somberly.

"I do know," she said reassuringly, "and it will make no difference. That's the kind of man he is."

And she was absolutely right. On our very first visit with him that same afternoon, he told me that Roni had presented an **'*interesting teaching case*'** for Pediatric Surgeons but that he would not perform that surgery.

"We'll watch him carefully," he said, " and I believe the hole will close on its own. I'm convinced the only lasting consequence of this situation is that he'll never be drafted!!!" This, in the middle of the war in Viet Nam, did not fall on deaf ears. And that was indeed the case.

As I was completing my year at the VA, I was offered a coveted position at the Out-Patient VA Hospital on 7th Avenue. It was highly unusual for an intern to be invited to stay on as a full-time staff Psychologist and, of course, I accepted immediately. Johnny and I found a tiny apartment on Gay Street, one of the Village's most historic meandering streets.

The apartment was advertised as a one-bedroom apartment although the total square footage could not have been more than 300 sq. Ft., maybe even less. It would simply have to due until we saved enough money to rent a proper apartment. Johnny built a bunk bed in the one tiny bedroom below which he and I slept. I enrolled Roni in PS 3 in the West Village, a delightful, child-centered, progressive school that was just a few short blocks from our apartment and Johnny got a part-time position teaching sculpture at an adult-education program in Great Neck.

RETURNING HOME

At the end of the first day on my new job, the head Psychiatrist approached me and told me I should be wearing a white medical jacket over my street clothes. I asked if it was necessary and he replied that it was —- to distinguish between the doctors and the patients. That very moment I knew I was in the wrong job. This was several years before the screening of "One Flew Over the Cuckoos Nest" and so in that sense I was prodigal. I may not have had the same combat wounds as my patients but I had my own combat wounds and I was not about to pretend I didn't. He also asked me to remove my make-up when I came to work, I should not be seductive with my patients! I told him I didn't think the job was the right fit for me and I'd be leaving at the end of the week.

In the mean time I searched for another position. I was lucky enough to be offered a position as a Psychologist at a Catholic Agency on the Upper West Side of Manhattan. I was interviewed by Sister Ann Marie, an interesting, very bright woman, savvy and seemingly unaffected by the changes and tumult that accompanied the '60s and '70s. That particular location housed an adolescent group home where I would work initially until I learned more about the plight of adolescents remanded by the court system and the services offered to them by the agency.

I made friends with the staff easily, all of whom (with the exception of their male Psychiatrist and myself) where social workers and nuns in the Order. As I said, it was a turbulent time in America; the Viet Nam war, issues of gender equality, sexuality, racial equality, environmental controversies and so forth. The nuns were not immune to any of these issues and had, for the most part, thoughtful, examined positions on them all. Several of them were in fact reconsidering their decision to join the order as so many young Americans were reexamining foundational issues in their lives. Others were considering joining the order, who, heretofore, had not considered it.

I had never been close to anyone who had profound religious convictions. The wit and wisdom of many of these women impressed me enormously and we quickly established a small group of friends and made it a point to go out at least one night every other week for dinner. I was utterly surprised and pleased with their candor as though they had known me all of their lives. We shared secrets and laughed at shared predicaments, and sometimes we even drank a bit too much.

My old friend Miriam had recently married a one-time heroin addict who had managed to get clean and together with several other former addicts, had founded a drug recovery program in Manhattan. Jimmy greatly admired Johnny who, like himself, grew up dirt poor on the mean streets of the Bronx and, who like himself, managed to get clean. Jimmy looked up to Johnny, 20 years his senior, and it was clear the two had much in common. The following winter, they invited us for Christmas Eve dinner at their apartment while Roni stayed overnight with my mother-in-law. It was a lovely evening.

We were all so pleased to have reconnected when, in the middle of dinner, Johnny leaned over to me at the table, saying almost inaudibly: "We have to go!" Before I could even respond he was standing up, putting on his coat and racing out the door. I was startled. We all were. Johnny had never been rude or so impulsive. I grabbed my own coat, saying nothing to our hosts and ran down the stairs calling for him to wait. Wait! It was all so bizarre since Miriam lived on a high floor and Johnny had not even bothered to wait for the elevator. I couldn't imagine what in the world had happened yet I knew something had indeed occurred.

"I'm having a heart attack," he blurted out to a cab driver who, fortunately, had just pulled over to allow his passenger to disembark. St Vincent's Hospital, the closest hospital, was only 4 blocks away from Miriam's apartment so I knew that for Johnny to take a cab for 4 blocks, something had to be terribly wrong.

When we entered the waiting room, Johnny was swiftly placed on a gurney and led into the emergency room, lights flashing, voices yelling over the loud speakers as I sat in utter terror. With out even realizing it, a nun in full habit sat down next to me and wrapped me in her arms, without saying a word. We sat that way, in silence for what appeared to be hours until a doctor finally came to speak to me. It was a major heart attack, he told me, and his condition was very precarious. The nun did not leave my side nor say a word until I was finally allowed to see Johnny in the Cardiac Intensive Care Unit.

For two months I would take Roni to school in the morning, race to St. Vincent's, go to work, pick up Roni and go back to St Vincent's for a brief visit in the evening. Roni was not allowed in the ICU all that time so I'd have him record a message in a small tape player, play it for Johnny when I got there and then have Johnny record a response. That's how they were able to communicate for the entire hospitalization.

The second event that stands out in my mind, was when I'd come to visit on one particular day when I heard Johnny cursing at the top his voice to "Get him the fuck out of here."

Johnny rarely cursed. He was a soft-spoken, courteous man who NEVER lost his temper, at least not for as long as I knew him. It was so unlike him. Johnny never yelled. NEVER. Had that not been the case, I could not have married him for a man's anger was too frightening to me.

I couldn't imagine what was going on until I got to his room and he told me to get the nurse out of his room. And than he told me that she had brought a priest in to administer the last rites! He was livid and, and I'm certain, terrified. His initial mistrust of priests since he was first arrested as a teenager, coupled with the lack of any preparation or discussion surrounding the Last Rites sent him into a tail pin. Who would not have responded in that very same way having been confronted with the very real possibility of one's own death? It was probably the lowest point in his long, protracted hospitalization.

The third event that shook me to my core was when I visited another day to find that Johnny had no teeth! I couldn't, for the life of me, know how a man's teeth could simply disappear. I approached one of the ICU nurses in a panic. Had a male staff member been called to restrain him? Had a goon walloped him? None of these, the nurse explained. He had "swallowed" his teeth while he slept.

"Swallowed his teeth," I screamed. "How's that possible?"

"That's why some people remove their teeth before they go to sleep," she relied. "They were fake. I'm sure you knew that."

I stood motionless, in disbelief. Of course I didn't know that, but how could I not have? All these years.......all the secrets we shared. My heart broke for this man who had to hide his shame from me, who told me the very first night I stayed over that he'd been in prison, twice; that he'd been an addict, told me that he'd seen my bitten nails (that I had tried to hide from him) and told me that my nails were "lovely". And yet what he couldn't share, what he had hidden so cleverly and consistently for more than ten years was a set of false teeth??? The thought that must have gone into keeping that secret, the planning, the self-loathing, it broke my heart. Did he think so little of me that I would reject him because his teeth were poor? Then I thought of Freddy Versace pirouetting around flaunting his false teeth. None of it made any sense to me and I was left with a broken heart for my husband who had to hide, for so long, such a meaningless and irrelevant fact.

I was no stranger to shame and secrets so the tragedy did not elude me. It occurred to me then that that must be the reason he always kissed me with his mouth closed. It also told me why when the delivery of our baby was taking so long and he thought he might fall asleep, he told me he was driving back to Pasadena to get some sleep. *Maybe he didn't drive anywhere,* I thought. Maybe he simply went to the van in the parking lot of the hospital to get some sleep where he could remove his teeth in private.

On one visit, after approximately two months in the Cardiac Intensive Care Unit, the doctor took me aside. He put his hand on my shoulder parentally, looked straight in my eyes as if searching for something……. then simply said:

"You're husband is as sick as a person can be and still be alive."

It was hard to process the information, to understand what he was telling me. "But he is alive. Right?"

"Yes but we can do no more for him here. We're discharging him first thing in the morning. "

"Then he's better if he can come home?"

"No. There's just nothing more we can do for him here."

I couldn't quite grasp the ambiguity. You're sending him home but he's not OK? Then why are you sending him home? I went into Johnny's room to tell him the good news that he's coming home in the morning. He looked rested and relieved that he was going home. I didn't tell him exactly what the doctor had said and didn't ask what the doctor had told him. He didn't offer that information either. I suspect I was in a state of complete denial. I kept playing those few sentences over in my head and just couldn't comprehend: "Then why are you sending him home?"

In fact I slept reasonably well that night and Roni and I talked about how terrific it was that his father was coming home. *The phrase "We're sending him home to die," never crossed my mind."* Instead, I suspected they knew he was better but didn't want to get my hopes up too high, in the event his full recovery took longer then expected.

I got up early the next morning to shower and take Roni to school then head to St. Vincent's. Our short walk to PS 3 was chipper and upbeat. I kissed him good-bye reminding him I'd be there to pick him up when school was over. From the school I walked directly to St. Vincent's to pick up Johnny. I thought about the nice reunions we'd all have and reminded myself to pick up a few special foods for Johnny.

Johnny's discharge was uneventful and even upbeat. I thanked everyone for saving my husband's life and told them that despite how nice they were, I hoped I'd never see any of them again. Even Johnny laughed a bit. When we got back to our apartment, I made Johnny as comfortable as I could and heated up some tea. He called me over to him and said lovingly: "We're quite a team." I agreed. We talked and talked about our plans for the future and cuddled tenderly till I realized it was almost time to pick Roni up from school. I called the doctor to tell him we'd gotten home and asked him if he thought I could leave briefly to pick up our son a few blocks away on Hudson Street.

"This is as good as it's going to be so you may as well get used to it and do what you have to do." I found the comment rude and incomprehensible. I still couldn't grasp why they'd send him home if he wasn't OK. I told Johnny I was headed to pick up Roni and would be back in about twenty minutes. I blew him a kiss and left. When we returned, I unlocked the door to our apartment with Roni just a few feet behind me. I could see Johnny was no longer in his bed. The bathroom door was open. Johnny was on the floor motionless.

I poised myself, as if catatonic, and in the most matter-of-fact voice turned to Roni and asked him if he wanted to visit "aunt" Becky just around the corner. Of course he knew her well since she was one of my closest friends. I told him to sit on the stoop just outside our door and I'd be right out. I called Becky, and again, in a totally controlled voice, asked her to pick Roni up at my apartment …to please keep him until she heard from me again. She knew something was wrong and asked me what had happened. "I think Johnny is dead!

THE STORM

GOING ON AUTOPILOT had always come easily when things had to be done, with the one exception of getting to Queens College all those years before. But this moment required it and I met the challenge, despite the anguish in my heart. First I called Johnny's friend, Jim Bradley, who came over immediately. Then the police came and told me they'd have to send the medical examiner before "the body" could be released. The term was so distasteful. Johnny was not "the body." And it was used over and over and over again. I had to let it go. Then I called Johnny's two brothers, Basil and Vincent who left work and came straight to the apartment. I called Becky back and told her what was happening and to please keep Roni until everything was resolved. I had to decide on a funeral parlor, I told her, and to wait for the medical examiner to release "the body."

    I finally decided, out of deference to my mother-in-law, it would be an Italian funeral parlor, a two-day wake with an open casket and any clergy they wished. While I knew Johnny would not want a priest, I also knew that, given the circumstances, he would want what would help his mother the most, and I suspected that would be a priest. The only thing I held firm to was that he would not be buried at St. Raymond's Cemetery in the Bronx, the cemetery where so many of his relatives were buried. He told me so often how long it had taken him psychologically to get out of the Bronx so I wasn't about to send him back there. And more importantly, I knew if I wanted to be buried with him, which I was adamant about, he would have to be buried in a non-sectarian cemetery.

I was clearly on autopilot; I was in a fugue state; but I was more capable than I'd ever been; goal directed, organized, utterly focused. I found a lovely non-sectarian cemetery on Long Island, Plain Lawn Cemetery, where I bought 3 graves, which I still have today.

The next few days were a long and airless black tunnel from which there was no escape until you managed to crawl through its length where, only there, you might or *might not* find air to breath.

I had already begun work at the Catholic Child Care agency before Johnny died and had already become extremely close to three of the nuns, Sister Adrienne, Sister Eileen and Sister Catherine. Since this was early 1973, the whole country was in flux. It was a time of great social turbulence, great change. I was closest to Eileen and the four of us went out after work fairly regularly to talk, to laugh, to share our inner struggles and to bond. I loved those evenings though occasionally we all drank a bit too much. Now I must remind you that I was Bea Marino at that time, Dr. Marino. It never occurred to me that they may not have known I was Jewish although looking back on that time, now, I can't believe that they hadn't known. We were so close and those evenings so honest. It was Johnny's death that caused me to wonder.

Every nun came to Johnny's funeral. While I am an atheist I occasionally adhere to several Jewish traditions like lighting the Menorah on Passover and following the rituals of mourning. I also speak a bit of Yiddish, the language my parent's often spoke at home (probably so my brother and I wouldn't know what they were talking about but, of course, we invariably understood). The point is, I certainly never tried to hide my Jewishness. To the contrary, it was one of the very few parts of me that I was truly comfortable with.

One of the Jewish traditions of mourning I decided to employ immediately. When someone close to you dies it is customary to cut a small piece of fabric and pin it to your shirt, a reference to the tearing of your clothes in grief. It's also customary to cover the mirrors in your home. This is no time for vanity. It's common to sit on wooden crates as opposed to comfortable chairs to remind yourself of the pain of loss. All of these practices made perfect sense to me and I was eager to follow them.

The Director of the agency for whom I worked was Sister Anne Marie, a short, overweight, dark-haired nun who was clearly very bright but also distant and a bit authoritarian. I remember vividly when Anne Marie came to Johnny's wake she stared, almost obsessively, at the cloth patch I had pinned to my shirt. I asked my close friend, Sister Eileen, why she thought Anne Marie was doing that. "I'll tell you later," she whispered.

After the burial, as is also customary, everyone came back to my tiny West Village apartment to "sit shiva." My dear Becky, whom I could always rely on in a time of need, did not come to the burial. Instead, she shopped for food for those who wished to come back to my home; she covered all the mirrors and gathered wooden crates to sit on. Becky was as close to a sister as I'd ever have and there was nothing I couldn't count on her for.

After the burial, many came back to the apartment as I'd anticipated. Becky had taken care of everything. When Sister Anne Marie walked in, she had the same look of astonishment on her face as she'd had when she saw me at the wake. Sister Eileen noticed my perplexity and took me aside for a moment:

"I thought you knew," she said quietly.

"Knew what?"

"That Anne Marie was born a Jew. She grew up in Brooklyn."

"A Jew??" I was astounded. "No. I'd never heard that."

"She grew up in an orthodox Jewish home," she told me. "Her father was a Holocaust survivor...... Eventually Anne Marie left home and converted to Catholicism and became a nun. Her father still lived in Brooklyn but refused to ever speak to her again. He died several months ago and made it clear that she was not allowed to attend his funeral. It was quite a scandal. I'm sure that's why she's been staring at you. She probably had no idea you were Jewish."

To say I was flabbergasted would be an understatement. Sister Anne Marie, whom I suspected was only a few years older than I, had apparently grown up close to me in Sheepshead Bay. It's remarkable that our paths never crossed, although her family's orthodoxy and my family's left-wing politics would never have connected us.

(It's an interesting dilemma since Israel, the very seat of Judaism was founded initially on a socialist model. As European Jews began immigrating to the area in the 19th century (and many earlier) they formed a communal living arrangement, the kibbutz, the corner stone of societal organization. It is, by definition, an egalitarian, collective, construct. People lived together, shared the fruits of their labors and benefitted equally from the profits of their work. Children were raised together communally. Everything was "ours." There was no private ownership. Of course, since its founding, in 1948, major changes have occurred and Israel is, today, a leading technological, democratic entity, with many, many privately owned companies trading on the Stock Exchanges around the world. However, many of the egalitarian underpinnings still exist. Healthcare and education are accessible to all. Racial diversity is inherent since Jews who were forced to flee ancient Israel two thousand years ago, the various "Lost Tribes of Israel, " have been returning to their ancestral homeland from around the world, many from Africa, India and throughout the Middle East since Israel's inception, many forced out of their countries because they were Jews.) ****

When I finally returned to work the following week, everything had changed. My work for the agency involved primarily individual and group Psychotherapy with the adolescent girls (who lived in one of the agency's group homes), consultation and occasional Psychological testing. I worked autonomously, although I suppose there was a hierarchy in place but one that was never made explicit, at least not from my perspective. I was the only Psychologist. There was one male Psychiatrist and many social workers, all of them nuns, if I'm not mistaken, including Sister Anne Marie.

One of my individual adolescent therapy patients, LuLu, was a beautiful, smart, young woman whom I'd seen regularly and had come to enjoy and respect. On one particular occasion she entered my office unusually distraught, announcing immediately that she thought she was pregnant. She talked about all that that meant. I asked if she'd seen a Gynecologist to confirm what she was concerned about. She said she was seeing one the following day. Shortly after seeing LuLu several more times, Sister Anne Marie called me into her office. It was the first time I'd seen her directly since Johnny's funeral and she abstained from any "small talk."

"Did you talk to LuLu about getting an abortion?" She asked directly.

"Excuse me?" I said, reflexively, taken aback, firstly by the question of how she knew what I might have spoken to LuLu about and secondly, by the violation of LuLu's privacy. "Sister, you know I can't discuss that with you."

"You know we are opposed to abortion....We will not allow any discussion or suggestion that would make an abortion more likely."

"Sister, as a general practice, I do not give my patients guidance as to what they should or should not do in any particular situation."

"But did you discuss abortion with her?" she persisted.

"Sister, you know I cannot tell you what we discuss in sessions."

"Dr. Marino, if you work for this agency then you must adhere to our principles, other wise you'll have to find another place to work." It was the first time since I had started working there that she referred to me as Dr. Marino. She was making a powerful statement, I suspected.

"Then I suppose you'll have to fill my position with someone else," I responded reflexively. To this day I have no idea why I took such a staunch posture. There are many other ways I could have handled the situation. But underneath I suspected she wanted me to leave because

I was a Jew and her father had just done to her the unimaginable. Imagine not being allowed to attend a parent's funeral! Imagine the PARENT forbidding it! I knew he was a Holocaust survivor but I'd like to believe that severing ties with ones own child is almost as out of the question as what the Nazis had done to the Jews----On the other hand, few people outside of Europe, certainly before and through the Holocaust, have any idea of the depth of Anti-Semitism that existed and the role of the Catholic Church in its creation. I say this fully cognizant that my family is primarily Italian and Irish Catholic and I love them all....and would hope that they can read what I'm writing in that context.

Jews, such as Ann Marie's father, must have grown up with the deadly Anti-Semitism that existed all throughout Europe and must have been one of its victims, although he, like so many other survivors probably NEVER spoke about it..... as he probably NEVER spoke about the Holocaust in general. SHE likely had no idea about this aspect of her Catholicism. Anti-Semitism was a way of life in Europe, the contempt for Jews, their exclusion from the larger Christian society and their repeated punishment as a result of the church's propaganda that the Jews killed Christ. So, I suspect, his daughter's decision to join "the enemy" must have felt to him like an ultimate and unpardonable betrayal. The few Christians who helped Jews (often saving their lives) did so in absolute secrecy. Had that not been the case, they and their families would have suffered the very same fate as the Jews (and some did!).

Now this was before the church opened its archives in the late 1960's wherein the general public had access to church doctrines, edicts and positions. And when it did, researchers of all religious persuasions including Catholic priests were astounded by the church's history of demonizing the Jews as Christ killers, as evil, of taunting the Jews and murdering them for the slightest provocation, real or imagined. For example, it was not uncommon for the town priest, such as in the town of Jebwabne in Poland, in 1941, to rile his parishioners

THE STORM

to the point where they gathered up all the town's Jews, forced them into a barn and set fire to it, burning them all alive. (Estimates of the number of Jews killed in this attack varies from 1,100 to 30,000, depending upon the source.) Many such events took place but were never made public, although the procedures seemed always to be the same: first you round up all the town Jews. (And if the family of one of those unfortunate Jews were to learn about it, there was absolutely nothing they could do. Their only choices were to make this travesty public or be shot to death along with their own immediate family, or keep silent!!!!). Jebwabne was not an isolated event. (See Buczacz in Poland in 1943 and a dozen other similar events). European Jews, such as Sister Ann Marie's father lived these horrific realities......so his daughter's conversion to the church that authored these events must have been simply unbearable. *

(*To understand the church's position you have to remember that Jesus was born to a Jewish mother and a Jewish father. By the time of the 3rd or 4th century ACE the new "Jewish Christians," as they were then called, had to find ways to distinguish themselves and their new religion from their old religion, "Judaism." In fact, they did so "brilliantly," with the most brilliant and creative public relations campaign that ever existed. The first stumbling block upon which all else hinged was the simple statement that Jesus was NOT Joseph's son. THAT was the groundwork upon which all else was built. He was, in fact, the son of god. And just how did that happen? It happened magically, "immaculately"! Once believing this, all else could follow easily. Now we must remember this was almost 2,000 years ago when little was known about science, physiology, biology, physics, the workings of the entire universe! People believed in any number of "gods" who were able to do any number of "magical" things, sun gods, wind gods, sea gods and so forth. Believing in those gods gave them some degree of comfort so the belief in an even more powerful god could not be so easily dismissed and it was upon this new god that the "Jewish Christians" formulated and developed their new religion. Still they had to account for the god of the Jews. Many people believe that the god of the Christians and the god of Jews is one and the same god but they then had to explain how this one god could abandon the Jews to the catastrophic events that befell them. That was another easy dilemma. They simply decided that the Jews killed god's son and were therefore evil. All else followed from this one assumption. And it was by demonizing the Jews, that their own new religion gathered steam. And by 350 ACE. (a mere 350 years later) Christianity was not only an established religion, it was the most promising religion of the day. (It was only several hundred years later, with the birth of Mohammed, that its supremacy was challenged).

To be honest, this topic is not my bailiwick. I have never read a bible, ANY bible, from cover to cover. I know as much (or as little) about the Old Testament as I do about the New Testament, or the Koran, for that matter. It doesn't interest me. The little I know I find pejorative, certainly to females. Most religions strike me as incredibly ambitious PR firms whose only real goals are wealth and power. I identify myself as a Jew because it was the family into which I was born, and I am fiercely protective of it, not because I know religion, but because I know history. Jews don't proselytize, they don't recruit, they don't promise eternal life…..but they also don't treat women as they do men. (I remember, as clearly as yesterday, going into a synagogue on some holiday and having to sit in the balcony even though there were available seats downstairs, closer to the front. When I asked why I could not sit there, I was told it was the men's section.)

ADULTHOOD

AFTER LEAVING MY position with the Catholic organization, I was hired almost immediately by a State Agency in New Jersey that represents Psychiatric patients and lost but a minimum of time in between jobs. In the interim, I called Dr. Steinfeld to let him know what had occurred and to arrange another visit with Roni. When I finally brought Roni in to see him, he put his arm on Roni's shoulder and simply talked to him:

"I bet you're wondering if what happened to your daddy will happen to you?" Roni nodded.

"There's nothing about what happened to your daddy that's like the reason you're here. You're going to be just fine. I have no doubt about it. You'll play softball, you'll play basketball, you'll run around like all the other kids. I have no doubt about it. The only outcome is that you'll never be drafted (and this in the middle of the Viet Name war!!!!!) In fact, you're doing so well that I don't think I'll need to see you again unless you and your mom think it's necessary. Then he hugged Roni in the most loving and considerate way. And he never, never gave me a bill!!!! What kind of a person does that? An Albert Schweitzer!

He reminded me of my Tanta Lena who had lived a few blocks from us in Brooklyn. She was low key, kind and very gentle. She and my Aunt Rhoda, my father's sister-in-law, were my closest relatives though they were very, very different. Tanta Lena was clearly from the old school, grandmotherly. She revered my father, as my mother did.

She was cautious with him and very deferential, the loving mother he had lost so many decades before. (She spoke with my parents in Yiddish so it's not surprising that she was referred to as Tanta Lena, Yiddish for "Aunt" whereas my Aunt Rhoda, born and raised in America, was simply Aunt Rhoda. While these descriptors may seem inconsequential, they, in fact, represented the difference between the old world and the new, the European Jew, engulfed in tragedy, poverty and ancient traditions and the American Jew for whom the sky was the limit.)

Tanta Lena was kosher and always made her own chicken soup which permeated her house with the most inviting aromas. What I remember is that I loved her, that she always smiled, at least when I saw her. And I always got a kiss from her. Always!

Tanta Lena and my uncle Jack lived with their daughter, Elsie, just three blocks from our home. She could not have been terribly old, maybe ten years older than my mother. My father had very tender feelings for her despite her orthodoxy because she was very maternal and very kind. What I remember most is a gold heart locket she gave me, probably for my fifth birthday which I never took off and kept in my mouth all the time, chewing it and sucking on it as if it were a nipple. I still have it, with all the teeth marks, the irrefutable evidence of a child terribly uncomfortable with herself and the world. It was the only piece of jewelry I ever got from anyone until I became a woman.

How does a mother not buy her daughter a little bracelet, a little ring, anything? How does a mother not fuss over her daughter, adorn her? How does a mother allow her daughter to get so obese?

The days and weeks and months following Johnny's death were excruciating. The only relief seemed to be having a visit from a girlfriend or from my Aunt Rhoda, a fascinating woman whom I adored. She and Uncle Lou were the parents of my cousins, Mark and David who lived in Brooklyn.

Although they didn't have as much money as my family, they seemed far, far wealthier. It was a time when women were just beginning to enter the work force and just beginning to flex their muscles.

ADULTHOOD

Lou and Rhoda were the embodiment of post World War II America, at least in terms of gender roles. Aunt Rhoda was the antithesis of my mother. She spoke to me directly, unashamedly, and laughed readily. She was, at least for me, approachable. Tanta Lena, on the other hand, was an immigrant, docile, ladylike and unknowable although I loved them both dearly. But I always felt safe with Aunt Rhoda. When I did something outlandish, which was not all that unusual, she laughed knowingly. I could confide in her whereas speaking to my mother was akin to speaking to the dead. I even think Aunt Rhoda envied some of my recklessness.  Maybe she even lived out some of her own sexuality through me though that concept would have been utterly anathema to me at the time. Aunt Rhoda was open, outgoing, quick to laugh and very smart, though without "higher" education. I think it may have been this lack of deference that made my father keep his distance. My father, I suspect, felt that his kid brother, Lou, whom he adored, could have done "better" had he married a more passive woman, as he had. Aunt Rhoda was direct and very outgoing. She was also beautiful. I remember a picture I had seen of their wedding where Rhoda is absolutely stunning. It's not coincidental that I was apparently the flower girl at their wedding, though I have no memory of it whatsoever.

Sometimes Aunt Rhoda and Uncle Lou would both come to the Village and the three of us would go out to dinner where alcohol and uncensored tales were the norm. Occasionally, Aunt Rhoda would come alone and the two of us would go out, as we call it today, barhopping. It was my only exposure to men in those days, though I never thought of dating.

I finally had the emotional resource to move out of my tiny apartment to a lovely one-bedroom apartment at One University Place, at the corner if Washington Square Park. It was far beyond my budget but a necessary move.

The apartment overlooked Washington Square Park and Judson and all the familiar sights of my adolescence. The apartment had a small Juliet balcony where, invariably, I stood to clear my head. Roni had the huge bedroom and I slept in the living room on the sofa. Most people thought that odd but there's no way I could have deprived Roni of a bedroom of his own given my early home experiences.

I remember taking my son down the block that bordered the park, teaching him to ride a two-wheel bike. It took less time than it took for me to put on my make-up. That's how extraordinary he is (although he seems to have a different recollection of this very same event.)

Other than talking with girlfriends and occasionally seeing my Aunt Rhoda, the only social activity I engaged in was playing chess at a small chess club on McDougal Street in The Village. There was always someone waiting for a game so it was a seamless process. Several times I was paired with the same good-looking guy who had also come to play. There was virtually no talk. We both took chess very seriously.

On several occasions after we'd finished playing, when I'd gotten up to leave, he'd ask if he could walk me home. I always declined, saying I had other plans, which I had not. On this particular evening when he asked me again, I was taken off guard and agreed. We walked the few blocks through the park and we exchanged small talk. His name was Thomas and I found out he had a Ph.D in Organic Chemistry and was on the faculty of NYU Medical School. I was understandably impressed but not interested in anything beyond chess. On another evening when he again walked me home, I asked him if he'd like to come up for a cup of coffee. When he came into my apartment, he made a point of telling me how lovely it was. And it was.

Just as I picked up my coffee that evening, my phone rang. It was the doctor's office where I'd been that week for a routine exam that included a PAP smear. His assistant wanted me to come back to the office as soon as possible. I asked why. She wouldn't say. I asked again and again she declined to tell me what the problem was. I began to worry. I finally said I would not come in until I knew what the problem was. She put the doctor on the phone.

"You have cervical cancer," he said abruptly. I dropped the phone. Thomas picked it up and instinctively asked all the questions of the doctor that were necessary. I couldn't believe someone was taking over my burden without even having been asked. He was extremely knowledgeable about cancer cellular changes and by the time he got off the phone we sat down and he interpreted all the information for me. I would have cryosurgery in the doctor's office, he said, freezing of the cancer cells to destroy them, no chemo, no radiation and that would be it.

On the day of the procedure Tom picked me up to take me to the office. When he arrived at my apartment he told me, almost incidentally, that he was in love with me; I would have dropped the phone again, had we been speaking on a phone. He said he wanted to marry me and, in the remote chance the cancer was more invasive than expected, he would adopt Roni and raise him as his own. His words were utterly foreign to me. I had not thought of men, nor dating, nor certainly remarriage. I suppose it was the tragedies of the past few years that combined to make me feel so totally vulnerable and it was in that context that he made me an offer I couldn't refuse.

By the time I returned to the doctor's office, I was in a very different frame of mind. The procedure itself was swift and uncomplicated, at least from my perspective. I was astounded. We married just a few months later at a friend's loft in Soho.

After we had been married for only several months, I expected Tom to go back to the Medical School where he had been teaching and from which, he told me, he had been granted a sabbatical. It's one of the things that so impressed me about him. He was so young to have gotten a sabbatical; his work must have been truly remarkable. I didn't ask a lot of questions about his work though I loved it when he explained complicated theoretical physics concepts. I looked up to him as I had to Johnny Marino.

On this particular evening, Tom had been drinking and though I knew he often drank too much, on that night he was *drunk*. I had several sculptures in my apartment that had been made by Johnny. Tom began a tirade about all the reminders of my dead husband; that it was like living in a mausoleum. The more he drank, the drunker and more abusive he got till he finally smacked me and demanded I get rid of all the sculptures. I told him I would put them out of sight. He wanted them destroyed; thrown out. I refused. He hit me again; Roni tried to intervene when he slammed Roni across the room. I grabbed my son and ran out of the apartment. When we got down to the street

Roni asked me where we were going. I told him that we didn't deserve to be hit and that I would not tolerate that behavior. Through his tears he looked up at me with the saddest eyes I'd even seen.

"Mommy," he said tearfully, "I've just lost one daddy and now you're going to make me lose another daddy." I was stopped in my tracks; despite the rage, the alcoholism, he found something in Tom that, at least for that moment, compensated for the hurt. I was so overwhelmed and confused. I knew my marriage had been a mistake but I never realized how much it meant to Roni, how much he wanted a Daddy. We sat on the curb of the street for some time as I tried to decide what to do. I held him tight and couldn't let him go. I finally decided to go back upstairs and give it another try.

Just before we'd been married, I had started my new job in New Jersey for a government agency and had gotten a larger apartment in Manhattan so I'd have my own bedroom. At about the same time, shortly after Tom and I married, he confessed to me that he was not on a sabbatical from NYU Medical School but, rather, on psychiatric disability. He told me that he had been married before, had a son, and that the marriage had been a mistake. As the marriage was crumbling, he said, he was teaching at the Medical School but *"found himself"* in a psychiatric hospital. Fortunately, he had disability insurance. He subsequently never went back to work. To this day I do not know the circumstances surrounding his hospitalization or his "disability," but I do know that he received a hefty check every month.

He had lied about so much and my critical judgment diminished the more desperate I felt. His drinking, jealousy and violence continued despite all interventions until I ultimately knew we had to separate. The apartment was in my name, paid for by me yet Tom refused to leave or even discus a separation. I called Becky, who could turn water into wine and whom I knew Tom disliked and feared. He had been privy to some of her miraculous doings that left us star struck and duly awed. She came over immediately and calmly but firmly told Tom he was going to have to leave, that she would leave for an hour or so and when she came back his suitcase must be packed and he would leave. He barely said a word, not a word! She did leave and when she came back his suitcase was indeed packed!!!. She had gotten him a studio apartment at Two 5th Avenue, one of the loveliest buildings and loveliest blocks in the Village. How? I have no idea. That is the truth. I have no idea how she does so many of the things that seem absolutely impossible to me. She's a miracle worker. She can do in the real world what most people can only do with magic and her loyalty to me was unyielding. By the evening, Tom had moved out and my life continued.

DAYLIGHT

RONI HAD EXPERIENCED such staggering loss since we returned to New York and I was just beginning to understand its depth. I had resumed my own psychotherapy to help ME deal with all that had occurred in these few short years… and that allowed me to step back and not engage in a power struggle with my son. Shortly after Johnny had died, his brother Basil, whom Roni and I adored, tried to fill his shoes. In no time at all, he too was dead, unexpectedly, from an ulcer that had ruptured. In less than a matter of months, my father died. The third brother, Vincent, was going through a divorce. On one occasion Roni had called him and they agreed to go fishing together the coming Saturday. Fishing was a family passion and Roni was very excited.

When Saturday came, Roni had all his fishing gear ready early in the morning. He waited and waited for his uncle to pick him up. When he did not, both he and I tried to reach Vincent, to no avail. Roni became more and more dejected and finally decided to go alone. I had to work so I didn't offer to go with him, a decision I've always regretted. It wasn't simply that he had to go alone. It was that I was still reeling from the very same losses and didn't have the ware with all to help him. I was a lost soul as well, depleted, terrified of my own shadow. And the more I worked to earn the money to pay for our lives, the more the capacity to keep us afloat receded, like the fat mirrors at an amusement park. The closer I got to the mirror of competence, the more distorted the image appeared. I might have looked just fine to the world but not to me. I was fighting for our lives!

STUMBLING HOME

During the years with Johnny, I had somehow reconstructed myself. I was whole, in love with my husband, my family and my life, competent and assured. I had excess. I had more love than I ever thought possible, more pleasure, more calm, more to give, enough to last me a lifetime. Or so I thought. And no sooner had Johnny died, I was back in the "depleted" realm. I was starving, barely able to function. I was a paraplegic again. My marriage to Tom was a testament to that. No sooner had a man come along whom I *believed* could help, I was back standing strong. I could toss away my prosthetics....until that source of "help" dissipated. And again I was without legs.

It's remarkable that when one is without legs, we can all understand the trauma, not just the physical trauma, like trying to catch a bus, like trying to run after a child who's disappeared in the playground, the emotional trauma as well, that I will NEVER be able to catch a bus, any bus, at any time. Yet as soon as the "as if" metaphor is replaced by a psychological reality, we are often unable to comprehend, unable to empathize, unable to experience the dilemma and we insist it's fabricated.

How do you insist, when a child cries about the ghost that's in her room, that there is no ghost. You can tell her from now until the cows come home that there are no ghosts in her room, that there's no such thing as a ghost, denying her reality, implying she's crazy or lying........... or...... we can begin to understand that her reality is different from ours. She is not being manipulative. She's not lying. She's not an "*actress.*" Yet, we also know that, in time, the child will agree there are no ghosts in the room. The problem is, until that time comes, we must find a way to believe, fully, that what the child experiences is different, at the moment, from what we experience. This is a remarkable dilemma that hinges on the impermanence of memory. The child's experience of "ghosts" in the room recedes. We don't see the recession but we know it occurs. We'd experienced it ourselves in our infancy yet can't recall it.... and we also may experience it in older age.

I know there came a time long after my father had died, when my mother believed, truly believed, that she had only one child, a son, a doctor, who lived in California, even though, at the time, she lived with me, and I stood not one foot away from her. After getting my job in New Jersey, after Tom and I divorced, I got Roni and me a lovely apartment on 14th Street and when my father passed away I moved my mother up to New York for an extended visit.

Now I can engage in psychoanalytic interpretations or I can understand that changes have occurred in my mother's brain, real, biological, anatomical changes that have resulted in her misperception, her misperception that she had only one child. Did it hurt, this statement she freely made when asked by a nurse how many children she had? Of course!! Yet I knew, even years before observable changes had occurred in her brain, that her perceptions were changing. One day, my ultra private, ultra conservative mother filled with shame and taboos, came into the living room with her panties worn over her trousers. In a million years this Rabbi's daughter, raised in a ghetto in Russia, would never have let the world see her "bloomers," as they were then called. NEVER! NEVER!

"Where is Sissy," she asked me as I stood directly in front of her, the name my family had called me my entire life. I looked at her and implored, "Mom, I'm Sissy." She laughed sweetly and simply said, 'Noooooo, you're not Sissy." She then asked me the name of the tall girl in the apartment with long brown hair, her own *GRANDSON*, Roni, whose hair had grown long, the way it was fashionable for young boys at the time to grow their hair. We all, as adults, have witnessed this process and so we know it exists. We don't imply that the person is intentionally lying when she says she has only one child, a son. We know there is a disease process at work because we've seen it progress with our own eyes. We probably can't remember being one year old and crying uncontrollably when we couldn't see "mommy," but we've witnessed enough babies crying for the very same reason and witnessed the child comforted as soon as mommy returns to know this is not a manipulation. It is a developmental reality.

So too is it a developmental truth that unless we have experienced something that has been experienced by others, that is verifiable, that is observable, we tend to mistrust it. At this time in my life, I was bereft. I felt like I assumed Roni had felt. The only real difference is that Roni was a young boy. He was also incredibly smart, handsome, resourceful and engaging. I assumed he could survive, whereas I, on the other hand, felt I could not. Neither was a lie or a manipulation. A fifteen year old who marries her boyfriend after knowing him for two days genuinely believes it is a marriage that will last. Why is it that we can look at this reality and fully believe that she believes what she's said, yet an adult, capable, competent, reality-based who says she feels totally incapable of enduring one more day is being 'theatrical".

Roni was struggling. I knew it but I was unable to help. He was 13 and without a rudder and had no male adults in his life he could count on. My brother lived in California, my wonderful brother-in-law Basil had recently died and my other brother-in-law was going through a divorce. The divorce from Tom was very difficult for Roni even though I knew he suffered from the relationship.

I knew the separation was hard for Roni. I tried to get him to see a therapist but he would have none of it. I asked Becky for advice. She told me about a young man who ran a youth program for kids whom she thought would be helpful and she gave me his name. I contacted him, Al, the youth worker. One evening when Roni didn't come home I called him. He came to my apartment and asked me a few questions about Roni: where he hung out, who his friends were, etc. etc. I answered as best I could but was certainly at a loss providing all of the information. It was about 9PM when Al left. By 1:00AM the doorbell rang. It was Al back WITH Roni. How he found him is another one of those miracles that I experienced in those turbulent times.

He stood in front of the door as I spoke to Roni who repeatedly tried to leave. This time Al wouldn't step aside from the door and simply said: "If you want to leave, you're going to have to go through me." I was appalled. Who is this guy I wondered to myself. That's no way to deal with a boy whose hurting! What are his credentials? Who is this man I've brought into my son's life? I called Becky again and asked her these very same questions as the standoff continued.

Forget his "credentials," she said dismissively. " He helps kids. That's what he does. There's not a kid south of 125th Street who doesn't know him and trust him. " A few minutes later they both walked into the other room and the "scuffle" continued. I called her again. "Let it go, Bea," she implored me. "Roni wouldn't abide by your rules but I'm sure he'll abide by his….." and, in fact, he did. It was the beginning of a transformation.

Roni became more and more involved with Al's "youth program" in the Village. It was akin to a one-man emergency room for adolescents. Al, the "director," was surrounded by boys 24/7. Though he had no degrees nor credentials the kids did seem to really like him. Most of what he did was done as a volunteer, unpaid for. At any particular time he could be found in the gym of the Church, the church that housed the "program", helping a kid with some intolerable situation that occurred in the kid's life. He had started the "program" several years before and since that church was his "home church," it was there that he began his work and engaged another adult to volunteer as he did. When I met him about 1979, I knew that with just a bit of help his program could be well respected and well funded. I volunteered to help write a grant for him, which I did and with great pleasure.

On one occasion after talking with Becky about men in her life and in mine, she asked me, almost coincidentally, what I thought of Al. The question seemed odd to me since I never gave it much thought. He struck me as an adolescent himself, but one who needed, for whatever reason, to be helpful to other male adolescents. "He's a kid," I responded flippantly. "The high top sneakers and all."

"But he's good-looking," she said.

"The way some teen-agers are good looking" I responded.

"Let's go to his apartment. I want you to talk to him and then tell me what you think."

"Becky, I have nothing to talk to him about! "

"Just do it for me."

The suggestion seemed superfluous, but, since I had free time that particular evening and the weather outside was lovely, I agreed. I'd never thought of Al in adult terms. I was almost ten years older than he and from another world. If I had any interest at all, it was only an academic one. But I agreed to join her for the short walk to his apartment. We walked the two blocks to where he and his wife lived and Becky knocked on the door. His wife answered. As she opened the door, I saw Al in the background with four or five "kids," wrestling on the floor. Becky asked to speak to him and he came to the door. The scene in the apartment was almost what I would have predicted, a house full of adolescent boys, with his wife, barely controlling her frustration and anger. The three of us spoke at the door for a few moments then left unceremoniously.

"So what do you think?" she asked me again.

"Becky, he's a kid." I didn't give the event another thought until several months later when Al called me to tell me it might be hard for me to reach him. If need be, he added, Roni always knows where to find him. I asked him if he was moving.

"Kind of, " he said. My wife and I split up."

"So where are you living?"

"On the roof!"

I was speechless. Not that I was surprised they were breaking up for I couldn't imagine any woman living in the environment I had visited. The fact that she had apparently lived with him for several years under those conditions was, in and of itself, remarkable. She must have been a very kind, patient woman, I thought, to myself.

"You're not really sleeping on the roof, are you?"

"Some nights…and some nights I sleep in the basement of the church."

"That's dreadful," I responded. "Look, if you need a place to stay for a few nights till you find an apartment, you can always stay at my apartment." The offer was actually a courtesy. He had done so much to help Roni. I knew that he had no money and no degrees, just a high school diploma. It was the least I could offer. When he showed up a few nights later with 4 kids I was totally shocked and at a complete loss to know how to respond. I saw that Roni was very happy that he was there so I simply welcomed them in and showed them all to Roni's room.

"It's a bit crowded," I responded "but I'm sure it will do for a few nights."

"My aunt offered me an apartment she's supposed to take possession of in Chelsea," he said. "So we won't be here long."

In fact, his stay at my apartment was more than a few nights but far less than it might have been, under the circumstances. When they all left I was relieved to have my apartment back, the quiet, the privacy, to have my life back, yet I felt badly for him. He was a man who willingly intervened in my son's life when he was in trouble and thus in my life when it was at a very low point. The question of why he did the "work" he did never crossed my mind.

AL

AL EVENTUALLY GOT his "own" apartment in Chelsea (which was actually in his parents name) and I eventually got a new apartment. Roni continued spending a lot of time with Al who occasionally came to my apartment for dinner. Sometimes Al and I even went to a film together. I suppose a stranger might have thought we were on a "date" but that would have been a mistake. I had no interest in him romantically, nor he in me. We were from two vastly different universes. He had no interest in the things that interested me nor I for what interested him. My only interest in adolescent boys was my interest in my own son, nor did I have any interest in sports, except, an occasional game of tennis. Couple all that with the almost ten year age difference and the vast educational and cultural differences and one can see that our paths were extremely different. While he apparently had tried college several times, he invariably dropped out.

I remember one evening when Al and a group of his 'kids" were out of town that my telephone rang. I picked up the receiver to hear a menacing, utterly terrifying voice:

"I can get you and your kid killed for five hundred bucks!!!!!" I froze. It wasn't a typical voice by any stretch of the imagination. It sounded like a voice drowning in phlegm, harsh, guttural, threatening. It wasn't the decibel level. That I'd heard repeatedly in my own home. It wasn't even an accent I heard. It was a sound like an animal might make when wounded, a roar. I thought it might have been the sound of a woman's voice but I wasn't at all sure. It was a sound completely unfamiliar to me.

Al happened to call me that night and I told him I was scared to death…Someone had called and threatened me and my son. I told him what had been said. "Oh!" he responded with a laugh. "That's just my mother…..That's just the way she talks." And apparently it was.

The following year my father passed away and left money for my brother and me. I contacted Manny to ask him where he wanted me to send his share. He said simply: "You keep it. You're the one who always looked after them.

As time went on, Al suggested on several occasions, that Roni and I move into his apartment since Roni was already spending considerable time there. In spite of the glaring red lights, we did, at times talk logistically about that possibility. I knew full well that I could never live as I'd seen his wife living those years before. We eventually agreed that **IF** I moved in, his "kids" would only come **over twice a week and _never_ overnight**. I also, at the same time, put our names on waiting lists for other apartments in lower Manhattan, **just in case**.

Given that much of my earliest years had been spent "living" in a coffin under ground screaming to be free, it's no surprise that I was extremely fearful of having my freedom so curtailed.

I also thought about my grandfather, Moishe, who had lost his wife, Chawe, whom he adored. Having been left with two young sons, he married Mary, a crippled woman who was herself a widow who had also lost a son. It was clearly a marriage of convenience though a marriage I never heard described in negative terms. They, in fact went on to have four children together, one of whom was their youngest son, my uncle Louis. My Aunt Rhoda was his wife and had

Moishe and Mary not married, I never would have had the love and support of one of the dearest women in my life.

As I look back on my early years with Al, I believed, at the time, that I had been spared the perils of history--- for after Roni and I moved in things did, in fact, improve.

For a time, our relationship became more harmonious and we had a sexual encounter. When I found out I was pregnant I knew immediately I'd have to terminate it since, at the time, I didn't feel secure enough with Al to bear his child. While things had improved, the improvement was so brief, certainly too brief to bring a baby into our lives. I sensed Al was disappointed because apparently his ex-wife had been pregnant on several occasions and had had several abortions. We never talked about these events since he was utterly incapable of talking frankly about his deepest feelings or needs.

As time went on Al began psychotherapy and started taking piano lessons. Being in the apartment was as different as it had been when he was there with "his kids" as night from day. It was a pleasure and it was in that context that we decided to marry, taking into account our agreement that *his "kids" would only come* **over twice a week and <u>never</u> overnight**.

Our wedding was lovely and my dear mother-in-law, Grace Marino, and the rest of the Marino family all showed up. Some were surprised that she came. She had buried her first son, my husband, several years before and yet, out of her devotion to me, she came to celebrate my new marriage.

Marriage presented advantages for both Al and me. I suspect it was something that we both considered as an attempt to prolong this period of quiescence. And it did just that. I paid off Al's mortgage on *his* apartment and bought us a car. ***(I never knew the apartment was actually his father's apartment....so I was actually, unbeknownst to me, paying off his father's mortgage though I didn't know that). I *enrolled him* in college, all of which I paid for as well. ***I tutored him, counseled him, paid for literally EVERYTHING and he eventually completed his Bachelor's degree after which he enrolled in a MSW program.

While no one, I suspect, would ever have described our relationship as "romantic," I had settled in and was enormously relieved that Roni had seemed to have overcome so many of the hurdles he had earlier struggled with. As a result he too decided to give college a try, which he too soared through culminating in his winning a coveted Washington Internship. All three of us seemed to have extricated ourselves from the demons we had all so painfully struggled with.

Though my relationship with Al was in many ways cohesive, he had virtually no interest in sex, at least with me and I had virtually no interest in sex at least with him. He was an adolescent to me. If anything, the absence of sex made life easier. But not the absence of devotion, allegiance or intellectual stimulation. I finally had to accept that this was my marriage. Had it not been for the fact that I had continued my own analysis, I don't know what my reactions would have been otherwise.

Despite these realities, there were also, as I said, periods of calm and satisfaction. On the second of the few times we ever engaged in sexual activity, I again become pregnant with his child and because our lives were less chaotic, I decided to keep the baby. During the pregnancy, I decided to purchase a house in the Hamptons where we could all go on week-ends which we did.

In terms of my pregnancy, Al and I talked about what last name

our child would be given since I had become increasingly aware of gender inequalities.

(In trying to locate my grandmother's grave, as my father had done unsuccessfully most of his adult life, I began searching genealogical sites and quickly realized that without knowing a woman's maiden name, the task was, in many cases, virtually impossible, especially if that woman never managed to emigrate, especially if that woman was a Jew born in Europe before or during WWII. It was in that context that I realized how utterly important ones last name was).

Al and I decided before we knew the baby's sex that if the baby were a boy he would have Al's family name as his last name and my family name as a middle name and if it were a girl, she would have my name as a last name and Al's as the middle name. Al understood completely.

Our beautiful daughter was born in early 1985, her first name, a tribute to my father's mother, whom he'd lost as a child and whom he'd longed for his entire life. Chawa's birth was magnificent and I couldn't have been happier. We would name her **Chawa Linatto Starr.**

As was common at the time, a child born in a Hospital in New York City would have the mother's last name written on the child's wristband to prevent the theft of the infant. Its only purpose was to know which infant belonged to which mother. My last name was "Starr" and so on Chawa's wrist that was the name that was written. It had nothing to do with the last name a child would ultimately use. Al had apparently phoned his parents just after our daughter was born and his father, living just blocks from the hospital, showed up immediately.

When Al's father entered the maternity ward to see his new granddaughter, he saw *my last name* written on her wrist and went into a rage. It was not until his father's horrific outburst that our initial agreement was terminated by me!

"What are you a faggot?" we heard a man scream through the hospital halls? ***"A pussy?"*** Al knew immediately it was his father, on the warpath. I didn't realize it as soon, but the minute I did, I called off all bets. I tried to calm his father down, to placate him, to appease him, explaining that the name he was seeing was not the baby's last name but my name to prevent infant theft, that the baby would be Chawa Starr **Linatto**. The entire nursery floor was focused on this ugly scene. While he did eventually calm down it was a life-altering event for me. I began to understand Al's need to surround himself with adoring, grateful young boys, why his older brother killed himself with alcohol and why his younger brother was profoundly psychotic.

It was not the first time I'd heard the father rail like that. He had done the very same thing, the very same words once before when we went to a wedding of Al's cousin. Al had gotten an ear pierced and was wearing a tiny gold earring as so many men were starting to do at the time. The earring was virtually invisible but the father's eyes were trained to recognize any infraction, any sign, however small, that he didn't see as sufficiently manly.

"What are you, a faggot? A pussy?" the father yelled. Had there not been other people around, I don't know what else the father might have said or done. As it was, both Al and I were utterly shaken and humiliated but neither of us said a word to the father.

Just days after our daughter was born and we took her home, Al, Roni, "Chawa" and I sat in our apartment's living room, sharing the joy of her birth. We all sat around our coffee table laughing and enjoying the moment. I had wrapped the baby in warm blankets and laid her in the deepest corner of the sofa, supported on both sides, as I sat next to her. She sat there, cooing and enchanting us all, the most beautiful sight in the world. I was so utterly enraptured, so at peace, so totally happy. At some point I had to excuse myself to go to the bathroom, which was just a few feet from where we sat. I turned to Al and told him to keep close eyes on the baby, that I'd be right back. No sooner had I entered the bathroom, I heard her cry. I bolted out of the bathroom and saw her lying on the floor, crying hysterically with Al looking on frantically but motionless, like deer in the headlights. She'd fallen off the couch, **right in front of him**! I grabbed her, picked her up and soothed her until she was calm and cooing again, apparently unhurt by the fall, thanks to the blankets in which she was swaddled. And Al, her father, was not three feet away.

I mention this incident because it was emblematic of one of the recurrent problems in my marriage. When Al was around "his kids" (Chawa, a female, could never qualify as one of "his kids,") he was utterly hypnotized by *THEM*, his attention inexorably focused solely on them, in this case the one male adolescent in the room, Roni.

Al's enchantment with adolescent boys had always been problematic…and continued to be for years after our daughter was born …..so when one of the buildings I had signed up for years before had an apartment that was available, I signed for the it, got the keys, had a few pieces of furniture moved and took a sigh of relief. Chawe and I moved into the new apartment seamlessly.

No sooner had I a few days of comfort in my new apartment, I noticed a lump on my breast. As it turned out the lump was cancer and I'd need to undergo a mastectomy several days later at Memorial Sloan Kettering Cancer Hospital in Manhattan. Al and Roni were at the hospital during the surgery and Al came each day until I was discharged. The recovery was painful and filled with stress but I never regretted my decision to have moved out earlier. As a matter of fact I always felt that had I NOT moved out the cancer might have killed me.

It's interesting to note that I have been hospitalized several times since we originally got together and he was always with me! I suppose one can assume that in these cases the need is clear, the situation unambiguous, and he can respond, as is necessarily. It's also interesting to note that Al's mother had many hospitalizations, serious hospitalizations throughout his childhood, for her diabetes and heart condition. I assume these were some of the few times in his family where the realities were clear, where nothing subterranean or insidious existed, where the father's delicate ego was not on the line.

STUMBLING HOME

(I'm reminded of something Al had told me years before....that as a boy, nine or ten years old, his parents would send him to Macy's to see his aunt who worked there and she'd give him two large shopping bags full of clothing she'd stolen for him to take home to his parents. When he told me that story he'd **always** emphasize the fact that they'd never sent either of his brothers to do that, that he was the **expendable** child, he was the least valued and could participate in a crime. Given the fact that of the three sons he's the only one who "survived," their neglect was probably a blessing in disguise, for as I said, his older brother killed himself with alcohol and his younger brother retreated into madness.)

While Al may have survived, he was certainly, terribly wounded. But unlike his younger brother, Al's wounds are "brilliant". The "public" Al is charming, gracious, funny, exactly like his father.... but the "private" Al is a very different species....and unless you have seen the "private" Al, you'd never know the truth of his authentic self. He's been able to remain "unknowable".... except the few times where his exposure seemed imminent. One of those times occurred while he was working for The Board of Education.

A journalist had heard something about an odd character who apparently had enormous power in The Board. She interviewed dozens of "kids" and parents for an article that ultimately appeared in the New York Post (Kind or Kinda Shady) and presented a very confusing picture. Many of the parents had only the most admiring things to say about him, as did their kids. A few thought he was dangerous but would not speak "on the record" fearing their sons would be penalized. Al carried enormous weight. The author of the article in fact found my name and contacted me for a comment, ...which I refused to provide.

I'd met Al's family many times and always remained guarded but cordial. They were a racist, anti-Semitic bunch that had no reluctance expressing their contempt for me as a Jew, yet I tried, repeatedly to win their approval, to no avail. I had even offered to take his parents to Italy, their **first plane trip** and first vacation to the country of their ancestors. I did, in fact, take them on that trip, the first of several, all of which I paid for from my considerable nest egg which had grown after my mother's death. (I also made them an elegant fiftieth anniversary party at a lovely venue in New Jersey. They seemed absolutely enraptured though their hatred of me remained unchanged.)

I'm reminded of an experience that occurred shortly before Al and I had married. Now mind you we didn't know each other that well yet and I certainly didn't trust my own perceptions or my instincts.

Al, his older brother and wife came to my apartment along with his parents. The brother came in and immediately saw my chess set and asked who played. I said I did and we sat down to play a game.

Chess, if you're not a player, is a strategic game. It's about the ability to think several moves in advance and formulate a game plan. In a few moves I knew that the brother was a reasonably competent player but certainly not a particularly strong player. I **decided to sacrifice** a piece to gain a strategic advantage. No sooner had his brother taken my sacrificed piece off the board when both he and Al jumped up, high-fiving each other, patting each other on the back, high-fiving again, hugging each other and laughing triumphantly. I felt like I'd been shot, not by the game but by the fact that Al was clearly rooting for his brother, he, the man I was thinking of marrying! The bravado was nauseating. I knew right then and there that this was a man who would never, **could never be** in my corner! But the worst part of this vignette, a conclusion I had to consider long and hard---that I've discussed in my own analysis ad nauseam .... is that I was so hurt by his display, so offended, that I literally felt I was thrown to the lions and would be eaten alive! Instead of that humiliation fortifying me, and making me more focused and determined, I was so hurt, so wounded that I could no longer concentrate on the game and wound up loosing! I should have won that game with my eyes closed....BUT NOT WITH MY UNCONSCIOUS IN OVERDRIVE! Now clearly this was only a game...but it resonated with me and was emblematic of our later relationship.

Over the next decade or two examples of his authentic self were everywhere, if you had the inclination to open your eyes. But even if you did not, in certain situations it was unavoidable.

Al had a tiny poodle whom he'd had from the animal's birth. He named him "giant." The major appeal of this dog was how absolutely adorable he was. Al relished putting him in the breast pocket of his jacket and taking a casual walk down the avenue stopping every few feet to respond to a stranger's enchantment. Eventually when our daughter married her wonderful law school boyfriend and moved to Westchester, she wanted to take "Giant" with her since her boyfriend also had a small poodle. It seems to have been a very happy time for the four of them. One day Al gets a call from Chawe. "Giant" (who's now older and frail) was dead!!!! Al, as it happened, was driving from work which was on the route to Chawe. He asked Chawe to put Giant in a box. He would stop by, pick him up and bury Giant in his yard in Brooklyn. Chawe was heartbroken. Al stopped by her house, picked up Giant and left hurriedly.

Months later, I happened to be at Al's house in Brooklyn. I asked him where Giant was buried so I could spend a few moments with him at his grave. Al looked at me as if I were form another planet.

"You didn't think I was really going to bury him, did you?" Of course I did!!! Why else would he tell that to Chawe. Why would he have her put him in a box? He, in fact, then told me **he threw him in the first garbage pail he found out of view of Chawe's home!!!** There was no burial. There was only the "gesture," like the vase he had brought me back from Europe decades before, broken in a hundred pieces because he didn't take the time to wrap it. Who puts a ceramic vase in a flimsy suitcase on an overseas flight UNWRAPPED??? Someone who cares more how HE IS SEEN THAN HOW YOU FEEL. Al's GESTURES are always impeccable.....but they are merely GESTURES They are made so he will look good, ..and kind...and thoughtful....and so caring!!!!!!

Now mind you one would think this event would have raised some flags…or at least presented a warning. And while it did, it's also true that I discounted those warnings!!!!!!I'm only a Psychologist! **Not a seer!!!**

Now getting back to Al's family: I can only assume that my Jewishness must have been such a thorn in their side, so much the talk of the family, so much the subject of incessant family conversations that it presented a veritable stumbling block for them all. While anti-Semitism was certainly known to me, it was apparently far more virulent than I had understood, especially as it existed in **this** family. Was this hatred all in response to what the church preached for centuries: that **the Jews killed Christ**, that they **killed little children and used their blood for the Passover meal,** both of which the church **finally "corrected" decades later** at the Second Vatican Council? Was it in response to the Protocol of The Elders of Zion, a proven **forgery?** Or was it in response to the centuries long policies in Christian countries of isolating Jewish families from their neighbor's and preaching hatred for the Jews from the pulpits? Did the church **correct** the **"Passion Plays"** enacted every year in Christian countries that demonized the Jews? I doubt that Al's family had ever known of any "corrections" made by the church.

Rumors have consequences, often murderous consequences.

TODAY

FROM THE MOMENT of my marriage to her son, almost sixty years ago, The Marino's have remained MY family and I love them all dearly. The older I get, the more aware I am of the differences between this family and Al's family.

I actually don't think Al's family is emblematic of other families, CATHOLIC OR NOT!!!. They are a unique subset of people from basically one Italian family who came to America *five* generations before, intermarried, settled in the Village, most in several neighboring buildings. They *never fully assimilated* and barely absorbed any of the lauded American ideals other than the quest for money and power, neither of which they were able to achieve because they failed to absorb the ideals of hard work and perseverance. Several were peripherally connected to "the Mob," (in lowly non-esteemed capacities) and all, it appeared at the time, were racists and Anti-Semites. (Blacks, Jews and Asians were particularly reviled). They were an angry, hateful clan who rarely achieved anything of any value and were left hating their neighbors and **hating each other, above all.**

What Al did do to express his allegiance to me after his mother's death was to tell me that he was going to convert *"to let them know I stand with you."* I was absolutely flabbergasted, particularly because I was not an "observant" Jew. But that wasn't the point. The point was a statement of allegiance and it was a powerful statement, and its meaning was never lost on me. I have never ceased to admire him for that statement although it seems to have been irrelevant to his family. When we met with the Rabbi who would convert him, I was awed. The only question the Rabbi asked was why he wanted to convert. A very short, simple question. Al responded just as simply saying it was to stand with me against Anti-Semitism! The Rabbi said **that was sufficient**, that he would call him up to the bimah, (stage) ask him that same question and he would give the same answer and that would be it! And indeed it was! This at the most splendid synagogue in the wealthiest part of Manhattan!

As it turned out, when our beautiful daughter got older she wanted to have a Bat Mitzvah which many of her Jewish girlfriends were having. We had the brief service at this same synagogue, with the same Rabbi officiating, followed by a large party afterwards. It might seem strange to some people that Al and I would have such an event. It made perfect sense, not as an expression of our Jewish faith, but as an expression of our awareness of the depths of Anti-Semitism and our eagerness to stand with the Jewish people against this ugly hatred.

As I've stated, I am not a believer. I have as many problems with Orthodox Judaism as I do with any other orthodoxy. But I am also aware that the Judaism I grew up with NEVER demonized anyone for ANY reason, certainly not for money or power. The Judaism I grew up with does not proselytize; it does not recruit or solicit members. It can be, for many, a timely, tedious process....becoming a Jew. It's not for everyone. It doesn't make promises solely to gain your devotion; it doesn't promise salvation, and it doesn't promise eternal life.

Years later, though Al and I had long since stopped living together, he hosted our twenty-fifth wedding anniversary party at one of the oldest Jewish restaurants on the lower East Side of Manhattan, a restaurant housed in the basement of an old tenement. Our daughter, Chawe, who had been living in Israel at the time, showed up completely by surprise. I can never express my love and gratitude as I opened the door of my apartment to see my beautiful daughter in front of me, all the way back from Israel for this party. And I will never forget being surrounded by my Jewish and Catholic families, feeling absolute gratitude and peace, my handsome, brilliant attorney son and his lovely wife making the trip up from Delaware for this party. What had I done to be so blessed with such amazing kids? I was "kvelling." *(glowing with delight and pride)*.

Our party was fabulous. Al had even written a hilarious "renewal of vows" that had everyone virtually falling off their seats with laughter. Most of the vows, incidentally, pertained to me, vowing that I be more accepting of his strange life style, more deferential, more adoring. I too had trouble containing my laughter. Needless to say, none of Al's family attended having long since cut ties with him and us. (Interestingly enough, after my father died and my mother began to noticeably decline, Al was the only person whom she recognized.)

As of this writing, Al and I continue to live seperately and I've filed for divorce. He continues to share his daily life with whatever kids need a place to stay, for that is *his* need. Having **retired** from the Board of Education several years ago, Al now works as a "psychotherapist " for an agency in upper Manhattan.

Throughout it all, the Marino family remains a cherished presence in my life. Likewise I have always (until just three years ago) maintained a house in the Hamptons where on any particular weekend friends and relatives joined us for tennis, the beach, pool parties, Bar-b-q's and fabulous games of poker.

And as for my children: After Roni had returned to college years before, he ultimately went to law school and is a practicing attorney today in Delaware and is married to his childhood sweetheart. They have a beautiful home in Delaware, a beach house on the shore and a huge boat where he's able to continue his life-long love of fishing.

Chawa, on the other hand, (who's fluent in several languages) lived in Israel for two years after graduating from College. She also went to Law School and married a lovely, successful, Italian and Irish law school classmate. She is today the lead attorney for a multi-million dollar tech corporation. (They have a beautiful home in Connecticut and I see them several times a month).

I'm pleased to say that my brother and his beautiful wife, Lisette, are in touch several times a month. While they live on the West Coast, the internet keeps us constantly connected. Manny is still a practicing Psychiatrist at 78. My relationship with him is very special. As he says often, I am the only person in the world who knows the truth of our early years as he is, likewise, for me. I have long ago forgiven him for taunting me as a child for I understand, full well, he was as much a victim as I, in some ways even more so.

I, on the other hand, now 77, am trying to adjust to days without the structure of work having suffered several debilitating falls requiring me to close my clinical practice. Had I been mobile, the absence of any real responsibility would have been a gift, as I also once loved to run and work out. Sitting on my "tush" has never been terribly appealing. But, above all and most surprisingly, I am remarkably at peace. I live alone and am grateful for every moment of solitude and quiescence that defines my life. Had you asked me forty years ago if I could live alone, if I WOULD WANT TO LIVE ALONE, I would have thought you failed to know me.

(Several years ago I got a call, out of the blue, from a man I had gone out with so many decades ago, during my *Sari* period! At the time we initially met, he was as handsome as could be, charming and very romantic. But this was now decades later. We had both obviously aged. He said his wife had just died and he had thought about me and how he could reconnect with me. A friend of his apparently helped him find my number and I invited him over. He picked me up and we went out for a drink. I sensed that nothing could possibly come from this meeting but he was as charming and as smart as I remembered him. The thought of participating in a romantic relationship was out of the question. But I knew that of all the men I'd known through six decades, he above most, would be most likely by me to be "let in." Maybe it was just curiosity. Maybe it was a barely observable inclination to partner with someone, to be part of a *REAL* couple, maybe it was a need to finally answer the question that existed in my heart for decades, whether I PREFER to live alone).

What I know most about myself today is that I am, and always have been, claustrophobic. I cringe at the thought of having to live in an environment I don't wish to live in, that I'm afraid to live in, that's of another person's design. If we are in complete agreement, so be it, but that is unlikely. And even then, what if he changes his mind, and no longer wants to **turn off the light**. I am still the little girl having to share a room with my mother, begging her, beseeching her to shut off the light. I am still the child who *didn't see what she saw and didn't hear what she heard*, although these "errors" are rapidly dwindling. My Jewishness and my love for my children and my family are virtually the only facets of my life that are utterly conflict free.

I recently heard someone say that if you're considering entering into a relationship with someone else, the only question to ask is **not:** *'WHAT DO YOU WANT?"* but rather, *"***What do you NEED?***"* A brilliant question! I'm reminded once again of the woman I'd met at a women's group who was single and had just bought her own vacation house in the Poconos. I was trying to understand her. Had she really bought her OWN house? It couldn't be just for her. Or could it? The concept was anathema to me. Why would an attractive woman CHOOSE to live alone? Did she NOT want to marry? Was marriage distasteful to her? Her stance fascinated me. Maybe this particular woman who bought her own house for herself had a very different view of matrimony.

Maybe marriage itself is like the "vaginal orgasm," a made-up concept that grows out of misinformation and a strategic need to preserve the imbalance of power in relationships in post-war America. Now certainly enough has been written about female sexual gratification in the last fifty years to assume that most people know how it is achieved, and for woman to be sufficiently more comfortable with themselves to educate their partners. Yet, I have my doubts. From the perspective of a Psychologist who had been in practice for almost forty years, I suspect that these concepts have been created to preserve what both partners felt they needed to preserve in the relationship to assure equilibrium.

It's so odd to revisit this at this point in my life, to look at my marriages as expedient, as preserving some necessary aspect of my life that needed to be preserved. In terms of my love for Johnny Marino, he seems to have been the only man with whom I was able to have a *romantic* love affair. *Maybe that concept is itself a fabrication.* In each case, I married because if I did not, I would lose something I felt was necessary for stability. And my marriage to Al was no exception. I needed him because Roni needed him. Together we were more stable than either was without one another.

I suppose if I had anything to do over, it would be to have had more children. I talk to my kids regularly, that coupled with my books and my occasional visits with family or friends creates a satisfying life, at least as satisfying as I am capable of creating and more satisfying than I would have predicted sixty years ago when I wandered into Judson Student House in that freezing, terrifying winter.

I don't think I've ever completely forgiven Al for the past, for repeatedly bringing his "kids" into our lives when we lived together, no matter how many times he promised, swore, he would not. It was always a war. I understand today that it was my fault as well. I saw how he lived with his first wife. I saw how he lived before he and I lived together but I believed him when he said that would not recur. My fault was in **BELIEVING WHAT HE SAID**. He did not HAVE TO surround himself with boys. It was a choice, perhaps a difficult choice but A CHOICE nonetheless! What complicated matters is that there was, as I've said earlier, a period, early on, when he was in therapy and was studying the piano. **DURING THAT PERIOD, AND THAT PERIOD ALONE**, he was able to respect our original agreement, so the notion that he had NO CONTROL is not accurate. As soon as he left therapy and stopped studying the piano he was back to being surrounded by his "kids"...... If, when Chawe was 3 or four or five and he said he would watch her, the truth is he MIGHT watch her unless he focused his ATTENTION on one of his "kids." I saw and fully appreciated how much he needed to be around these boys, how much he needed them to need him. He was rarely ever alone. It's apparently too painful for him. "His ego is inextricably connected to "them," whoever 'they" were, and they are all interchangeable. I was living in a room with my mother again, where I had no rights. When I finally understood that I moved out.....*and this coming from the mother of the son whom he had helped in just that circumstance.*

We were both so wounded, so damaged. It took a long time for me to grasp that he wanted what he wanted and would pursue his wants at any cost. I had to accept that our relationship was limited, painfully limited. I was not a priority, nor **ever** had been. I was not interested in most of the things he was interested in, nor he in what interested me. And so we each went our separate ways.

Out of this abyss, instead of feeling depleted, I found myself craving books, literally craving reading...and I do so relentlessly. History has become my passion, 20th century history to be exact. I wish I could say that I also exercise, use my treadmill, etc. but that wouldn't be true. I read and read some more. I quilt, I fix anything that needs fixing..... .....and read again.

When I returned to college years ago in California, I read what I was expected to read and apparently did well enough to get my Ph.D, to teach in respected universities, publish and present numerous clinical papers in respected periodicals and conferences. But today is different. I read, study and write solely for me!

I read and learn because it fills me up. It excites me...and the more I learn the more I want to learn. It enriches my **SELF**. Ah...... after all the costumes and accents and false lives, there is a **SELF**..... and she does what millions and millions of other "ordinary" selves do. She pampers her, feeds her, adorns her **SELF**, for she has value.

CLOSURE

AFTER ALL IS said and done, I know that I love my son, my daughter, my daughter-in law, my son-in-law, my family and my extended family. Retiring my clinical practice after 40 years is without a doubt, the most difficult aspect of my life today. I miss my work with patients but have returned to writing, research and books. Books are my dear friends and I pursue them relentlessly.

After years spent experiencing Anti-Semitism, first hand, its lethal and diabolical edges, it is the focus of most of what I read. As a Jew, born in Brooklyn just after Germany invaded Poland and, with both of my parents still having family trapped in Europe, it is no surprise to me that it is a seminal event in my childhood.

I recently read a fascinating physiological study determining that DNA, which had been previously thought to be determined solely on the basis of genetic inheritance and immune to learning and psychological events occurring after birth, is indeed affected and altered by those very events.

Once it was assumed that a woman, tortured in Auschwitz but subsequently able to escape would not have her DNA altered by those experiences; that any children she may subsequently have had would not have been effected by those experiences, genetically. But any child who grew up like I did would always find this assumption to be dubious. Growing up I did not know this supposed physiological "truth." I did know that a child raised by survivors (such as a boyfriend of mine had been) was very different from children raised by parents who had no connection to the Holocaust, or so we were taught.

My only question is what of a child raised by severely abusive parents, is there serious trauma? Are their genes not altered because it was "the run of the mill abuse" as opposed to a "Holocaust?" As a Psychologist, I suspect that ALL trauma impacts our genetic inheritance. It's just that, thus far we've only been able to study the effects of clearly observable trauma. We are unsophisticated, even though we've travelled to the moon, can send a text that's received in a nanosecond. We are ignorant of the real workings of the universe and ourselves, despite what we've learned over the last centuries. We don't even know with any certainty if, in this vast universe, other life exists.

I doubt that anyone would argue that someone imprisoned in *Sobibor*, who witnessed her parents dragged away to their deaths would argue that this event was not TRAUMATIC and would probably have a life-long impact. However, what of the daughter of an "upstanding" religious family who beat her at will, who imposed arbitrary standards based only on the demands of their religious community, for whom punishment was severe and idiosyncratic, who's psychotic mother beat her to purge her of the demons the mother truly believed infested her psyche, whose psychotic mother was only "trying to be of help?" Does that daughter grow up unscathed?? I doubt it.

And what of young Africans brutally seized, torn from their families, their homes, their lives and transported in slave ships to a new, hostile, utterly unfamiliar world over which they had absolutely no control, assuming they even survived the kidnapping and the harrowing passage. Would I have even wanted to survive that horror? I suspect not. For the life of me I cannot imagine their torment, their fears, their unimaginable loss. When I think of those young men, all those "nameless" young men, I fully understand how prisoners of Auschwitz might have thrown themselves on the electrified wire that imprisoned them.

And we Americans, who profited from slavery, whether directly or indirectly from their capture, their imprisonment and the forced labor they had to endure, have never atoned. To the contrary we often hear *"I had nothing to do with it. I never even owned a slave!......"* Nonsense! You didn't have to own a slave to profit from his capture. You saw it happening. You or your family or their family before them, benefitted from his slavery. But let's even assume you were living on another planet when these horrific events occurred. Where is the religion you tout, that you will fight for? Are you not your brother's keeper?

To the extent we are not actively involved in undoing the horror we Americans created, we are no better than the bystanders who saw what was happening to Jews in Nazi Europe and did nothing to help.

We've developed a category in clinical assessment, Children of Holocaust Survivors for we know that what the parent endured will affect that parent's offspring. Where are all the groups "Children of Slaves," "Descendants of Slaves?" Where are all the books written about what these descendants have endured, WILL endure, where is the legislation so that we all might purge this unimaginable crime from American history. Where is the mandatory education so we understand that *"Well, I didn't own a slave...I wasn't even alive then,"* is a meaningless statement. When a young black male is arrested, born to a single mother, whose father is no whereto be found, whom do we blame? Is this family fragmentation not A DIRECT result of the family fragmentation WE created years and years before? When we wrenched that young Black African from his home, shackled and agonized, did we not anticipate there would be consequences? Were we fools or did we just not give a damn? I suspect we were both. When over the last several hundred years we saw and created the disparity between the Black family and the White, did we care or again did we not give a damn? Where is the religion we taut every day when we need it to undo some of the crises we've created.

It is absolutely remarkable to me how some people account for the "haves" and the "have nots." When a Jewish man succeeds it's because he's a "cheater, slippery, amoral". When a Black man does not succeed it's because he's "lazy." We NEVER, NEVER look at the world in which they lived. We NEVER look at the world in which they were forced to live!

Slavery and the Holocaust are events that will ring out for remedy, I suspect, until the end of human history.

THE END

www.ingramcontent.com/pod-product-compliance
Lightning Source LLC
Chambersburg PA
CBHW071236160426
43196CB00009B/1079